Beginning with a celebration of life, *Flight of the Osprey* is a gripping and perceptive travel memoir about a couple's inspirational passage through the fifth decade of their lives.

You will discover:

- Life as a vagabond—personal glimpses into life aboard a 42-foot sloop as her crew circumnavigates the globe.

- Healing is never an easy journey—the process has more than its share of abrupt reversals, detours, starts, and mad dashes.

- A grand travel adventure in the gentler world of pre 9/11—not a logbook of heroic posturing.

- A gripping account of relationships and experiences that crosses the neatly defined nonfiction concepts of adventure, travel, and drama.

- Letting go is a difficult but necessary precursor to moving forward with life.

- Unexpected lessons taught by visiting the diverse cultures of 50 other countries.

Testimonials:

- *I am frequently called upon to help the families cope with the grief over loss of a loved one. It was an inspiration to read about a couple who were able to deal with their worst nightmare and move on with lives while holding sacred the memory of their son. For those of us who have faced such a tragedy, and for those who unfortunately will, this book is a must read.*—Eugene S. Lapin, Director of Cardiovascular Services of Multicare Health Systems.

- *What begins as a classic sea adventure to discover new landfalls becomes a couple's journey to discover uncharted territories with their souls. A compelling tale of love, loss, and spiritual discovery.*—C. Mark Anderson, clinical psychologist.

- *Excitement and philosophical insights are constant companions as the author takes us places we can only hope to someday visit.*—Jerry D. McKellar, nationally acclaimed artist and sculptor.

- *A fascinating and well-crafted account that captures the mystique of long distance sailing and the essence of exotic ports.*—Terry Hammond, navigator aboard Australia's America Cup challenger *Gretel.*

Flight of the Osprey

Flight of the Osprey

✦

A Journey of Renewal

An absorbing travel memoir exploring love, loss, and spiritual discovery.

Kurt Mondloch

iUniverse, Inc.
New York Lincoln Shanghai

Flight of the Osprey
A Journey of Renewal

Copyright © 2005 by John Kurt Mondloch

iUniverse books may be ordered through booksellers or by contacting:

iUniverse
2021 Pine Lake Road, Suite 100
Lincoln, NE 68512
www.iuniverse.com
1-800-Authors (1-800-288-4677)

ISBN-13: 978-0-595-36962-1 (pbk)
ISBN-13: 978-0-595-81370-4 (ebk)
ISBN-10: 0-595-36962-6 (pbk)
ISBN-10: 0-595-81370-4 (ebk)

Printed in the United States of America

Contents

Preface xiii

An overview of *Flight of the Osprey* from 1995 until 2002.

Osprey's World circa 1995–2002 xix

CHAPTER 1   The Tragedy 1

The unsuccessful search for Tyler & Ashley in the Himalayas of India: October–December 1995

CHAPTER 2   The Aftermath. 15

Unforeseen repercussions from the deaths of Tyler & Ashley: January 1996

CHAPTER 3   The Birth of a Dream 17

Our circumnavigation of the world was inspired by history and fueled by passion.

CHAPTER 4   Shakedown Cruise. 20

Embarking on the vagabond life of full-time yachtsmen: spring and summer 1995

CHAPTER 5   The Initiation 25

Introduction to the moody offshore weather of the North Pacific: August 1995

CHAPTER 6   The Seafaring Life 29

Enjoying the good life in California prior to the search for Tyler & Ashley: September–October 1995

CHAPTER 7   The Awakening 34

An insightful voyage to Mexico after the memorial service for Tyler & Ashley: February 1996

CHAPTER 8   The French Connection 42

Osprey's 2800-mile trade wind passage from Mexico to French Polynesia and beyond: April–July 1996

CHAPTER 9   The Coconut Milk Run 58
Island hopping through the Cooks, Niue, Tonga, and Fiji: August–October 1996

CHAPTER 10   Gale Warnings 68
Coping with a major gale en route to New Zealand: October 1996

CHAPTER 11   Home of the Kiwis 71
Immersing ourselves in the incomparable delights of New Zealand: October 1996–
April 1997

CHAPTER 12   Down Under 79
Touring Australia in a grand manner: May–August 1997

CHAPTER 13   More than just Bali 87
Exploring the far flung islands of the Indonesian archipelago: September–October
1997

CHAPTER 14   Strait of Malacca 97
Dealing with pirate fears in the Strait of Malacca and Malaysia: October–
November 1997

CHAPTER 15   Thai Takeout 102
The many faces of Thailand in pre-tsunami days: December 1997

CHAPTER 16   The Indian Ocean 108
Appreciating the unique ethnicity of Sri Lanka and the Maldives: January 1998

CHAPTER 17   The Arabian Peninsula 114
Sailing with the NE monsoon into the Arab lands of Oman and Yemen: February
1998

CHAPTER 18   Red Sea Flashbacks 119
Bashing upwind in the Red Sea from Eritrea to Egypt: March–April 1998

CHAPTER 19   Egyptian Lessons 126
Tracing the path of the Pharaohs in Luxor, Cairo, and the Suez Canal: April 1998

CHAPTER 20   The Contested Lands 135
Timely history lessons in Israel and Cyprus: April–May 1998

CHAPTER 21   The Carpet Guys 145
Soaking up the Turkish culture: May 1998–March 1999

CHAPTER 22   Come Fly with Me 155
Riding the rails in Great Britain: November 1998; skiing the powder in Chamonix:
January 1999

CHAPTER 23   Greek Salad 159
Lazy sailing days in the Greek Islands: April–June 1999

CHAPTER 24   Italia 165
Bonding with quintessential Italy: June–July 1999

CHAPTER 25   Spanish Eyes 169
Checking out the offerings of Spain from the Mediterranean to Portugal: July–
September 1999

CHAPTER 26   The Pillars of Hercules 176
Moroccan road trip from Tangiers to Marrakech: October 1999

CHAPTER 27   Canary Island Jump-off 180
Gearing up for the Atlantic Rally for Cruisers: November 1999

CHAPTER 28   Atlantic Crossing 183
Osprey's 2700-mile trade wind passage from the Canaries to the Caribbean:
November–December 1999

CHAPTER 29   The Windward Islands 188
Revisiting the Caribbean from Martinique to Grenada: December 1999–January
2000

CHAPTER 30   Carnival in Trinidad 196
Going native at Trinidad's world-class Carnival: February–March 2000

CHAPTER 31   The Haves and the Have-Nots 198
Encountering the many faces of Venezuela: March–April 2000

CHAPTER 32   Winging It over South America 202
Traveling lessons en route to Machu Pichu and Lake Titicaca: April 2000

CHAPTER 33   Island Time 207
Savoring the beautiful anchorages of Los Roques, the Aves, and Bonaire: May–June
2000

CHAPTER 34   A Florentine Celebration 212

Celebrating our daughter's Florentine wedding and our new bonds with Italy: June–September 2000

CHAPTER 35   The Spanish Main 216

A trade wind sleigh ride to the San Blas Islands of Panama: September–October 2000

CHAPTER 36   The Ultimate Ditch 223

Osprey's Panama Canal transit from the Caribbean to the Pacific: October 2000

CHAPTER 37   Hanging Out in Central America 227

Poking along the Pacific side of Panama and Costa Rica: October–November 2000

CHAPTER 38   The Overlooked Middle 232

Discovering civilized anchorages tucked into the coasts of El Salvador and Guatemala: November 2000

CHAPTER 39   The Mexican Riviera 237

Prime cruising waters from the Gulf of Tehuantepec to Zihatanejo: November 2000–February 2001

CHAPTER 40   Crossing *Osprey's* Outbound Track 243

Completing our 40,000-mile circumnavigation of the world at Bahia Navidad, Mexico: January 7, 2001

CHAPTER 41   Manana Land 246

Inland jaunts from Puerto Vallarta to San Miguel de Allende: January 2001

CHAPTER 42   Hemingway Live 248

Sorting out Papa's legend in Cuba: February 2001

CHAPTER 43   Sea of Cortez 251

Following Steinbeck's lead in the Sea of Cortez: February–April 2001

CHAPTER 44   The San Carlos Saga 257

Osprey and our wanderlust left in the Sonora desert for an eight-month stint of dry storage: April 2001

CHAPTER 45   Minimalist Reentry 260

Reentering the USA lifestyle translates into a difficult transition for travel addicts: May–December 2001

CHAPTER 46   Getting It Together in Baja 262

Readjusting to the cruising life after the shocks of reentry and 9/11: December 2001–February 2002

CHAPTER 47   Breaking Free 266

Spirited sailing down the Sea of Cortez from San Carlos to Cabo San Lucas: March 2002

CHAPTER 48   Taming the Baja Bash 269

Motor sailing in benign conditions from Cabo San Lucas to San Diego: April 1– April 8, 2002

CHAPTER 49   Graveyard of the Pacific. 271

About as good as it gets sailing north from San Diego to Port Townsend: May 2002

CHAPTER 50   The *Osprey* has Landed .275

New beginnings for the *Osprey* and her crew.

Preface

o o o o o o o o o o o o o o o o o o o o o o o o o o o o o o o o o o

I am not the same having seen the moon shine on the other side of the world.

—Marijanne Radmacher

1995 should have been a year to relish. My wife and I were starting a circumnavigation of the world aboard our 42-foot sloop *Osprey*. As with many dreams the implementation of our plan relied on a heavy dose of reality therapy. I sold my dental practice and PL left her counseling job. Cars changed hands, furniture was stored, and the house was rented. Our children, Kate and Tyler, were college educated and following their own personal journeys. With a good deal of fanfare we said goodbye to family and friends. PL and I felt confident and bulletproof as we sailed from Seattle and into the first chapter of our new life. Less than six months later we would dejectedly return to Seattle to face the most shocking scenario a parent can imagine. Our son was missing.

In September of 1995 PL and I were enjoying the offerings of San Francisco and getting into the cruising mode. About that time we started to hear news from Kate that something was amiss with Tyler and his girlfriend Ashley. Tyler and Ashley were in the midst of a three-month backpacking trip around the world, but they were overdue for their rendezvous with Ashley's aunt in Nepal. Our nerve endings started to tingle even though we had confidence in our son's ability to deal with the inevitable hassles of international travel. Concern grew into genuine worry when PL and I sailed into San Diego and learned that Tyler and Ashley were still missing. We flew back to Seattle in October to deal with the mysterious disappearance of our son and his companion. *Osprey* and our cruising dreams were put on indefinite hold in San Diego.

In late October Tyler and Ashley failed to board their scheduled flight back to Seattle. Ashley's father and I decided to fly to India to personally organize a search for our missing children. In a distant mountain village in northern India, Ralph and I discovered the backpacker hotel where the kids had stayed and the bank where my son had cashed a traveler's check. We found no further trace of Tyler and Ashley. Even though Secretary of State Warren Christopher and Congressman Norm Dicks graciously provided diplomatic contacts at the US Embassy and the India Ministry of Home Affairs in New Delhi, Ralph and I dejectedly returned to Seattle a few weeks later with little good news to report.

The onslaught of winter weather in the Indian Himalayas was not far away, so a critical decision had to be made. Our families feared kidnapping or foul play far more than the siren song of ashram cults. We needed professional help. We hired Kroll Associates, one of the largest investigative agencies in the world, to organize an international search for our lost children. Until the possibility of a hostage scenario was ruled out, Kroll advised our families not to speak to the local media. A partner in Ralph's law firm established the Ashley Palumbo and Tyler Mondloch Search Committee. Donations from concerned family and friends helped to fund the massive search. The Kroll investigation was an excruciating four-month ordeal that exacted monumental costs economically, spiritually, and physically. The love and generosity of hundreds of supporters helped us through those agonizing months.

On January 9, 1996 an overseas phone call delivered devastating news. Our families received notification that Ashley Palumbo and Tyler Mondloch lost their lives on September 4, 1995 while trekking in the Himalayas of northern India. Kroll Associates confirmed that Ashley and Tyler checked out of a small hotel in the village of Chatru on the tragic day and began the hike back toward the town of Manali. A shepherd confirmed seeing two backpackers, a tall Caucasian man and a short Caucasian woman, attempting to cross a flooded tributary of the Chantra River. It had been raining heavily and the water was at flood stage. The monsoon-swollen river was tearing a path of destruction and carnage as it swept down the mountains and through the rural villages. Both kids were carrying all their gear—their packs were heavy and the high mountain weather was miserable. Tyler and Ashley would have been anxious to be back in Manali.

Tyler successfully waded through the treacherous glacial river and waited for Ashley on the far side. As Ashley attempted to follow Tyler's lead, she fell into the icy water. Tyler leaped back into the raging current attempting to save her. The force of the rushing water swept both of them off their feet and carried them away. Their bodies have never been recovered.

In India local people such as the shepherd fear the police and never want to be involved in government investigations. If the shepherd had not been questioned by one of Kroll's operatives, Tyler and Ashley would have disappeared without a trace. Since the operative was a trusted fellow Indian, the shepherd related his story. The tragic drama unfolded so quickly and lethally that the shepherd was unable to help.

A memorial service for Ashley and Tyler was held on January 17, 1996 at Saint Mark's Cathedral in Seattle. The cathedral overflowed with wonderful people paying tribute to Tyler and Ashley. Kate had lost her brother, we had lost our son, and our dreams were shattered.

The loss of a child can obliterate the parents' relationship and destroy their lives. PL and I struggled through the dark times and eventually emerged into the daylight together. The challenges of global cruising presented us with new and unexpected perspectives as we struggled through the many stages of grief. *Flight of the Osprey* is not a logbook of heroic posturing, but rather an exploration of the essence of the human spirit. Accepting our son's death has been an ongoing process with its share of reversals, detours, abrupt stops, and mad dashes—not an easy journey.

We still grieve for Tyler, but time has soothed some of the pain and we are at peace. Our daughter and her husband are happily married and they have given us our first grandchild. We completed our circumnavigation of the world, but after almost seven years we returned home very different people. *Flight of the Osprey* is a story about those times.

Acknowledgements

To my son Tyler, a shooting star and my inspiration.

To my wife PL and my daughter Kate, the swirling planets in my universe.

Osprey's World circa 1995–2002

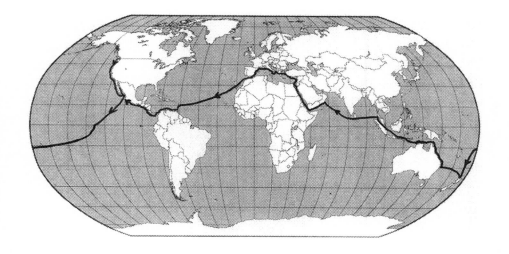

1

The Tragedy

Time holds the final claim check for everything we gain or attain in this lifetime. All our possessions, along with the people and feelings we love, are at best only loaned to us for a very short time by eternity.

—Frederick Lenz, **Surfing the Himalayas**

The circling vultures are etched in my memory. As I got my bearings in New Delhi, it became quite apparent that the loathsome predators were just part of the chaotic scene. Every neuron in my brain went into sensory overload as India assaulted my senses. Blaring horns and claxons frazzled my nerves. The stench of open sewers, industrial pollution, and diesel exhaust permeated the stagnant, humid cloud that enveloped the capital of India. The crush of sweaty bodies on crowded streets was of little consequence compared to the gnawing dread that ravaged my guts. I was terrified about the disappearance of my son as a tangled web of fear, helplessness, and depression haunted me. I felt impotent, insignificant, and irrelevant. It was a time to dig deep into my soul, but time was running out. What the hell was I going to do?

I was a long ways from home with very few answers. Although I had recently retired from dentistry, I was still the same overachieving first-born who thought he had it all together. My persona as a bearded, turbocharged fireplug had always served me well. I relished challenges so I morphed from a thirteen year old Eagle Scout into a successful professional. I considered myself a good husband and caring father. Along the way the feds licensed me as a commercial pilot and a master of auxiliary sailing vessels. My decision to retire and explore the world on my own nickel had very recently catapulted me out of the mainstream and into the unexplored backwaters frequented by vagabonds. At his stage I had constructed the rugged exterior of a human being, but I had yet to explore my bones.

1

PL, my strikingly beautiful wife, is ideally suited for her vocation as a counselor. My mate is not only a well educated woman with a vibrant personality, she is also the stabilizing influence in our relationship. A mellow middle child with three siblings, she sees the world as a community to be embraced rather than as a challenge to be faced. She is a loving mother and wife who tolerates my whims and embraces my wanderlust. Her passions are her friends and family. PL's unenviable task was to stay in Seattle and investigate our son's disappearance while I traveled to India to organize a search.

The appearance of two concerned fathers in New Delhi and our subsequent launching of a full scale missing person investigation insured an added measure of respect and cooperation from Indian authorities. Just prior to our British Airways flight into New Delhi, Secretary of State Warren Christopher sent a note assuring us of continued assistance from the US State Department.

According to the Indian authorities Tyler and Ashley were not in jail, there was no sign of kidnapping, foul play had been ruled out, and they apparently were not living in an ashram. We knew Tyler and Ashley had traveled to Manali but from that point on they seemingly vanished.

A free-lance former CIA operative assured us that the American Embassy in New Delhi was providing an unprecedented level of help. He also counseled us that we should not go off to Manali on our own. Our subsequent security briefings from Kroll Associates warned that northern India featured the third highest incidence of kidnapping in the world. The final reality check, rammed home by the intelligence agent, tagged India as a country noted for sporadic violence and endemic corruption. He reiterated that personal safety was a major issue and bribery was a way of life.

Paul Thoreaux's book, *Traveling the Great Railway Bazaar*, aptly described our frustrating situation:

> *It becomes increasingly apparent that this missing person scenario in the eastern countries is nothing new. These are the children whose pictures appear in the far-flung US consulates around the world under the heading of 'Lost US Citizen'.*

When our flagging morale needed a boost, our friends and families back in the States were there for us. While we were in New Delhi, Ralph and I received daily briefings on the progress of the Ashley and Tyler Search Committee. PL, Kate, and the rest of the Search Committee were pulling out all the stops.

Organizing a search in India is a daunting task. The chances of completing a phone call are much better on international satellite circuits than trying to call across town in New Delhi. Supposedly valid telephone numbers are either nonexistent or buzzed with an infuriating busy signal. Faxing in India is a study in perseverance. Email was still in its infancy and not a part of our communication regimen. The muggy climate is oppressive. Rudyard Kipling rightly considered heat the central fact of India.

On the positive side the US Embassy graciously assigned Himish Bhatnagar to be our full-time translator and guide. Himish, a personable Hindu, spoke many of the dialects unique to northern India. He introduced us to the intricacies of the Hindu religion.

Gurcharin Singh, the Joint Secretary in Ministry of Home Affairs, lent his prestige to our effort and sent us off with a sealed document directing superintendents of police to expedite the missing persons investigation. The Chanckyapuni Police Station in Delhi televised a picture and description of Tyler and Ashley on the local TV channels. The police also distributed hundreds of our missing persons posters that depicted our kids in full color.

Ted Cubbisson, the Consul General at the US Embassy in Delhi, became our lifeline for information and personal contacts. We received copies of cable traffic flashed to various officials in the State Department. Ralph and I were assured that the Secretary of State and Congressman Norm Dicks were very invested in our investigation.

Ted and his stunning wife Connie graciously invited Ralph and I to be their houseguests for the duration of our stay in India. We were treated like family. The days of the Raj still endured at Connie's home where she employed a cook, assistant cook, laundry woman, valet, driver, nanny, and gardener. With time on her hands and goodness in her heart, Connie made it her personal mission to track down our missing children.

Since Ralph and I were in the land of gurus and ashrams, the Cubbissons suggested a visit to one of Delhi's famous psychics. Following Ted and Connie we hesitantly wandered down a steamy back alley and eventually located a small, obscure office housing Dr. Nalin Nirula, consultant. Initially Ralph and I were skeptical but we were desperate for information and prayed for encouraging news. The psychic's mystical séance conjured a vision of our children stranded somewhere in the Indian Himalayas, perhaps at a monastery.

The Dornier turboprop winged over a high alpine plateau en route between Shimla and the outskirts of Kulu. Compared to the insidious pollution of New Delhi, the Himachel Pradish district of northern India is literally a walk in the park. The sprawling pine forests are reminiscent of the high desert of central Ore-

gon. The forested slopes descended into terraced hillsides and eventually meandering valleys. The phenomenal scenery unfolded on the threshold of the
mystical Himalayas where massive mountain ranges reached to the sky—the stuff
of legends but the everyday staple of the resident farmers and itinerant monks. I
was finally feeling a bit of optimism percolate into my spirit.

Our first stop was a frustrating visit to the local Superintendent of Police, the
SP in Kulu. The khaki uniformed police lounged around the station and paid us
no mind. Their nonexistent work ethic is spawned by years of socialism and nep-
otism. In his own good time Mr. Sharma, the SP, arrived in a chauffeur driven
jeep accompanied by two machine gun toting bodyguards. Ralph and I desperately needed this gentleman's cooperation if we hoped to look through any
records. Our sealed letter from the Ministry of Home Affairs turned out to be our
silver bullet. After a quick read, the SP became a changed man. The lethargic
police outpost snapped to attention as Mr. Sharma took immediate action. One
of our missing persons posters of Tyler and Ashley was prominently displayed at
police headquarters that afternoon.

All the stations in the SP's district were directed to immediately launch
searches of all the guesthouses and hotels and report back within the week. Even
Malana and Pulga, remote villages favored by bohemian westerners who vege-
tated in a stuporous atmosphere of no cops and cheap drugs, received a team of
the SP's police on a surprise passport sweep.

India is bursting with a population surpassing one billion souls. The high
tech, vibrant city of Bangalore seems to be India's key for unlocking the twenty-
first century. Yet in most of India, the dynamic social and economic fabric disin-
tegrates outside the environs of the high tech office complexes. Overpopulated
India is plagued with an antiquated infrastructure that was born after the fall of
the Raj in the late 40's and endured until the demise of the Soviet Union in the
early 90's. The system favors plodding bureaucrats. That legacy was our nemesis.

Ralph and I sifted through grungy bundles of almost indecipherable copies of
Form C, the infamous paperwork each tourist is required to fill out when regis-
tering at a hotel in India. Himish talked it over with the SP's clerical guy who was
pounding away on an ancient typewriter. No computers and no printed hard
copies are to be found in the hill country. We were left to sort through hundreds
of smeared, carbon paper generated copies stuffed into dusty plastic garbage bags.
After hours of scrounging through the paperwork, we were still no closer to having any clues.

The school children in Kulu, sporting classic British style uniforms, descended
on their school about mid-morning. The kids are well groomed and happy, a

marked contrast to the knots of displaced men who frequented the cafes and shops. The women, clad in bright saris and stoic demeanors, did most of the work. Although India has a major population problem that grows exponentially each year, children seemed to be treasured and well treated—especially the boys. Unfortunately the pine scented mountain air and the pungent smells of the open-air marketplace failed to mask the acrid smell of urine and feces in the open sewers, a problem common to most Indian towns and cities.

After our initial assault on the Kulu SP's office we hired Bhoomi, a local guide, to drive us around the hill country of Himachel Pradesh in his small jeep. Doing a masterful imitation of a grand prix start, Bhoomi fired up his Marudi Gypsy SUV and we roared across a ramshackle bridge. Bhoomi nonchalantly negotiated the treacherous and narrow pot-holed road up to the mountain towns of Jari, Kasol, and Manikaran. Himish thought nothing of the insane driving performance, but Ralph and I were numb. Our butts hurt and our survival juices were on high boil. Our process of interviewing backpackers in far-flung places was about to begin.

Most Hindus are either followers of Vishnu or Siva. Siva is known as the destroyer and reproducer but even more important, Siva was also the god of choice for both Bhoomi and Himish. If Bhoomi spied a temple dedicated to Siva, our rig came to a grinding halt as Bhoomi and Himish piled out to pay their respects. Perhaps it was this devotion, or perhaps it was the dashboard-mounted figurine of Siva riding the bull Nandi, but we did survive our driving adventures unscathed other than the psychological trauma of driving with a true kamikaze.

The Rainbow Restaurant in Kasol was a hangout for a number of young trekkers and travelers, mostly from Israel, Italy, and Canada. A few of these unfortunate souls looked like most of their brain cells had packed it up—so much for cheap and available dope. The road through the Parvati Valley ended at Manikaran. At that juncture we walked across an antique suspension bridge into the village of Gurdwara, a whimsical setting dominated by sulfur hot springs and a Sikh temple. The locals not only use the hot springs for bathing, but also for cooking their meals. A few expat freaks, clad in loincloths and turbans, seemed oblivious to the world as they languished in the hot pools. Sacred cows had the run of the place. After paying our respects to the resident Guru and receiving *prasad,* a communion of deep fried bread, Ralph and I visited the local police station. The constables were considerate, but not motivated. Backwaters such as Manikaran produced very little in the way of cutting edge police work.

Every official in India continued to assure us, from these village cops to the ministers in New Delhi that if our children were dead, in jail, or in the hospital, we would be notified.

Connie was paranoid about Delhi Belly, India's version of Montezuma's Revenge, so she sent us off to Manali with a huge case of food from the embassy commissary. Since Ralph and I were tiring of Connie's well-intentioned cracker and jam rations, we risked a simple omelet and cup of butter tea at a nondescript inn out in the countryside. As we we learned, an omelet is probably one of the safer foods to eat in India. If you cannot peel it, boil it, or completely cook it, think long and hard about eating it. Since the origin of any meat in rural India is suspect, Ralph and I always ordered boneless chicken. The concept of heart disease has yet to make any inroads on the Indian habit of lathering their food with butter. Indian chai, a sweetened milky tea, was definitely an acquired taste. We consoled ourselves with Kingfisher beer.

In November winter has not yet invaded the hill towns of the Indian Himalayas. We enjoyed brilliantly clear mornings and warm days. Between sunset and sunrise there were hints of frost. Farmers worked ancient terraced fields in a pastoral countryside dotted with teepee shaped haystacks. Rustic farmhouses featured picturesque drying corncobs on their slate roofs. Spectacular sunsets painted the towering Himalayas in swatches of brilliant orange and glistening gold. The Kulu Valley was flat out gorgeous.

Manjiras, bells attached to a pair of wood rods, and drums served as our wakeup call after our rather fitful sleep. Our hotel was wedged against the west escarpment of the Kulu Valley, and we were cradled in the shadow of the absolutely awesome Himalayas. Many substantial homes with seemingly impossible access were perched on the surrounding hillsides. Unfortunately our "deluxe" rooms at the Kulu's Shobla Hotel lacked certain amenities, such as heat. The fall nights in the hill towns get downright nippy, so my pile jacket came in handy. Since electricity was sporadic at best, my flashlight became an essential item for deciphering a menu, reading a book, or shaving. I was homesick, tired, and disgusted.

Ralph, Himish, and I each paid 500 rupee ($15) for our rooms, but Bhoomi slept in his little jeep. We paid $15 a day for Bhoomi and his weathered 4x4, but Himish confiscated the keys at night so Bhoomi would not siphon out the gas and sell it.

As Bhoomi careened the Suzuki through assorted small villages in northern India, he was much more concerned about colliding with a sacred cow than causing the demise of a pedestrian. After all, killing a cow involves finding the owner and then negotiating hundreds of dollars in compensation. The accidental death of a male may cost the guilty driver $150. A girl's death, no matter how regrettable, would bring little monetary compensation to the surviving family. In India if you are deaf, inattentive, or not adept at riding a bicycle, you probably will not live to a ripe old age. Traffic laws mean little to Indian motorists, but a heavy hand on a blaring horn seems to be the hallmark of veteran drivers. Bizarre driving habits are part of the fabric of India and they bring new meaning to the Darwinian maxim of survival of the fittest.

The mountain scenery on the climb from Kulu to Manali is reminiscent of rural Switzerland. The steep foothills are carpeted with pine forests and the precipitous narrow roadways seem to be perched on the very rim of the deep gorges. The turbulent Beas River raged through the canyon far below. The remote countryside is sprinkled with Hindu and Buddhist temples. Himachel Pradish deserves its reputation as one of India's most beautiful states.

Each day I was torn with yet another variety of conflicting emotions. The lack of any positive leads soured my perspective on life. Intense, disjointed emotions are certainly not the most ideal ingredients in a marital relationship. PL and I had both withdrawn into ourselves and each of us harbored our own fears. Not knowing the fate of our son was a cancer that ate into every fiber of our souls and left us physically and emotionally ravaged.

Phone calls and letters from friends and family helped to fill the hollow void in my spirit and the huge outpouring of love and support soothed my raw nerves. The folks back home were doing everything they could and I was humbled by their generosity and understanding.

Manali struck me as a frontier hill town. Clutter and haphazard planning were the norm. Whereas the drive to Manali is quite picturesque, the town itself is classic rural India. A conglomeration of trucks, busses, and motorbikes negotiated the narrow streets already jammed with people and cows. Dilapidated wooden shacks were interspersed with unfinished concrete apartments adorned with rusting iron frameworks. Other than as a jumping off place for treks, it seemed a day or two in Manali would be enough for anyone.

Prior to leaving the States, American Express notified us that Tyler had cashed two of his traveler's checks at the UC Bank in Manali. When I presented the directive from the Ministry of Interior Affairs, which demanded full cooperation with our investigation, the manager of the UC Bank in Manali rummaged through his filing cabinets. The harried banker finally found a record of Tyler's transactions, dated August 26 and August 27. Since the bank required identification and a local address when any tourist cashed a check, Ralph and I stumbled on to another clue. Tyler and Ashley had stayed at a local backpacker hangout, the Greenland Hotel.

At $3 a night, the Greenland Hotel is not exactly in a prime location, but after threading our way through a series of footpaths and past some rather forlorn shacks, we found the place. One of Tyler's favorite admonitions was advising his listener to "savor the irony." The irony I now savored literally jumped out at me. In the grubby pages of the hotel register amidst all the conservative entries of backpackers from Germany, Israel, France, England, and Italy, one very unique registration almost leapt off the page. "USA" was printed in huge block letters and was set off with a jazzy sketch of a shooting star. Tyler's trademark scrawl completed his personalized registration. I was absolutely blown away with our good fortune. Much later I would come to realize that the dynamic signature was Tyler's parting gift to me.

Our next step was to visit the police station in Manali, present our special directive from Delhi, and then start sifting through more Form C copies in hopes of locating yet another hotel where the kids might have stayed. In the dusty, ramshackle open air police station, Ralph, Himish, and I sat at a spindly card table and sipped Chai while a local cop accessed his filing system of Form C garbage bags. Our threesome split up the mound of tattered Form C copies and waded through months of questionable records. As we learned later, most backpackers stayed at hotels that do not get too overwrought about registration with a Form C. Ducking the government paperwork translated into cheaper accommodations for the kids, a nonexistent paper trail for the guesthouse, and no subsequent taxes for the conniving guesthouse owner.

After days of interviewing shopkeepers, innkeepers, guide services, and backpackers, we had exhausted our list of possibilities. Ralph and I decided to take a hike around the local foothills. About midday we came upon an old village perched on the edge of a roaring mountain river and cradled in the shadow of the snow-capped Himalayas. The breathtaking scenery and primitive surroundings easily explained why an extended trek in the region would have appealed to Tyler and Ashley.

Jim Wickwire, a world-class mountaineer from Seattle, had earlier suggested that Tyler and Ashley might have ventured into Ladakh—a rugged land boasting the world's highest mountain passes. At the time we dismissed the thought because of Ashley's susceptibility to intense sun and high altitude. But perhaps the psychics we had consulted in Delhi were more perceptive than we thought. Little Tibet occupies the trans-Himalayan Zone, a boundary between the peaks of the western Himalayas and the vast Tibetan plateau. Once a traveler is up and over the Rohtang Pass, a spiritual world of remote mountaintop monasteries awaits the seeker.

The prevailing religious theme in this area of the world admonishes each of us to find our individual path. As our life unfolds we are driven to our fate, whatever that end may be. The monasteries and ashrams of India offer believers a unique view of the world and lend a surreal aura to this complex country. It is not just the mysticism that makes India so distinctive. India is also plagued with a never-ending series of natural and man-made disasters. Fires, floods, earthquakes, and train wrecks are part of the national heritage.

When we arrived back in Kulu, the SP advanced a theory that perhaps our children managed to catch a bus overland to Nepal by negotiating a fifteen-day visa extension at an obscure outpost. As he pointed out, the areas are immense and there many options, such as Manali to Leh and on to Kashmir, or perhaps Manali to Shimla and on through the maze of interlacing roads in the Indian province of Utter Pradesh. The SP went on to say that he was in Manali after the floods in early September, and that even though the road was torn out in places, stranded busses provided shuttle service on their respective patches of road. Mr. Sharma encountered a number of trekkers who were seemingly undaunted by the floods and hiked their way back to Kulu. The Rohtang Pass route to Leh was closed to traffic, but army helicopters were dispatched to rescue any tourists stranded between Leh and Manali. Snow had come early in the year, so Rohtang Pass was open only for commercial traffic after the floods.

Violent flash floods in early September had obliterated many sections of the winding mountain road leading to Manali. Women, dressed in rainbow colored saris, wielded shovels and hammers, and handled the roadwork. After the rock was broken up with sledgehammers, other women hoisted the gravel filled baskets onto their backs and then dumped their appallingly heavy loads into the huge chuckholes. Not much in the way of mechanical equipment, but labor was cheap and plentiful. With no anti-pollution laws dictating environmental standards, fifty-gallon drums of oil were left smoldering at the roadside as the female crews poured some of the goop over their crushed rocks to create very low-tech asphalt.

Tata is the name synonymous with heavy transport in India. No pickup trucks need apply. Wildly painted Tata busses and trucks were stuffed full of people and produce as they belched diesel smoke and hurtled around blind curves with the driver's hand firmly planted on the horn. Regional roads featured broken down sections of aging blacktop, one-way in size but serving impatient two-way traffic.

Many of these glorified paths seemed to be adjacent to a vertical cliff of chilling height. Indians, armed with a stoic disposition bred through the centuries, jammed into these wallowing busses as though they were being vacuum-packed. A bus ticket costs the same whether you occupy a window, aisle, floor, roof rack, or even the ladder at the rear of the bus. Chaos seemed to be an essential ingredient in the national character.

At this stage the stress and frustration played havoc with my normally upbeat persona. I felt punch drunk. Even though Ralph and I attended many high-powered meetings with very connected officials, we were running out of ideas. Nobody could provide a definitive description of the late summer weather in Manali until…I asked Bhoomi. Bhoomi was actually in Manali during the horrendous floods of early September. He maintained that it was impossible to drive from Manali to Kulu for about a week because of the washouts on various sections of the road.

Our next destination in Himachel Pradesh was Dharamsala and the adjacent village of McCloud Ganj—a mountain top settlement perched 5400 feet above the valley floor and renowned for its collection of expat eccentrics, dropped out freaks, assorted mountaineer types and, of course, the Dalai Lama. McCloud Ganj also happened to be the centerpiece in a puzzle conjured by the famous psychic who we had consulted back in New Delhi. Because India is renowned for alternative lifestyles and religions, our Western skepticism was pummeled by the promises of Eastern mysticism.

After Ralph and I jammed in the minuscule back seat of the subcompact 4x4 and Himish and Bhoomi hopped in the front, we rocketed through the mountains dodging pedestrians, cows, goats, donkeys, trucks, busses, and road repair crews. Bhoomi relied on speed, god Siva and his blaring tape of Hindi music to negotiate all the obstacles. Our eight-hour marathon road race was especially memorable because drivers in the backwaters of India consider headlights an unnecessary drain on their vehicle's battery—headlights are only used sparingly, if at all. I was beyond caring at that point.

Whereas the Kulu Valley is one of the most picturesque locations in India, the Kangra Valley is enveloped in a perpetual haze of industrial smoke and diesel exhaust—shades of New Delhi. As our screaming little jeep charged towards the hill station, we could see monkeys scampering across the terraced fields of maze and oxen dragging wooden plows through the wheat fields.

At first glance I figured an outhouse had been inadvertently planted on the roadside. Then a bedraggled figure stepped out with a hunk of tattered rope in his hand. The drooping rope was strung across the narrow road and tied to a stump. That was my introduction to a low budget tollbooth. When our rig pulled up, the tollbooth guy jerked the rope up to block the road. After a rupee or two was passed his way, the rope dropped and we were on our way again.

Just after dusk we arrived at our hotel. Since we already had nagging doubts about the quality of accommodations in the hill towns, this rundown resort did not hold many new surprises for us. If nothing else, we made it to Dharamsala in one piece

The pale morning light held little warmth. Unable to sleep, I bundled up in my pile jacket and hat and took a predawn stroll down the McCloud Ganj's main drag. The stark peaks of the Himalayas towered above Dharamsala's pine forests. Oblivious to the chill, scarlet robed Tibetan monks roamed the hillsides. This was the land of Buddha and the never-ending search for enlightenment. Although intellectually I acknowledged the Buddhist concept that pain is inevitable but suffering is optional, I was not there. I was demoralized and I did not have a clue of what to do next.

Mr. Sengh, the SP in Dharamsala, reiterated the now familiar refrain that if our children were dead, in jail, or in the hospital, we would have been notified. The SP encouraged us to seek out John Kennedy, an expat American married to a French woman and living in McCloud Ganj. Their Ekart Guest House was head-quarters for "The International Council for the Research in the Nature of Man". As the recently christened Premananda Deve and Lakshui Devi, these folks were apparently into yoga, meditation, and psychic reflection. Unluckily they were also into padlocked doors. In the end, the best we could do was to leave one of our posters.

An itinerant Buddhist monk appointed himself our guide. Our guide and his companions lived in fifteen assorted monasteries immediately outside McCloud Ganj. Northern India, Kashmir, and Tibet boast many such monasteries—each offering a matchless setting and the attendant opportunity for revelation and insight. With his flip-flops flying and his long robes flapping, the holy man negotiated the steep footpaths like a mountain goat. Panting after him, Ralph and I eventually located the director of the Tibetan Library. Yang Chen spoke eloquently about the serenity that pilgrims seek by embracing the Buddhist philosophy. Her library offered ongoing religious and philosophical courses. Seekers are welcome to spend a day or a year or a lifetime seeking the road to enlightenment. Unfortunately she had no news of our missing children.

Good karma kept us from any roadway mayhem as we drove back to Kulu. Although our search had come to a dead end at Manali's Greenland Hotel, we were still optimistic that good news might be awaiting us back in New Delhi. We said goodbye to Bhoomi and his Hindi tapes and then walked out to our waiting airplane. As we strolled into the small airport we noticed an identical plane, sans windshield, parked on the ramp. A bird had smashed into the windshield of the daily inbound flight from Delhi and knocked the pilot unconscious. Luckily the turboprop landed safely with a very tense copilot at the controls and a senseless pilot slumped in his lap. After days and days of being slammed with disappointing news, I felt like the hapless pilot.

Back in New Delhi Himish resumed his duties at the consular office. Connie took it upon herself to debrief Ralph and I. We recounted our motoring traumas at the hands of Bhoomi. I was still in awe that Bhoomi could blow through little villages without killing or maiming anyone. As we told Connie, our driver would scatter grandmas, toddlers, goats, cows, and dogs with abandon and panache, never slowing for an instant. Stops were only made for petrol, tea, god Siva, and toll roads.

India has a selection of nasty bugs just waiting to ambush the unwary traveler. Thanks to Pepto-Bismol, Connie's care package, and judicious restaurant selections, Ralph and I managed to avoid any major bouts of Delhi Belly. Besides a good measure of luck, each of us had also had all our "jabs" back in the States. Connie insisted that Mefloquine, the most broad range anti-malarial drug available, was just going to bring us schizophrenia and delusions. She maintained that the medical community in her native Columbia was so advanced that she was given a one-time inoculation that would protect her for a lifetime. We decided to take our chances with mental illness as opposed to a dose of malaria.

Connie's driver, Mr. Chalal, chose to make the search for Tyler and Ashley his personal quest as well. Since Mr. Chalal lived with his brother at the presidential palace, our empathetic driver was able to rally a number of his cohorts to our cause. Our dragnet grew because this brotherhood of drivers seems to have connections all over Delhi. Typically we would split up and show our missing persons poster to a sympathetic assortment of backpackers and locals. The backpacking youngsters were helpful but could not recall seeing our kids. The response from the locals was a more certain, "yes, *sahib*" accompanied by an affirmative head bob. After hearing the same refrain over and over, we figured the locals wanted to make us feel good, but their information was rather suspect.

Tyler and Ashley sent postcards from Goa prior to traveling to Manali. Desperate for any scrap of information, Ralph and I decided to backtrack to the popular backpacker hangout on the southwest flank of India. We hoped to make contact with some other young people who had perhaps discussed future travel plans with Ty and Ash. It was a long shot at best, but we were fresh out of options.

Goa is an incredibly beautiful tropical destination—a drastic change from what Ralph and I had experienced up to that time. Long strands of sparkling sandy beaches and a backdrop of luxuriant emerald green jungle reminded me of Kauai. Unlike the persistent haze over New Delhi, Goa lazes under a cobalt blue sky. In the upscale, modern airport Harrier jet fighters were parked adjacent to our 737 and guard towers surrounded the airfield. The generals knew a good thing when they saw it. No reason to be stationed in Delhi with its circling vultures and open sewers when you could be sipping a G & T in the land of sand and surf.

The Portuguese were the colonial power in Goa, but the Indian government ejected them in the early '60's. If nothing else, they outlasted the era of the British Raj, which ended in the late '40's. As a result of the Catholic influence there are many historic churches in Goa, but in typical Indian fashion, the churches languish in various stages of disrepair.

Not many saris here—skirts for the ladies and slacks for the men. In Goa I did not see gigantic chunks of rock or mounds of straw or bundles of firewood being packed around on the backs of the women. The ladies of Goa definitely had it figured out because the former Portuguese outpost is the only state in India with community property laws. Vespas and motorcycles were everywhere.

The Leela Beach Resort dispatched a car and driver to deliver us from the airport to their tastefully appointed hotel, a 40-kilometers drive away. Once again the one common thread binding all of India together seems to be the male passion for driving with sheer abandon. Apparently the Hindu belief in reincarnation is a sort of safety net.

Ralph, through contacts at his law firm, enlisted the aid of Colonel Ramachandran, chief of security at the Leela Beach Resort. The colonel was an imposing presence—a tall and lanky Indian with a handlebar mustache, silver hair, and the ramrod bearing of his British military heritage. Even though the colonel smoothed the way with the local cops, both he and the local SP had little to offer.

Ralph and I rented mountain bikes for the 15-kilometer ride to Colva Beach, the backpacker village where Tyler and Ashley had stayed. Our plan was to talk with the young people who hang out on the beaches and in the bars that dot the shoreline. As we pedaled down a long stretch of deserted shoreline towards Colva, we suddenly heard the piercing scream of a jet engine. A fast mover was headed our way. We tore down the beach and away from the oncoming commotion just as a hail of gunfire shredded the jungle behind us and a jet fighter rocketed across the beach just above the tops of the palm trees. I felt like a ground hugging cruise missile had just punched me out. Fortunately for us, a late lunch is a tradition in India so we bided our time until the fateful hour. At the appointed time the fighter pilots who had been flying strafing runs over our return route all morning flew home to lunch. We saddled up and pedaled back through the free-fire zone post haste. The colonel later explained that the warning signs were not always visible, but the Indian Air Force needed a strafing range and the isolated coastline worked for them.

Goa draws young westerners into an inexpensive, Margaritaville atmosphere that features a convivial population of backpackers, hippies, dropouts, expats, and voyeurs. Kids live cheaply here. Although Ralph and I finally located the hotel where our children had stayed, we could not locate anyone who recognized their pictures or anyone who could provide the information we desperately needed.

My best memory of the place was watching a young couple, obviously very much in love, bounding through the surf hand in hand and oblivious to everyone else but themselves. I am sure calling home was the last thing on their minds. I prayed that Tyler and Ashley were living a similar dream—two great kids on a grand adventure with the world at their feet.

The lonely flight back to Seattle was a bitter reminder that Tyler and Ashley were still missing. I was exhausted, depressed, and sick at heart. Deep down I knew the worst had probably happened. Throughout my adult life I was the one in charge and in control. No more.

Back in Seattle Kate, PL and I found that we were dependent on the generosity of friends and family members. Our spirits were battered and broken. As charitable and caring as people were, I found this dependence and vulnerability difficult to accept.

My awakening had begun.

2

The Aftermath

In one of the Stars I shall be living. In one of them I shall be laughing. And so it will be as if all the stars were laughing, when you look at the sky at night...You, only you, will have stars that can laugh!

—*Antoine de Saint-Exupery,* **The Little Prince**

Kroll never discusses an investigation, whether the case is active or closed. During the first week of 1996 our families were blind sided by Kroll's demoralizing description of the fatal accident that swept Tyler and Ashley into a raging mountain river. It is extraordinarily difficult to accept the grim reality of losing a child and each of us grieved in our own way. Tears did not wash away the pain. Other than a brief summary of events leading up to the untimely deaths of Tyler and Ashley on September 4, 1995, we will never know all the facts surrounding a tragedy that changed all our lives. Since we are not encumbered by a lot of conjecture, perhaps we have been allowed to move on with our lives and put the events to rest.

The permanently endowed *Ashley Palumbo and Tyler Mondloch Memorial Scholarship*, administered by the University of Washington, has been established to honor the memories of Ashley and Tyler. The Palumbo family and our family select recipients who share the adventuresome spirit and intellectual curiosity personified by Ashley and Tyler.

After the memorial service Arish Turle, a principal in Kroll Associates, penned a very personal and poignant letter to our family. Arish reminded us that Tyler displayed monumental courage in a situation where nothing less would do. In his military service Arish marveled at the conspicuous gallantry of soldiers willing to die on behalf of their comrades and he assured us that Tyler's selfless act of bravery touched him in the same way.

Arish praised Tyler as a fine young man who was following his heart and his dreams. Our son was living life on his own terms. At the time of the terrible accident, Tyler and Ashley were acting prudently and correctly, but the events spun out of their control. As Arish sagely concluded, we should continue to follow our dream because Tyler would expect no less from us. Although we were sifting through many tangled emotions and agonizing memories, Arish's letter reminded us of what we were really all about.

We recently received a very touching letter from one of Tyler's high school friends. She shared some of her fond recollections of our son and then wisely observed, "He was in fact a piece of each of you, until love made him who he was."

Kate followed her bliss and continued on with her graduate work in art history. PL and I also followed Arish's insightful counsel and his advice changed our lives in ways we could never have imagined. The demons of our loss still haunted us, but the dream of sailing around the world brought us comfort and purpose. We returned to San Diego, provisioned our sailboat, and sailed off into our new life.

3

The Birth of a Dream

The first circumnavigation of the world launched in 1519 when Ferdinand Magellan's Armada de Molucca set out with five ships and 260 men to explore the unknown reaches of the globe. Only 18 men and one ship survived the brutal three-year voyage—Magellan was not one of them.

If you are a sailor, it is always good form to know where you are—both physically and philosophically. Although my internal compass and a bit of dead reckoning have served me well, long voyages require a bit more precision. Mariners can estimate parallels of latitude by the duration of the day, or by the height of the sun or assorted guide stars. The precise altitude of celestial bodies can be measured with a sextant. Gauging the meridians of longitude, however, is a different ball game. Longitude is a function of time. In order to determine longitude at sea, the navigator needs to know the exact time aboard ship and also the exact time at another place of known longitude at that precise moment. In 1762 John Harrison solved the greatest scientific problem of his time when he presented his portable marine chronometer to the world. With the precise time and a bit of mathematics, seafarers could now accurately compute longitude.

In the early 1980's PL and I sailed aboard a 40-foot cutter from Seattle to Hawaii. During the 16-day passage, we navigated with a sextant and steered the sailboat with a simplistic wind vane system. Despite few electronic gadgets, our four-person crew did just fine. I was hooked.

Ten years later I crewed on an ultralight 70-foot sloop from San Francisco to Hawaii. Unlike most monohull sailboats, this sailboat planed at blazing speeds and chalked up a very fast 10-day passage. The onboard GPS, a relatively new innovation at the time, insured spot-on navigational fixes. The big sloop was jammed with the latest electronic wizardry. My outing aboard the hot rod racing sled was fun but I am bonded to *Osprey,* a sailboat of a more mellow persuasion.

Our well-traveled sailboat has been a lucky talisman for PL and I. She has served as both a magic carpet and a security blanket. Since offshore sailing passages involved less than ten percent of our time, *Osprey* also served as a very homey apartment when we were moored. Ernest K. Gann wanted a boat that drinks six, eats four, and sleeps two—we found a lot of wisdom in those words.

In the last decade technology has swept through the cruising community at an unprecedented pace. Sophisticated gear helps, but long voyages on relatively small vessels are still reliant on a favorable combination of wind, wave, and weather—not to mention compatible crew. Many aspiring sailors seem to be long on equipment but short on expertise. True seamanship is about coping with the mercurial moods of the sea and keeping your crew safe. It is easy to forget that the ultimate tried and true navigation unit actually lurks between a sailor's ears.

Although we carried a sextant as a backup, scores of cruisers feel that such a practice is equivalent to stabling a horse on the off chance the family car fails. Hard-core sailors in traditional vessels still roam the oceans, but the times have definitely changed. Scores of the exotic venues from bygone days now edge closer to just being out there rather than truly out there.

We have found many guidebooks and cruising guides to be outdated, overly optimistic, whimsical, directive, and limited in scope. Our travel addiction feeds on the unexpected—a natural high that expands our senses and notches up our awareness.

Sailing off into the sunset has been an escapist notion for many centuries. Initially our sailing trip was meant to be a celebration of life. The death of our son jarred the very foundation of our lives and radically changed the entire premise of our circumnavigation. Our journey of renewal became an exploration of the human spirit—a time for deep introspection and consummate soul searching. The grand adventure evolved into a philosophical exploration of our place in the universe. Along the way I learned to let go

During the search for our missing son, we learned from Kroll that the world is a conflicted, fascinating, and sometimes dangerous place. The planet is filled with intriguing people and exotic landscapes as well as violent terrorists and scarred countries. Occasionally we encountered uncomfortable or potentially frightening situations, but we never feared for our lives. We have been fed and housed and befriended by people from all over the world who own little, share all they have, smile unabashedly, and love their countries.

Although it is satisfying to count coup as a circumnavigator, our trip around the planet was not a death defying frontal assault on the oceans of the world. Our trip was the embodiment of a dream. It was all that we could have hoped for and we learned a lot about ourselves in the process. PL and I returned healthy and content with a story to tell.

4

Shakedown Cruise

They are enmeshed in the cancerous discipline of 'security.' And in the worship of security we fling our lives beneath the wheels of routine—and before we know it our lives are gone.

—Sterling Hayden, **The Wanderer**

In the spring of 1995 PL and I moved aboard *Osprey*. It was time to savor our new personas as people of leisure. The weather was fine and the lifestyle was agreeable, but we deemed our new quarters a bit cramped compared to our house. Over the course of the summer, the constant hit of meeting new people and exploring new locales eclipsed any nostalgia we may have felt for our old life. Our social life became a blur as friends stopped by to talk it over and wish us well. We were flying high and the horizon looked deceptively clear. At the time, the concept of letting go was an aspiration but we had a long ways to go.

During our short stay in Seattle, Ashley and Tyler invited us to an outdoor concert featuring their favorite group, "The Grateful Dead." After our cross-generational dose of culture, PL and I enjoyed a wonderful dinner with Ashley and Tyler as we toasted their college graduation. To this day I vividly recall those special times because after we wished the kids well on their upcoming adventure around the world, they would pass out of our lives. I treasure our final hugs as Tyler's twinkling blue eyes casually assured us that he would take care.

After weaning ourselves from the siren call of Seattle, PL and I sailed across the Straits of Juan de Fuca into the relaxed embrace of the San Juan Islands. Over the next few months we logged 1200 miles during our roundtrip sailing trip to and from the north end of Vancouver Island.

Gliding past the shrouded, misty peaks of Jervis Inlet *Osprey* sailed into the heart of the place, Princess Louise Inlet. We stared slack jawed and wide eyed at the beautiful panorama of sparkling snowfields, sheer cliffs, and towering waterfalls. Oysters were ours for the picking as we waded through a rocky pool at the foot of majestic Chatterbox Falls. As a brilliant sunset dusted the surrounding mountains in a patina of gold, we feasted on grilled oysters and chilled beer.

The only real mishap of our entire shakedown occurred as we entered the marina at Campbell River, a fishing town tucked into the rugged terrain of Vancouver Island's east coast. At the time I figured we were in prime form, our mooring technique was sorted out, and PL and I could assure ourselves of good harbor face whenever we tied up at a dock. On this morning harbor face was the least of our concerns. Our white sloop was looking good as we shot through the thirty-foot gap separating the jagged rocks of the breakwater from the dozens of huge fishing boats moored on the inside. We rounded the north jetty of the stone breakwater with a combined 2-knot southerly ebb current and 15 knot northerly breeze pushing us downwind much faster than I had planned. Since the narrow channel was only 8 feet deep and because *Osprey* draws 6 feet of water, a little deceleration was in order. I casually shifted our engine into reverse…no reverse, nothing, *nada*. As *Osprey* continued to rocket down the ever-narrowing channel, our options were becoming more limited by the second and trouble was brewing. Our alternatives were to collide with a fishing boat, drop the anchor while flying down a very narrow channel, or lasso a moored fishing boat as *Osprey* flashed by.

PL opted for a lasso technique. Rob, a crusty fishing boat skipper, snubbed our hastily thrown line to the gigantic cleat on his purse seiner. *Osprey's* forward progress was not only abruptly halted, but she was also spun around 180 degrees and then unceremoniously slammed up alongside Rob's massive boat. Rob's mechanic friend Wayne sorted out our problem. Apparently all three bolts that coupled our transmission to our propeller shaft had sheared off—basically the transmission was not hooked to the propeller. Forty-five minutes and $25 dollars later, Wayne had installed new coupling bolts and we were back in business. PL and I celebrated our deliverance with an awesome dinner at the spectacularly beautiful April Point Lodge across the way. To complete our therapy we biked around Quadra Island the next day.

At slack tide we motored north through the infamous Seymour Narrows, a narrow passage that can generate 16-knot currents and huge tidal overfalls when the current screams through at full throttle. Before us lay the far reaches of Johnstone Strait with its fickle weather and huge semi-submerged logs, appropriately named "deadheads." Orcas seem to favor the place and we were not disappointed. Although Johnstone Strait streams as far north as Queen Charlotte Straits, I decided to duck out of the choppy seas and take a short cut to our friend's small cabin next to Green Point Rapids. I wistfully watched the parade of passing yachts as they cruised north through the protected waters of the famous Inside Passage. Although my pipe dream was a grand tour of the planet, just the thought of sailing in the far reaches of British Columbia or Alaska seemed like an almost insurmountable challenge at the time.

A sunburned meadow overgrown with wild flowers and blackberries and the hum of thousands of bees was our introduction to the abandoned native village of Mamaliliculla. Coastal Kwakiutl Indians inhabited the village until the early twentieth century when the Canadian government shortsightedly outlawed any traditional native celebrations. Former inhabitants enjoyed an unlimited bounty of shellfish so generation after generation had thrown their empty clamshells on the settlement's beach. Time and wind and tide ground the shells to bits. The bleached white shoreline gleamed mystically in a landscape dominated by huge evergreen trees and granite shorelines.

Towards the north end of Vancouver Island there are relatively few recreational cruising boats in the early spring. This is a maritime world dominated by tugboats, fishing boats, and an occasional cruise ship. The stunning beauty of the place brings with it an ethereal serenity. Morning curtains of fog rolled back by midday, and then the warm spring sun bathed the secluded coves and bays. As we sailed further north the stark wilderness and massive trees lent an evening chill to the quiet shores of our remote anchorages. At Lagoon Cove, Marie showed PL how to harvest and prepare sea asparagus for our salads. As the weeks rolled by our crew seemed to lose track of time.

"*Osprey—Osprey—Osprey*, this is *Marita Shan*. We need your help!"

I was startled by the surprise radio call since we had seen very few private yachts roaming around our neck of the woods. The emergency broadcast was from Paddy and Tashi, Canadian sailors who we had met just a week prior. *Marita Shan* was four miles to the north of us with a blown diesel engine and little wind. After I pulled alongside the wallowing ketch, Paddy assured me that his diesel was a lost cause. Motor oil was sprayed all over the engine room and the overheated engine was emitting an unhealthy crackling sound. Under normal circumstances 42 foot *Osprey* would be hard pressed to tow a huge ketch ten feet longer and twice as heavy, but I was feeling lucky. The seas were unusually calm in Johnstone Strait, the current was slack, and the wind was light. Dusk was just a few hours away and with no other help in sight, PL and I decided to tow our new friends to the tiny logging village of Port Neville. Just about sunset the small dock fronting the village post office hove into view. After we secured *Marita Shan*, Paddy called for "the good stuff" so we sat down on the ramshackle dock, sipped single malt, and talked it over. As it turned out Paddy and Tashi would be our cruising companions for the next three years.

As our homeward bound shakedown cruise edged south again, the improbable look of a European style cabin perched on a raft of logs caught our eye. Cordero Lodge is a touch of Germany in the sparsely populated wilderness to the south of Green Point Rapids. Good wholesome German food, a few German songs, and a round of schnapps add up to just the right touch. After dinner Reinhardt, our genial host, motioned us to the outside deck. It was time for the finale of the evening—feeding the resident bald eagles. Like miniature fighter planes the eagles soared above Reinhardt, just waiting for their chance. As chunks of sausage and fish hit the water the eagles swooped down, snatched their share of the evening's meal, and then returned to a towering cedar tree to enjoy their feast.

Desolation Sound is on every Northwest yachtsman's short list as a prime cruising area. Located within the deep fjords of British Columbia's isolated West Coast, Desolation rewards the weary boater with pristine anchorages, eye-popping scenery, and warm water. The trademark yellow fuselage of a Kenmore Air seaplane flashed across the treetops and then splashed down close to *Osprey*. Long time friends Denny and Andrea disembarked for a short stay aboard. The four of us swam in the shimmering waters of Laura Cove during the day and talked it over during the evening happy hour. *Marita Shan* sailed in a few days later and surprised us by hosting a sumptuous seafood dinner in our honor. Paddy briefed me on the fate of his diesel. Apparently the postmistress at Port Neville contacted a logging outfit on Paddy's behalf and explained *Marita Shan's* predicament. The crew boss dispatched a mechanic and eventually Paddy and the mechanic jury-rigged the ailing diesel so *Marita Shan* could get underway. A machine shop in Campbell River, Paddy's hometown, finished the job of resurrecting the engine.

At Bliss Landing, just a few clicks south of Desolation, PL and I visited with our friends Page and Mo who had just built a new cabin. After dinner and a rehash of our trip, another story came to light. One-year old Emma and her proud parents were also dinner guests and the story concerned them. As the story goes Page and his son had just finished building their cabin a year before when Emma's very pregnant mom stopped by for a visit. Emma decided to be born right then and there—the ultimate house warming present. Members of the

Canadian Coast Guard and the standby medical helicopter crew were there to cheer as she made her special appearance.

After saying goodbye to Page and Mo, we sailed south, caught a northerly wind in the Straits of Georgia and ended up in the beautiful Canadian city of Vancouver. Vancouver, one of our favorite cities, boasts a cosmopolitan atmosphere and vibrant lifestyle. PL and I pedaled our bikes along the winding paths through Stanley Park and strolled through the huge farmer's market on Granville Island. The Vancouver Rowing Club treated us royally. It seemed we were wrapped in the gentle embrace of the endless summer.

As *Osprey* rode the ebb tide out of Vancouver Harbor, we sheeted in her sails and caught the sea breeze in the southern Straits of Georgia. Soon we would be sailing into the familiar waters of Washington State's San Juan Islands. Towards evening we rounded a starkly beautiful headland on Stewart Island just as a resident pod of orcas came to call. The curious killer whales not only swam around our boat, but also under it. I took our up close and personal whale watching encounter to be a good omen—my former fast track lifestyle was becoming just a distant memory.

5

The Initiation

Believe me, my young friend. There is nothing, absolutely nothing, half as much worth doing as simply messing around about with boats.

—*Wind in the Willows*

A fledgling eaglet tentatively flutters its wings just as a blossoming adolescent girl shyly flaunts her new femininity, but maturing into a magnificent eagle or a beautiful woman requires time, perseverance, education, guidance, and a good measure of luck. This rather steep learning curve is also very applicable to the world of blue water sailing.

Over time PL and I encountered scores of new challenges. With patient counsel, veteran world cruisers shared their insights. I came to appreciate subtleties that escaped me before and I became less attached to my former views. It finally dawned on me that perhaps I could learn more if I was not the one doing the talking, but that would all come later.

In early August four of my friends joined me to sail *Osprey* from Puget Sound to San Francisco. Tyler was on his three-month around the world backpacking adventure, Kate was busy with graduate school, and PL was finishing a series of continuing education classes.

Although I had never sailed *Osprey* down the west coast before, I had sailed to Hawaii twice aboard other yachts as well as owning, racing, and cruising sailboats for twenty years. Conrad, Mark, Terry, and Don were also excellent sailors, but none of us had extensive offshore experience. During the next week we all learned a few valuable lessons in sailing and coping as we introduced *Osprey* to the blustery waters of the North Pacific.

The 800-mile sailing vessel trip to San Francisco is typically done either by harbor hopping down the Pacific Coast, or sailing an offshore route. The inshore route allows a series of stopovers at interesting ports and the vessel avoids the higher winds and seas of the outer waters. The disadvantage of the "hop" is prevalent fog, innumerable crab traps, and considerable boat traffic. With the advent of GPS navigation, the 125-degree meridian of longitude paralleling the Pacific Coast of the western United States is equivalent to an interstate highway for commercial vessels—the big boys set their autopilots and away they go. Wary small boat skippers in the know wisely avoid the charging behemoths.

I gambled on the offshore route, not only because the crew wanted to sail, but also because the Pacific high-pressure ridge was in an ideal location to provide northerly winds for the trip south. Even the current and swells were going our way.

As our crew settled into the onboard routine after leaving the hype of the farewell party, the first surprise occurred—the forecasted light afternoon westerly morphed into a blustery 30 knot headwind and the attendant short, steep, sloppy seas. Instead of a mellow evening sail westbound through the Strait of Juan de Fuca, our jostled crew ducked into the coastal town of Port Angeles to regroup and enjoy a peaceful night at the dock. Next day the winds died. After a frustrating day of motoring through the placid waters of the strait, we reached Cape Flattery. The first fitful puffs of breeze filled the sails as the long Pacific rollers gently lapped the hull. A breathtaking sunset painted the western cliffs of Tatoosh Island in brilliant crimson as *Osprey* came alive under the press of the building evening breeze.

I steered south past the fading images of the Olympic Peninsula as *Osprey* plunged her shoulder into the deep blue seas of the Pacific—the bottle green waters and fickle breezes of Puget Sound disappeared in our wake. A blanket of twinkling stars enveloped us in a magical spell as we glided across the crests of the gentle ocean swells.

Under her full spread of mainsail and Genoa jib, *Osprey* was in her element and her crew was beginning to relax. The next day came and went. Just before nightfall, Mark caught a fine silver salmon. I called for a celebration so our very contented crew toasted yet another fine day offshore with a fresh salmon feast.

With an excellent weather window bringing us premier sailing conditions, the crew's confidence grew so naturally I broke out our huge spinnaker. As *Osprey* raced through the sparkling seas, the ship's company was jubilant. We intended to dine like Vikings and sail boldly into the bosom of the sea.

Our comeuppance happened about 120 miles due west of the Columbia River, an area renowned for nasty weather. Rather than a massive spinnaker flying in a steady breeze, *Osprey* was now charging along under a much more conservative set of sails, but the wind continued to rise and spindrift started to blow off the tops of the towering seas. The sleigh ride continued as *Osprey* reached the latitude of Newport, Oregon. The seaside town was 150 miles off our port beam, but a world away in terms of a readily available safe haven.

Osprey careened down the faces of the now rather impressive rollers and the miles slid by under her keel. We found ourselves 190 miles due west of Port Orford, California in a developing gale. The bruised sky finally produced a sliver of cold moon with just enough light to silhouette the massive breakers that occasionally washed into the cockpit.

I decided the time was right to change course and sail closer to the coast. Since the weather was a bit on the nasty side, our crew was about to perform a jibe maneuver in heavy air. The concept was to control the jibe, a tricky tactic at best given the miserable conditions. The basic jibe maneuver involves a downwind tack—the boom, with its attached mainsail, is shifted from one side of the sailboat to the other as the boat races along propelled by the wind and waves coming from behind. Dealing with the raging wind that literally pinned the boom to the port side of our hard charging boat upped the ante considerably. A controlled jibe is not too tough in light air, but fraught with hazard in stiff winds and confused seas. Our initial jibe was textbook—controlled, quick, and effective. A curling wave caught the stern of the boat causing a violent second jibe—uncontrolled, lightning fast, and terrifying. The massive boom arched across the cockpit and slammed to a stop. Fortunately the recently installed boom brake worked as advertised. King Neptune had just served notice that we best pay attention.

The next evening, as the seas became larger and more chaotic, any thoughts of using the autopilot faded and reluctant volunteers tried their hand at steering the boat through the frenzied seas. As the ink black night gripped *Osprey* and her crew, the spiraling wake streamed a trail of phosphorus—the tail of comet captured in the obsidian waters of the raging Pacific. Since none of us had been able to sleep because of the violent motion and horrendous pounding, everyone was huddled in the cockpit in their soggy foul weather gear and safety harnesses. Suddenly *Osprey* dove off the crest of another huge graybeard and a brilliant light enveloped the cockpit. Although the consensus at the time was that the crew was seeing the end of the tunnel and someone was coming for them, in actual fact it was just the halogen flood light above the cockpit coming to life because of an electrical short in a very wet switch.

One week after *Osprey* and her crew had blissfully left the calm waters of Puget Sound, we triumphantly sailed under the Golden Gate Bridge. We had learned a few object lessons in seamanship, as well as receiving a good dose of humility. There was a lot more to come.

6

The Seafaring Life

○ ○

Never turn back and never believe that an hour you remember is a better hour because it is dead. Passed years seem safe ones, vanquished ones, while the future lives in a cloud, formidable from a distance. The cloud clears as you can enter it.

—*Beryl Markham,* **West with the Night**

Months before *Osprey* arrived in San Francisco, I had met David at Bliss Landing in British Columbia. As any cruiser would do, I helped David sort out some electrical problems on his boat. After all was said and done, David was very appreciative. He subsequently gifted us with free use of his condo slip at Pier 39, one of the nicest marine facilities on San Francisco Bay.

PL flew into San Francisco just after my crew left. We set up residence at Pier 39 right in the middle of the action at Fisherman's Wharf. San Francisco is another one of our favorite places, so it was easy to become immersed in the pulsating beat of the city.

For the next month PL and I embraced our roles as tourists on a holiday. We indulged our palates on the exotic cuisine of Chinatown and the tasty seafood at Fisherman's Wharf. We also spent days just wandering through fascinating museums and strolling along the bustling waterfront. Our mountain bikes served us well on our trips around the city.

Eventually the *Osprey* crew opted for a change of pace. Early one morning we strapped our packs to the back of our bikes and headed out. Our next order of business was to squeeze our bikes aboard the northbound ferry across San Francisco Bay. Our destination was the wine country of Napa Valley. Although there are over 200 wineries in the 30-mile long valley, PL and I knew our livers could only tolerate so much tasting. The trick was to pick and choose. Using assorted B

& B's as our temporary bases, we pedaled the historic Silverado Trail and immersed ourselves in a wine tasting extravaganza. Our packs bulged with the souvenir wine goblets as we worked our way through the valley from one end to the other.

The young guy who ran the gondola ride at Sterling Vineyards gave us an ultimate accolade when he saw us park our bikes and stow our packs; "Hey, you two bohemians really have it together!" We liked that.

Rejuvenated from our bicycle jaunt through the wine country, we stowed our collapsible bikes aboard *Osprey*. Next up on our list was motor out of San Francisco Bay and explore the inland waterways of the Sacramento River. On September 5, 1995 *Osprey* sailed under the Richmond-San Rafael Bridge and entered the muddy waters of the river. Although our side-trip was intended to explore the popular deltas and sloughs inside the levees, I still recall the inexplicable unease of that day.

The previous night I dreamed of soaring spirits and an unsettled universe, of a complex puzzle with missing pieces, of icy premonitions. I dismissed the dream as one would switch off unsolicited news on the radio, but the unrelenting vision persisted. A mystical presence had perhaps skirted the periphery of my consciousness and then flown off into eternity. Far away in India and unbeknownst to us, Tyler and Ashley died that day.

The day before PL's forty-ninth birthday we found ourselves at anchor in a mosquito-infested slough. The locals raved about Potato Slough, but the birthday girl was not happy. PL and I soon backtracked out of the fabled slough and back down the river. We found ourselves a mooring buoy on Angel Island—a naturalist's paradise in the midst of San Francisco Bay. By and by we sailed into Marin County and the charming waterfront town of Sausalito. As we were fueling *Osprey* at the local marina, I chatted with a friendly couple fascinated by our cruising plans. Fate one again intervened in the form of Jack and Mary Lou, who offered us their empty berth at Sausalito Yacht Harbor. From our newly acquired moorage, PL and I had a ringside seat to all the activity in the town plaza. Our gracious hosts gave us a personal guided tour of Mill Valley and Sausalito. Later we joined them for an evening of fine dining and good conversation. At the time our world was still a kaleidoscope of colorful evenings and sun-kissed days—it had yet to implode.

Tyler and Ashley were now overdue in Nepal. Since PL and I were accustomed to Tyler's impromptu travel adventures and erratic schedules, we just assumed the kids had to adjust their itinerary for one reason or another. PL and I were confident they would turn up. Ashley's father, from his law office in Seattle, saw a more ominous situation developing since none of his international contacts had linked up with our son and his daughter. Our friend Herb, working in conjunction with Congressman Norm Dicks, was making inquiries through US State Department channels.

After passing under the Golden Gate and sailing south, our next port of call was the yacht harbor at Santa Cruz. Our only concern at that stage was the upcoming verdict in the OJ Simpson murder trial. In retrospect, the hype about the earth-shaking verdict paled in comparison to the cataclysm about to engulf us.

Our immediate goal was to visit Monterey. Since the prospect of riding our bikes along the treacherous coastal highway bordering Monterey Bay seemed a bit dicey, we decided that hopping aboard the local Greyhound made a lot of sense. As we explained our dilemma to the travel agent, a kindly voice with an Australian twang interrupted our conversation. "Mate, what kind of yacht are you on?"

I told the fit looking older gentleman that we were sailors. Almost instantaneously a set of twinkling eyes lit up his weathered face. "Since you are sailors, I'll be happy to give you a ride."

That chance meeting introduced us to Terro, the former navigator on Australia's America Cup challenger *Gretel*. Terro, a dynamic septuagenarian, became a role model for us. Terro later confessed that if we had been power boaters he would not have been so generous.

As our new friend related stories about his ongoing sailing adventures, we discovered a brilliant man who embraced life with the enthusiasm of a youngster. Terro and I immediately clicked—kindred souls who shared a passion. We spun tales back and forth nonstop while our ladies scoped out the action in Monterey. Although visiting the first rate Monterey aquarium would typically be a day well spent, my ongoing chats with Terro eclipsed the offerings of the fish tanks. Terro promised to stay in touch and, true to his word, he eventually hosted us at the Royal Queensland Yacht Squadron in Australia. Terro was also destined to be *Osprey's* navigator during our trans-Atlantic crossing.

Santa Barbara, with its Mediterranean architecture and Southern California ambiance, was the site of our twenty-fifth wedding anniversary. To celebrate, we biked to the tiny village of Mendocito, famous for the superb Italian cuisine at Palazzio. Butcher paper covered tables and a couple of oak wine vats wedged into an alcove in the white plaster wall caught my attention. Our Italian stallion waiter explained the system. I really warmed to the concept of standing in front of the wine vat, opening the spigot, and filling my wine glass with good Chianti. A basket of color crayons at our table allowed us to keep score of our vino intake on the butcher paper.

As PL and I sipped the delicious wine and toasted one another, our paper tablecloth became filled with colorful diagrams and pictures as we blithely sketched our future. We were beginning to redefine ourselves outside the confines of our former lives. It felt good to just enjoy the moment without investing in its permanence or lasting reality.

Since we were in a festive mood, we called Seattle to tell Kate that our Silver Anniversary gifts to one another were discrete tattoos—a butterfly for PL and a compass rose for me. She applauded us. Now all four members of our immediate family shared a unique badge of distinction. As we reminisced about our close family, Kate reminded us that her Irish twin was a very capable guy and she was not unduly concerned. Our daughter is a young woman of remarkable insight and we valued her sound advice. I am sure we were all in denial and did not want to acknowledge a very frightening reality.

Normally the laid-back Southern California lifestyle would have a lot of appeal, but this was not a normal time. A week after our anniversary Tyler and Ashley were still unaccounted for and we were becoming very worried. Although our sail to San Diego was one of our most ideal passages in months, even the bow wave riding antics of our porpoise escorts could not shake our fears. San Diego is the winter gathering place for yachtsmen intending to sail south into Mexico, but we were not in the mood to socialize

The news from Seattle was not encouraging, so in late October 1995 we moored *Osprey* at Cabrillo Isle Marina on San Diego's Harbor Island, signed a long-term lease, and flew back to Seattle. PL and I had no idea when we would return to the boat or what our future plans would entail. Our sole purpose was to find Tyler.

Back in Seattle The Ashley Palumbo and Tyler Mondloch Search Committee had been organized and was pulling out all the stops. The committee networked with friends and relatives to provide logistical, legal, and financial backing for our international search. The committee sorted through mounds of conflicting information and became the conduit for our search effort.

We relied heavily on friends and family to sustain us emotionally and physically while we maintained our vigil. At times PL and I shared Kate's apartment in

Seattle, where the three of us tried to solve the mystery of the baffling disappearance.

Even with Kroll's expertise, finding Ashley and Tyler was not to be. Our family was devastated with grief, but we tried to carry on as best we could. Kate decided to continue her graduate school studies and immerse herself in the academic world. In late January of 1996, PL and I said goodbye to the people who had been so supportive of our family throughout the ordeal. We assured them that returning to our life aboard *Osprey* was the right thing for us to do. As the new chapter of our life began to unfold, PL and I knew that the pages would be splotched with tears.

7

The Awakening

We returned to San Diego, but the open wounds in our souls were slow to heal and our world became rather insular. The cold reality of losing Tyler engulfed us as we tried to get on with our lives. Grief is a bitter medicine. I blundered through the stages of disbelief, denial, anger, and acceptance but the path was elusive. Acceptance is an ongoing process with its share of reversals, detours, abrupt stops, and mad dashes—not an easy journey.

Our good friend Conrad offered to crew for us from San Diego to Cabo San Lucas. Conrad was well aware of our fragile emotional state since he had lost his son in a tragic accident a few years prior to Tyler's death. We were moved by the depth of Conrad's empathy and comforted by his frank discussions about the emotional turmoil that ensues when a parent loses a child. Conrad not only crewed aboard *Osprey* during our spirited sail to San Francisco, but he was also aboard for the trip from San Diego to Cabo San Lucas, and eventually for the Pacific crossing from Puerto Vallarta, Mexico to the Marquesas in French Polynesia. As PL and I slowly extracted the deep splinters of pain from our hearts, we became more appreciative of the unparalleled opportunities that were unfolding before us. New friends in the cruising community provided us with solace and stability.

On January 26, 1996 Conrad, PL, and I sailed from San Diego bound for points south. Since the winter migration of southbound cruisers had left two months prior, our crew encountered few other sailing vessels along the way.

The winter northwesterly breeze continued to increase over the next few days, as did our learning curve. Cedros Island, on the Pacific side of the Baja Peninsula, is notoriously windy. As we surfed down the faces of some rather impressive following seas, a tremendous blast of wind tore across our deck—*Osprey* broached into an uncontrolled jibe as the boat violently slewed across the face of a wave. The boom brake once again did its job but the preventer, a block and tackle affair meant to restrain any movement of the heavy boom, literally tore a three-foot section of aluminum toe rail from the deck. Fortunately no one was hurt, but *Osprey* had received her first real battle scar. The unexpected ambush was another one of those cosmic wakeup calls urging the skipper to get it together.

After three rather blustery days we ducked into Turtle Bay, our first encounter with a Mexican fishing village. I naively assumed that we could pull up to a fuel dock and top off our tanks just like we did back home. I learned quickly that it was a different ball game south of the border.

We anchored *Osprey* just off Freddy's dilapidated fuel pier in Turtle Bay and then went ashore in our dinghy. I squinted at our Spanish dictionary and hesitantly asked Freddy, "*Quiero cargar diesel, por favor.*" Eventually some rather dirty fuel was filtered into our portable jerry cans. In broken Spanish I pointed out to Freddy that his fuel pump's meter did not get turned back to zero. "*Lo siento, senor.*" After my introduction to grungy fuel, questionable business ethics, and inflated prices, Conrad and I lugged the heavy plastic diesel jugs back to our dinghy. Then it was a matter of a wet ride through the chop to deliver our hard won booty back to *Osprey*—a routine that would become very familiar as we cruised the developing countries of the world.

We were getting hungry so our threesome hopped back into the dinghy and went ashore to check out the dusty little village. Jesus, a self-described guide and amigo, just happened to run into us. Our new amigo assured PL that he knew of a woman who could launder our salt encrusted clothes. Under orders from PL, I motored our small inflatable back out to *Osprey* and then returned with a duffel bag of dirty clothes and a huge jug of laundry detergent. After I treated Jesus to lunch at a tiny cafe, the amigo guy went off with our laundry assuring us it would be ready by early afternoon. Conrad, PL, and I continued to check out the local digs but there was not a lot to see. After siesta time came and went, we were becoming anxious about our clothes—it was time for us to leave. As our trio was debating the next move, a young man shuffled our way bearing our bag of laundry. After forking over a large sum of pesos, we were reunited with our missing clothing. We sailed out of the harbor as PL happily unzipped our laundry bag and lifted out our immaculately folded garments. Interestingly enough not only were the clothes still dirty, but also our only jug of laundry detergent had gone missing. Welcome to Mexico.

As we continued sailing down the coast the next day, I figured that I still had a bit to learn about heavy air sailing and dealing with the local Mexicans, but I felt comfortable with our anchoring techniques. We rode the afternoon westerly breeze down to Asuncion, a modest village tucked into a protective bight and shielded from the prevailing winds. Anchoring in about four fathoms, we soaked up the spectacular sunset and marveled at the roar of the surf on the beach—suddenly our depth sounder alarm startled us with a series of shrill, loud beeps. A quick look at our depth sounder showed 8 feet…not good! But then the sounder registered the expected 24 feet, then 8 feet, and then 6 feet. I figured we were in danger of imminent grounding, but about that time a playful seal poked its head above the water and the mystery was solved. A couple of seals had decided to play tag around and under *Osprey*. As the game continued, the depth sounder alarm fired off each time the cavorting seals swam past the thru hull transducer.

Conrad's custom-made fishing lure, a white squid with a gold inlay, proved just the thing for catching tuna as we continued our sail down the coast. As luck would have it the lure also attracted pelicans, so instead of our standard albacore catch of the day we reeled in a very surprised pelican. Fortunately for all of us the hook had only snagged the pelican's back. After we extracted the barb from the wildly flapping bird, the miniature pterodactyl flew away a much wiser pelican.

A few days shy of Cabo San Lucas we stowed the sweats and pile and broke out our shorts and T-shirts. January off the coast of Baja is definitely a different proposition than the winter offerings of Seattle. We coasted close to shore past Punta Tosca as the dry mountains of the Cape, dwarfed by Cerro Picacho, appeared off our port beam. After rounding the famous rocky arches of El Arco in the wee hours, Cabo San Lucas emerged from the mist like a storybook fantasy. Our tired crew was finally able to bask in the tropical sun after the chilly 700-mile cruise from San Diego. There was no doubt that Cabo is a major upgrade from Turtle Bay, but just like our experience early on, the local hustlers seemed to know when new gringos arrive. Whether it is the newcomers doe eyed innocence or the pale skin, the vendors instinctively know that you would love to have a chilled beer and a taco or two so they are more than happy to lead you to their establishment. And while you're at it, would you be interested in a time-share?

The exorbitant moorage rates at Marina Cabo San Lucas are typical of Los Angeles, but the red tape is unique to south of the border. I was initiated into the infamous paperwork cha-cha so typical of Mexico. Bureaucrats in many foreign ports love their stamps and triplicate forms, but Mexico is definitely one of the leaders in promoting endless paperwork and frustrating rules. Veteran cruisers just shrug off the governmental hassles and play the game. The alternative is not to cruise in developing countries.

After our amazingly complicated check-in Conrad flew home. Back in Margaritaville I was unceremoniously introduced to the secret pass word that all veteran cruisers know by heart, *M-A-I-N-T-A-I-N-A-N-C-E*. On any vessel, large or small, various pieces of gear will fail from time to time and electronics seems to lead the list. Even though *Osprey* is well equipped and pampered, she is no exception. In our case the automatic antenna tuner on our long-range single side band radio failed—no tuner, therefore no long distance communication. I enlisted the aid of an expat electronic technician who tore into the tuner module and announced that a few of the transistors had failed.

Where to find new ones? Not in Cabo but perhaps in LaPaz at his friend's shop, over a hundred miles away. I was desperate so PL and I rented a car and headed north along the jarring hunks of broken asphalt that serve as a highway in rural Baja. We eventually found the out of the way electronics shop in LaPaz. I handed the shopkeeper our wish list and he started rummaging around his dusty shelves. Eventually he found just the bits and pieces we needed. *"Muchas gracias"* was definitely the operative word. PL clutched the little transistors, I fired up our Baja wheels, and we were out of there.

Roaring surf and barking sea lions lulled us to sleep at our Cabo anchorage. Offshore massive cruise ships coincided their daily arrivals with the blossoming sunrise over the Sea of Cortez—quite a sight, but eventually the thunderous barrage of noise from the cruise ships as they did their anchoring thing frayed our nerves. When the next gigantic white floating circus disgorged its hoards of tourists, we sailed for Isla Isabella. PL and I were looking forward to a bit of solitude.

Isla Isabella is over 200 miles SE of Cabo and about 20 miles from the Mexican mainland. This offshore volcanic rock pile is home to thousands and thousands of frigates, boobies, gulls, terns, and cormorants. A couple of local fishermen looked up from their net repair to graciously point PL and I in the direction of the resident bird colonies. We gingerly stepped around the scores of haphazardly arranged blue-footed booby nests that were at ground level. As we stared down at our feet, dozens of fuzzy little white hatchlings blinked back at us. Frigates clacked their beaks warning us to keep our distance from their perches. Our crew eventually fled back to *Osprey* to escape the overpowering stench of bird droppings and fish guts. Jacques Cousteau filmed a documentary about this miniature Galapagos. The Frenchmen aboard Cousteau's *Calypso* must have been tough guys just to deal with the pervasive stink day after day.

Our midday siesta was cut short when PL spied a pair of brown eyes peering into the window above our bunk. I grabbed my flare gun and hustled up on deck, ready to repel boarders. The intruders turned out to be a local fisherman and his three children. They were standing on their tiptoes inside their small dory trying to satisfy their curiosity about our boat. After some mutual nodding and smiling the fisherman muttered, "book." PL offered a magazine as well as pencils and balloons for the kids. The local shook his head in frustration. "*Playboy,*" he finally blurted. School supplies were one thing, but PL was not prepared to go the extra mile for dad.

Later in the afternoon a shrimp boat anchored next to us. With a bit of sign language, a smattering of Spanish, and a smile my clever mate charmed the shrimpers—before long a bag of fresh shrimp came our way. We reciprocated with a tin of Spam and a few packs of Marlboro cigarettes. Before we sailed south, wily cruisers advised us that a stash of Marlboro hard packs would serve us well in the Third World. Despite our nonsmoking guilt complex, we found that the Marlboro man is a well-received gift just about anywhere.

Banderas Bay, the gateway to Puerto Vallarta, was a welcome sight after sailing across the unprotected lower reaches of the Sea of Cortez. As a gentle breeze ghosted us into the sheltered waters, a majestic humpback whale and her baby leisurely crossed our bow. Mother whale apparently bonded with *Osprey,* so she happily swam beside us with her baby tucked safely under her long protective flipper. When the little humpback tried to duck under its mom for a closer peek at us, the ball game suddenly changed. The startled cow performed an awesome snap roll, tucked the youngster back under her flipper, and then she and her curious little calf were out of there.

As PL and I were savoring our magical whale encounter, a familiar Canadian voice burst from our radio, "*Osprey-Osprey-Osprey*, this is *Marita Shan*—welcome to Puerto Vallarta." Tashi and Paddy welcomed us to the La Cruz yacht anchorage and into the embrace of our new cruising family. After sadly recounting our tragic news, PL and I put on a brave face and listened to the updates about cruising Mexico. With dozens and dozens of cruising boats filling the anchorage and scores of others moored in the marinas in PV, there was no shortage of new folks to meet.

We discovered that the name of a cruiser's boat takes the place of the yachtie's last name. Our crew was now known as the *Ospreys,* PL and Kurt. No last names or stuffy titles intrude on the culture

After settling into the cruising scene in PV, our choice was to embrace the new and intriguing lifestyle or to withdraw from the yachting community and explore other paths. Some days the soul searching was a private affair, yet on other days only the input of friends would do. In the end our choice was to get on with our lives. Sailing across the Pacific would hopefully rekindle the sparkle in our eyes and the fire in our bellies.

Since it was almost two months before our April departure for the South Pacific, a Mexican road trip seemed like a good idea. With a few amigos and a venerable Volkswagen microbus, our little group chugged into the west central highlands. After being relieved of *mucho* pesos at the assorted tollbooths along the way, our wheezing VW finally arrived in vibrant Guadalajara, the second largest city in Mexico. With its huge array of shops and museums and theaters and restaurants, as well as an ideal climate, Guadalajara has attracted a large community of expat gringos. Although our backpacker class hotel was a bit on the seedy side, everyone's spirits were resurrected in the restaurants at Playa Tapatia. After a couple days of gorging ourselves on delicious Mexican food and seeing the sights, it was time to make tracks back to PV. The new Costco store on the outskirts of town was our last stop. We jammed the microbus with goodies that PL would eventually stuff into the lockers of our boat. Years later we would discover some of those same cans tucked into assorted nicks and crannies aboard *Osprey*.

Rather than stay in port waiting for our South Pacific departure in April, *Osprey* and *Marita Shan* cruised south for a few weeks. After rounding the notoriously blustery headlands of Cabo Corrientes, we sailed south to the popular cruiser hangout of Bahia Tenacatita.

Managing our dinghy in the breaking surf off the long sandy beach of Bahia Tenacatita was our baptism into the art of a surf landing. Learning to use our two stern mounted dinghy wheels in a high surf environment was a study in going with the flow. In essence the classic cruiser technique is to lower and lock the aluminum struts which support the large pneumatic dinghy wheels, tilt the outboard motor up to clear the oncoming beach, and then pray that your surfing karma is with you. The intrepid sailor attempts to time the beach approach so the dinghy catches the face of an incoming wave and surfs up on to the beach. In theory the dinghy skids onto the beach as the passengers scramble out and unceremoniously drag hundreds of pounds of boat and motor up on to the dry sand before the next huge wave engulfs the landing party. To reverse the process the dinghy is nosed back into the surf line and the crew paddles furiously until the water is deep enough to fire up the outboard. If all goes well the wheels clear the sand, the motor screams to life, and the dinghy leaps over the unforgiving breakers into the calm waters behind the surf line. As in life, some days are better than others.

Tenacatita is renowned for its jungle ride—you supply the ride. The Disneyland sort of jaunt is actually a winding three-mile long dinghy ride up the narrow Rio Boca las Iguana. Under a long canopy of overhanging mangroves, we entered a primal world of egrets, herons, and kingfishers. Just about the time PL and I were getting into the *African Queen* mode, we zipped out of the thick jungle into the far western lagoon. Happily our destination featured a small coastal village that obligingly offered good seafood and cold beer.

We sailed as far south as Bahia Navidad, the port where we would officially complete our circumnavigation of the world six years later. The folks in the small coastal town of Malaque were celebrating their version of Carnival, so we got into the spirit of the moment by dressing up in outlandish costumes, dancing around the village square, and madly throwing candy to the local children. PL and I continued our cultural immersion by hopping aboard a rickety bus and visiting a few dusty country villages. Not much activity in the towns—exactly the reason local expats decided to live in manana land.

At the local watering hole Jean of *Jambo lll* lamented that she had lost one of her anchors in the bay. Since Jean was from our hometown and she was sailing back by way of Hawaii, she had our admiration and certainly our help. I clambered into my scuba gear and PL fired up the dinghy. She putted about the bay dragging me at the end of a long rope. After scoping out my fair share of Bahia Navidad's sandy sea floor and sucking down two tanks worth of air, I spotted Jean's anchor. Soon she was reunited with her long lost anchor. Jean was the first in a procession of very competent women skippers that we would meet in our travels.

After the festivities wound down, we sailed north back towards Puerto Vallarta. A day before our return, we anchored *Osprey* at the remote fishing village of Ipala in the lee of gusty Cabo Corrientes. Although reported to be a drug running center in the '80s, the cove was now deemed safe for overnight stops. A skiff packed with school-aged children visited us in the tiny harbor. The kids came away with quite a stash of our pens, pencils, and tablets.

Being a good citizen only gets you so far and it certainly does not carry over to anchor recovery. PL, our anchor specialist, usually just pushed a foot switch to retrieve the anchor and chain, but this time our beefy electric windless struggled to get the job done. Finally our anchor cleared the water, but one of the flukes had snagged a huge hunk of rusty anchor chain. I decided that the best method of dumping the superfluous chain was to snag the twisted mess with our boat hook, dangle over the bow, hyperextend my limbs, and try to shake loose the uninvited bundle of junk. Since I was still in the formative phase of cruising, my techniques were not particularly elegant nor were they always successful. I was still on the bottom of the learning curve, but at least I was beginning to shed the viewpoint that I had all the answers.

Back in PV the annual spring kickoff party, which caters to new cruisers planning to sail "The Coconut Milk Run" to the South Pacific, was underway. Veteran sailors, as well as specialists on weather, boat repairs, and offshore survival skills offered seminars for us—a star struck audience of anxious neophytes.

> A Spanish proverb summed up the situation for most of us aspiring South Pacific cruisers: *It is not the same to talk of bulls as to be in the bullring.*

After our circumnavigation PL and I had the pleasure of conducting such seminars ourselves, but at the time my only contribution was a dental survival guide for cruisers, "Dentistry 101 for the Cruising Yachtsman." In the South Pacific cruisers showed up in our cockpit for consultations, checkups, and some very basic dentistry. Since I was usually the only game in town, cruisers always seem to know where *Osprey* was anchored. The dentistry for wine concept worked for me and there were no pesky dental insurance forms to deal with.

Conrad flew back into PV carrying our rehabilitated toe rail and a new boarding ladder in his hands. After we bolted the repaired section of toe rail back on to the hull, the battle scar from our accidental jibe off the coast of Baja was no more. Conrad, PL, and I crammed every available space with groceries, filled the water and diesel tanks, and sailed from PV on April 6, 1996. We were bound for the South Pacific and points west.

I was torn with many conflicting emotions. The bitter taste of anxiety and the haunting spectrum of nightmares were my uninvited shipmates. Although the upcoming adventure promised new and exciting landfalls, I was still trapped in the dismal world of a grieving parent. Perhaps I was just running away.

8

The French Connection

To affect the quality of the day…that is the highest of the arts.

—*Thoreau*

Our 23-day voyage to the Marquesas Islands of French Polynesia introduced us to long-range passage making on the high seas. Although coping with periodic doses of 30 knot reinforced trade winds got our attention, the 2800-mile journey was relatively uneventful. With three of us aboard the night watches could be split into four-hour shifts so each of us could luxuriate in eight hours of uninterrupted sleep. During the day our crew idled away the hours tweaking the sails, repairing bits and pieces, catching an occasional tuna, reading, or simply watching the vast ocean roll by.

Although it is an acquired taste for many people, I found long ocean passages to be mesmerizing and addicting. I was able to loosen my grip on the intense sorrow that still haunted me. Nights in the far reaches of the Pacific were surreal and mysterious. Overhead thousands of stars twinkled under the immense canopy of the endless sky. I was convinced that the occasional shooting star was the embodiment of my son watching out for us. On moonless nights the dim red glow of the cockpit instruments and the red-green-white probing colors of our tricolor masthead navigation light were like guideposts in the middle of the black featureless ocean. The tantalizing glow of our bright tricolor light was a beacon for wandering frigate birds that would soar beside the light for hours during the dark Pacific nights.

Cooking on our gimbaled stove as the boat rolled, pitched, and yawed in the heavy trade winds added a new dimension to chef's challenges. Conrad baked fresh bread. The crunchy loaves were so delicious that they disappeared before they had time to cool. PL continued to produce gourmet fare from her small gal-

42

ley, a high point of our day. The designated cook always wears a heavy rubber apron to prevent being scalded by a hot entrée that may suddenly slosh out of the pan. Plates and tables are strictly calm weather accoutrements, so at sea our meals were eaten from substantial plastic bowls balanced on our laps.

The weather was balmy and the NE trades just happened to be going our way. The downwind sailing in steady trade winds was a fine ride, just as advertised. Then the fluky weather of the equator's doldrums interrupted our westward passage. Being becalmed for two days was definitely a recipe for frustration as *Osprey* wallowed, the sails drooped, and the crew prayed for wind. Suddenly huge green blobs invaded our radar screen and these moldy looking creatures packed a punch. Towering black clouds surrounded us as torrential rain, bursting thunderclaps, and violent lightning strikes announced our arrival into the Intertropical Convergence Zone, the ITCZ.

Sailors who have not crossed the equator are known as Pollywogs. After an equatorial crossing, King Neptune bestows the title of Shellback on the intrepid voyager. Eventually the warm kiss of the SE trades lifted our spirits as *Osprey* crossed into the Southern Hemisphere and caught the fresh tropical breeze. Our crew of newly minted Shellbacks watched the Northern Hemisphere disappear in our boiling wake as we sailed into the enticing waters of the South Pacific.

From the eastern islands of the Marquesas to the western island of Bora Bora, French Polynesia spans a good size chunk of the South Pacific. The French protectorate includes over a hundred islands scattered across a section of ocean the size of Europe. Our course mirrored the westward track of the sun. After exploring the Marquesas Islands, we eventually sailed through the Tuamoto Archipelago, and then on to the Society Islands of Tahiti, Moorea, Huahine, Raiatea, Tahaa, and Bora Bora.

After days of corkscrewing down the faces of some rather lumpy seas, an apparition materialized to the west. In the blossoming glow of the tropical sunrise, the emerald green mountains of the Marquesas appeared on our horizon. Renowned as some of the most remote islands on earth, the sheer cliffs tower almost 4000 feet above the Pacific. Robert Lewis Stevenson compared the landscape to the pinnacles of some ornate and monstrous church.

The island of Hiva Oa was our first port of call in the South Pacific. Even though Captain Cook may have discovered a favorite harbor over two centuries ago, cruisers tend to feel a bit territorial if another vessel shows up. As *Osprey* poked into the harbor of Baie Taahuku, I was astounded to see a couple dozen other cruising sailboats anchored in the lagoon of my dreams. After we dropped the anchor Conrad, PL, and I flopped into our bunks for the first uninterrupted night of sleep in weeks. Next day my territorial tendencies melted away as we met some of our new cruising neighbors. Over the course of the next six years we would periodically meet these same fine people in far-flung harbors around the world.

It was time to scrub down the boat and organize all the paraphernalia that had been scattered around during our bouncy trade wind passage. PL had piles of very ripe laundry that needed attention, but the only laundromat consisted of a cement slab with two concave pits. A spigot of water was attached to the adjacent concrete wall and a hole in the side of the pits acted as a drain. On the other side of the concrete wall was an outdoor shower just in case one was so inclined. Inhibitions evaporate when the prospect of a long leisurely shower with unlimited water in a non-rolling environment suddenly comes your way. After three weeks at sea, the stream of water was deliciously cold and a welcome relief from the hot and muggy weather of the tropics. Besides scrubbing away an accumulation of salt, I also flushed away many of my former notions of how things should be. For the first time in a long time I was feeling good.

Although taxis and buses do not exist on these small islands, many of the locals drive brand new Toyota 4-wheel drive pickups. We eventually learned that the nice rides are rolling examples of French subsidies. The work ethic did not compute with the locals. The favored activity seemed to be chatting with one another under a shady coconut palm while sipping Heineken beer and chomping on Cheetos. Although heart disease is endemic among the huge natives in the Marquesas, canned New Zealand corned beef is still the favored entrée. Fishing, or for that matter eating fish, does not seem to be part of the islander culture.

Our threesome hitchhiked our way around the island. The people were friendly and seemed happy to help us out if they could. After I checked in with the local French gendarme, it was off to the grocery store, post office, and bank. The prime exports from the Marquesas are the gorgeous collectable stamps, but making a purchase at the understaffed and disorganized post office challenged our patience. The priorities at the local bank seemed to be their two-hour lunch break and a slow, languid pace. These were valuable insights into just how things really work, or do not work, in the South Pacific.

During our three-week exploration of the Marquesas, we gorged ourselves on papayas, bananas, mangoes, pineapples, breadfruit, and grapefruit-like pamplemousse. Unlike the locally grown fruits and vegetables, imported food is very expensive and there is little to choose from. PL boycotted cereal for $8, but she finally forked over $5 for a dozen eggs. The French government subsidizes staples like butter and baguettes, so for thirty cents I would spring for a fresh baguette. Instead of a newspaper box, a common fixture in French Polynesia is the gaily-painted tubular baguette box. Each morning the local citizens stroll out of their house and extract a fresh baguette from their *boites de pain.*

Herman Melville and Jack London were both captivated by the exquisite scenery of the Marquesas. Paul Gauguin lived out his days with a native girl as he sketched the tattooed locals. As PL and I strolled the sandy shores of the tropical paradise, everything seemed to be right with the world. Then the no-nos and mosquitoes swarmed us. We slathered on every manner of repellant from Jungle Juice to Skin-So-Soft, but none of it fazed the no-nos. It became quite apparent why most folks avoided the beaches. Although the French provided free inoculations at the local clinic to prevent the extremely disfiguring tropical disease of Elephantiasis, the only sure-fire protection against the marauding no-no was to wrap our bodies in some sort of a cocoon when they were about.

Geoff, an expat Parisian, subsisted in a broken-down little shack at Baie Hanameau. The resident beachcomber pronounced the place paradise as he lighted coconut husks in an effort to smoke out the hordes of circling mosquitoes. Since it was a hot and muggy day, Geoff invited us to bathe in the cool waters of his mountain fed pool. Red and white hibiscus, fragrant Tahili Tiare, stunning Birds of Paradise, and assorted trees of lime, lemon, and pamplemousse surrounded the bathing area—there was even an overhanging Banyan tree…magic. But as I toweled off on the sandy beach, the infamous no-no itch assaulted my feet and ankles. I mumbled a hasty *"Adieu"* to our host as our crew raced for the dinghy.

"Watch out for the hammerheads," the French hermit warned as we dragged our dinghy out through the surf.

Over the next few days I spread our entire stock of calamine lotion and A & D ointment over my sorely bitten legs, but the itch just kept on coming. I attribute my eventual recovery to PL's nursing talents and the therapeutic properties of gin & tonic. If nothing else I learned not to go scampering around bare footed on South Pacific beaches.

More recently there is trouble in paradise. The TV show *Survivor* has altered the way of life on Hiva Oa. Apparently *Survivor* was due to be filmed on location in Jordan just prior to the terrorist attacks on 9/11, but after the brutal suicide mission Hollywood figured the Middle East was probably not a good choice. Since the passive inhabitants of the Marquesas are the antithesis of fanatical religious zealots, the island of Hiva Oa answered the siren call of Hollywood. Taioa Bay has been the home of Daniel and Antoinette for the last thirty years. Crusty old Daniel had cultivated the area around his small shack so he could offer all manner of homegrown fruits and vegetables to visiting cruisers. Daniel also ran a hose from a hillside stream to a spigot on the beach so yachts anchored in his cove could replenish their fresh water supplies. Small wonder that Hakuai Cove became known as Daniel's Bay.

Under pressure from the authorities, Daniel had to relinquish his cove to the 200-person crew of the Aussie and American *Survivor* staff. A luxury cruise ship from Los Angeles provided air conditioning, accommodations, and food for the staff, actors, and production crew. Ashore a bulldozer demolished Daniel's beach place and men in white ghost buster suits sprayed insecticide so the resident no-nos would not bother the film crew. Cruising yachts were banned from the bay and the small local markets found their shelves emptied by the eager eaters from Hollywood. After the onslaught was over, Daniel was gifted with a brand new prefab two-room house but the face of Daniel's Cove had been changed forever.

Rose's Keikahanui Inn at Baie de Taiohue on Nuka Hiva hosted our farewell dinner with Conrad. As we feasted on our peppered rib-eye steak entrees, we toasted Conrad as a fine shipmate and a good friend. PL and I would miss his spiritual insights and his nautical expertise. Conrad empathized with us during our brooding moments and rejoiced with us when the cloud of despair drifted away.

Next morning, while Conrad endured a kidney jarring truck ride up a pot-holed jeep trail to reach a small mountainside airstrip, we weighed anchor. At this juncture PL and I now had only each other to sift through the emotional upheaval of the past, deal with the present, and plan for an uncertain future.

After a bumpy four-day, 500 mile sail to the Tuamotu Archipelago, *Osprey* was practically on top of Isla Manihi before I sighted the low-lying palm trees. Unlike the jagged mountain peaks of the Marquesas, the Tuamotu Archipelago is a scattered collection of 78 islands, which are only a few feet above sea level. Not many accurate charts exist of this area and many of the original navigation charts were drawn a century or two ago. As other cruisers had warned us, even though our onboard GPS was right on, the atolls could be slightly lost by a mile or two.

In the tropics it is prudent to negotiate dicey reef passages with the sun at your back between midmorning and early afternoon. The sunlight exposes many potential hazards in vivid colors. Midnight blue water is very deep. As the color spectrum shifts to lighter hues, a wary navigator's pulse kicks up a few beats. Shoaling water runs the gamut from a safe navigable depth of dark turquoise to the iffy shoal draft depth of pale green—a subtle warning that any mariner takes seriously. Yellow tinged water is synonymous with very shallow coral heads and the promise of an unceremonious grinding halt.

Boats enter the inner lagoons of atolls through natural breaks in the encircling barrier reef. A few of the atolls feature wide and deep entrance channels, but typically the entry is tortuous and shallow…and dangerous. Experienced sailors negotiate atoll entry channels at slack low water. A blasé approach can lead to a disastrous encounter with breaking surf, surging currents, and unforgiving coral.

Hitting a coral head, or bommie, is a dangerous business. Many sailboats have been lost in the Tuamotu because of inattention, sudden weather changes, or just bad luck. The Tuamotu is a "black hole" as far as accurate weather information is concerned. The first sign of weather trouble is usually an unexpected wind shift to the north, a warmer and lighter breeze, and a rising barometer. Soon a violent squall rolls in bringing a wind shift to the south with intense wind gusts—a recipe for disaster if the yacht happens to snag its anchor chain on a bommie, or if the crew has anchored too close to a lee shore.

Even though the Tuamotu atolls are relatively isolated, there are small communities with schools and stores and churches. The *Aranui*, a freighter from Papeete, makes the rounds. The freighter delivers all manner of supplies, so the natives lived relatively normal lives even though they are far removed from the more populated islands of French Polynesia. The Tuamoto rates as one of our favorite destinations and score our rare Shooting Star Award—Tyler's signature accolade for the best.

The sandy bottom and clear waters of Manihi's picturesque inner lagoon have created a fine, secure anchorage. Ashore coconuts are easy to gather, and if you are quick, the skittish coconut crabs make a tasty entree. Even in this remote village, the subsidized baguette was alive and well. Manihi is renowned for its black pearl farms. Since the Japanese-owned pearl farms have come to town, the locals have acquired motor scooters and speedboats, as well as satellite dishes and televisions. Even with their new affluence the self-sufficient residents of the arid Tuamotu are friendly and outgoing, much more so than the natives of the Marquesas with their welfare mindset.

PL befriended four young men who were pearl divers. The guys arrived in their small skiff and offered to trade black pearls for liquor—it was their day off and they were definitely in the party mode. We shared pictures of our family and told them about life in the United States. In turn the party animals gave us the lowdown on sharks. The native divers maintained that black tip sharks would swim away from us, but that we should swim away from white tip sharks. Their parting admonition was to "leave the water quick" if a tiger shark is about. As we heard time and again it is best not to encounter tigers and great whites, the aggressive territorial eating machines. After an enjoyable visit, PL came away with a handful of black pearls and the boys happily sped away with a bottle of firewater.

Snorkeling in the Tuamotu is simply the best. Giant clams with their brilliant magenta, cobalt blue, or emerald green lips peeked from behind the coral beds. Black-tip reef sharks, parrot fish, angelfish, puffer fish, needlefish, sea bass, and perch swam along with us—a crystal clear, 85-degree aquarium.

One of the few downsides of living in the tropics is dealing with the inevitable coral cuts or insect bites. The hot muggy climate is not conducive to fast healing, and exposure to the salt water actually inoculates the inflamed area with microscopic coral spores. PL encountered this problem first hand when a raw insect bite became infected and a large abscess developed on her hip. After sifting through every medical text on board I came up with a plan. The very intense regime of treatment involved draining the abscess, administering antibiotics and anti-inflammatory drugs, dressing the wound with topical antibiotics, and catering to my first mate's every wish—the princess treatment proved to be the most effective therapy.

Rangiroa is the second largest atoll in the world with a circumference of 100 miles—lots of room to roam. Passe de Tiputa is an easy entry compared to challenging access of the smaller atolls. The lagoon, with its shimmering azure water, is the quintessential picture perfect South Pacific anchorage.

Our collapsible mountain bikes were just the ticket for exploring the villages scattered around the atoll. The heartwarming sight of a tiny motor scooter sagging under the bulk of a huge grinning islander, together with his three children and their assorted fishing poles, set the tone of the place.

Rangiroa is action central for cruising sailboats and so our group of new friends expanded rapidly. Now in the middle of the Pacific, our cruising family added an Australian boat, *Dolphin Spirit* with Laurie and Carol and son Ryan. Dorothy and Gary from *Gigolo*, as well as Sue and Steve from *Pilgrim*, made up the California contingent. Washingtonians included Heather and Dave aboard *Promises* and Tammy and Steve of *Skybird.*.

We absorbed ourselves in the world of moray eels, eagle rays, reef sharks, and all sorts of exquisitely colorful tropical fish. Our copy of *Fishes of Polynesia* became dog-eared as we researched the fish we had spied during our snorkeling expeditions. The ultimate snorkeling hit was our drift dives on the eastern side of Passe de Tiputa. The trick is to catch the incoming current just before slack water so the water is smooth—not much point in getting bashed on a coral motu.

To cap off our week of underwater exploration, PL and I temporarily retired masks and flippers for our party clothes as we joined a Tahitian feast at the upscale Kia Ora Village. Sensual Tahitian dances, tropical drinks, and delicious French entrees made for a very memorable evening. The Southern Cross, rather than the more familiar North Star of the Northern Hemisphere, glimmered in the enormous tropical sky above our dance floor.

In western Mexico most of the sailboats are home ported on the West Coast of the USA and Canada. In the far-flung anchorages throughout the Pacific we encountered more of a cross-section of the world cruising fleet. As the number of American boats shrunk going west, our cruising family began to include sailors from England, France, Germany, Italy, Norway, Switzerland, South Africa, Australia, and New Zealand. Many of these veteran global cruisers considered a circumnavigation of the world a reasonable approach to life. In this rather unique fraternity, time is not an issue and letting go just comes with the territory—I was beginning to get the picture. The Aussies and Kiwis insisted that it would just get better as we cruised west across the Pacific. They were right on.

The weeks rolled by, but eventually the lure of the big city lights enticed us to see what Tahiti was all about. After our blissful days of island hopping, it was culture shock to arrive in bustling Papeete with its noisy traffic, expensive stores, and clamoring citizens. The new downtown quay is packed with an international collection of cruising sailboats. The yachts are all jammed together side-by-side, sardine style, and each is Med-moored at a right angle to the city pier. We noticed that one end of each vessel was tied off to the jetty and the opposite end secured to the vessel's own anchor.

The Med-moor technique originated in the crowded harbors of the Mediterranean. The challenging time-honored Med-moor is renowned for securing a maximum number of boats in a minimal amount of space. North American cruisers are used to expansive docks and side tie moorages, but it is a different playing field in the rest of the world.

Anxious to join the hard-core ranks of the world cruisers, I paid close attention as an expert European sailor performed the Med-moor maneuver. After plunking his anchor into the harbor, the suave yachtsman shifted his sailboat into reverse, revved up his diesel, and casually backed towards the concrete quay as the anchor chain rumbled out of the boat's chain locker. Since Euros seem to favor the wedge approach, my French mentor nonchalantly jammed his boat between two other yachts and then tied the stern of his vessel to the quay. After tensioning his anchor chain, my new hero lowered a *passerelle,* or gangplank, onto the pier and, with a dash of Gallic aplomb, strutted ashore. Well, our learning curve soared to new heights, but *Osprey* did eventually end up tied stern-to and sandwiched between two other boats like a Vienna sausage stuffed in a tin can.

Med-mooring is merely an introduction to the mystique of international cruising. Once we left North America our familiar 110-volt electric shore power was replaced by a very foreign 220-volt shore power source and a bewildering array of connectors. Rather than the familiar embrace of rubber fenders against a dock, long range cruising boats spend their time either at anchor or Med-moored next to an unforgiving concrete pier.

Papeete is a bustling place—definitely not an island time operation. PL restocked our refrigerator with fresh meat, tasty fish, and beautiful vegetables, but at a price. Almost anything our heart desired was available in Papeete, however the astronomical costs convinced us that we did not want a lot. Fortunately our lockers were still jammed with canned goods from Mexico. The ultimate, cheap dining bargain in Papeete was *les roulettes*—innovative vans that offered all sorts of delicious, inexpensive food. The four wheeled portable cafes pulled up to the quay, flipped up their hinged canopies, and dinner was served.

Picking up our mail at American Express was a major event—Internet cafes and email still did not compute for the *Osprey* crew. We pulled up a chair at a shore side bistro, ordered a latte, and then read and reread each treasured letter. Although the sentiments were genuine and the letters welcome, I found that I was unconsciously loosening my attachment to our former world. I felt strange and a little disjointed, but almost relieved. I was becoming more a creature of the moment.

Some cruisers opted to forward international mail to the local harbormaster. I thought about the idea until Papeete's harbormaster showed me his file cabinet of forwarded mail. He opened the beat-up cabinet and suddenly torrents of torn, smudgy, and ancient letters from all over the globe fell on the floor. Cruisers always have the option of sifting through the mess and I suppose the postal gods could smile on you.

Sunday Mass was our magic moment in Papeete. The first service was in Chinese and it was so intriguing that PL and I decided to stay for the French version. A lively Polynesian choir boomed out their special brand of music. The dynamic priest seemed to be the personification of Jesus Christ. Both of us sat dumbstruck watching the bearded young man preach. As we tried to absorb the gist of his French homily, the Mass continued and the hymns became more spirited. The priest raised his golden chalice to the heavens. Then, in a vibrant French baritone, he consecrated the wine. A tropical downpour suddenly materialized, replete with thunder and lightning. We just waited for the roof to peel back and for the priest's ascension to heaven. As the torrents of rain sluiced down the gutters, I dug deep into my pockets when the collection plate was passed. I wanted to cover all our bases after the astounding service. After Mass we hung out in the church waiting for the rain to stop. The dramatic ceremony had captivated us. The only blip on the mystical morning was that I forgot to close the overhead hatches aboard *Osprey*. Not only was the church inundated with the downpour, but also the inside of our boat was soaked from the priest-induced cloudburst.

The next week the crews of *Promises* and *Osprey* decided to attend the Protestant church. As we strolled towards the church, PL and Heather noticed all the women wore white dresses and the men sported tropical suits. Most spectacular of all were the ladies' hats. The straw hats were big and beautiful and adorned with ribbons, flowers, feathers, and other tropical delights. Our ladies opted for the princess look—stunning garlands of fresh cut flowers woven into floral crowns.

PL and I rented an overpriced beater Fiat to check out the island. The missionaries have been busy in Tahiti ever since Captain Cook made landfall. Massive stones that once formed the island's huge *marae* temple complex have been broken up to pave the local roads. But even though the London Missionary Society has given it their best shot, there are not many native Tahitians industriously fishing or farming these days.

If a sandy beach did not attract no-nos, then it seemed to attract a number of fascinating hedonistic specimens. Topless French and *demi* (islanders of mixed European and Polynesian extraction) women idled away the hours lazing in the sun and preening both themselves and their children. In Polynesian society many families raise the youngest child in the family as a girl, whether they are born male or female. The *mahus* dress like women and perform traditional female duties. The tourist brochures never mention Papeete's *mahus* or the transvestite clubs, but they are part of the social fabric of the islands.

The blasé Euro approach to smoking is well ingrained in Tahitian life. "*Defense de Fumer*" is posted inside busses and cafés, but the supposed prohibition does not stop the locals from firing up their beloved cigarettes. A sage writer observed that having a smoking area in a restaurant is like having a pissing area in a swimming pool.

The great heart-shaped island of Moorea, dominated by Mt. Muaroa and sculpted by Cook's Bay, was a welcome break from the relatively fast pace of Tahiti. The volcanic peaks and spectacular bays bear a striking resemblance to

James A. Michener's mythical island of Bali Hai. We clicked off a lot of miles on our bikes as we pedaled past the huge pineapple plantations and sprawling cattle ranches of the Opunohu Valley. Pumping our way up the last few kilometers to Belvedere lookout paid off with an awesome view of Cook's Bay and a very tiny *Osprey* far, far below our perch. Bracing ourselves against the heavy wind gusting across the peak and down into the bay, it was easy to imagine the havoc a *Maramu,* or southerly gale, could wreak if it ripped into the anchored cruising fleet.

Snorkeling is impressive in Cook's Bay, to a point. We were less than thrilled by our chance encounters with a number of orange tufted zebra fish and camouflaged stonefish, two of the most toxic and deadly fish in the tropics. These notorious critters are renowned for inflicting painful and debilitating stings on unwary folks who inadvertently step on them. Reef sandals prevent such nasty outcomes, so very bright and very French rubber booties became part of our standard swimming attire.

It is a given in the cruising community that no matter how expensive the yacht or sophisticated the equipment, eventually something will break—usually at the most inopportune time. The major offenders are electric autopilots, water makers, generators, and refrigeration systems. When our number popped up unexpectedly, it was our refrigeration compressor that packed it up. I thought our ice cube days were over until I met Dave on *Blue Ribbon*. Dave expertly handled refrigeration repairs, which had financed his cruising lifestyle for the past 17 years. Dave ordered a new compressor from the States and assured me that eventually a yachtie would pick it up in Papeete and deliver it to us at our anchorage in Moorea. Amazingly enough, in the finest tradition of the yachting community, our new compressor actually showed up aboard Jack's sloop *Newsboy* a couple of weeks later.

In the meantime we greeted every new boat we meet with, "Hi, our names are Kurt and PL, do you have any ice?"

Since Huahine is only six miles wide and ten miles long, PL and I decided to pedal our bikes around the island and check it out. Unlike the more touristy Society Islands, Huahine favors pineapple plantations over T-shirt shops. At an intimate little bistro on the windward shore of Huahine, an elegant gray haired lady accepted our invitation to share a table. Monique nodded appreciatively as she learned about our adventure. In blazing French she directed the waiter to bring a bottle of good French Bordeaux to our table. As we toasted one another, she animatedly shared her story. Monique was a retired photojournalist on her own personalized grand tour of the world. Although this intriguing woman traveled alone, she assured us that she was neither lonely nor in a hurry.

Her goal, "Gather memories for her old age." Her favorite city, "Paris."

Huahine boasts an extensive barrier reef that encourages a lot of exploration. Our inflatable dinghy was our passport to the remote coves and pristine undersea gardens inside Huahine's barrier reef. About the only downside of Huahine was the grumpy local gendarme who was stationed in Fave town. The concept of island time eluded the homesick Frenchman.

One of my finest sailing memories is gliding across the crystalline blue water inside the huge protected lagoon at Raiatea. The rippled seas of the lagoon lapped against the hull as *Osprey* ghosted along in the gentle warm breeze. It was certainly a radical departure from the jarring, bumpy seas we typically found on our interisland passages.

As we savored tasty French seafood at the Apoiti Marina in Raiatea, an expat Frenchman by the name of Claude introduced himself. Claude is a schoolteacher who settled in French Polynesia because of…well, the money. With a multiyear teaching contract at 170% of his pay in France, the lifestyle is an attractive choice for a guy like Claude who lived aboard a sailboat in the harbor at Uturoa. Since only about 5% of the locals attend college, most of the professional and managerial people in French Polynesia are imported from France. That explained the nasty cop in Huahine.

After dinner we hopped aboard Claude's truck for a ride through the lush countryside to the tiny seaside village of Opoa. By and by we got our own personal tour of the largest marae in the South Pacific, Taputapuatea. For the ancient Polynesian Maohi, Raiatea was known as Sacred Havai'I—center of royalty, religion, culture, history, and heraldry. Claude went on to say that the massive black stone temple complex had been in use until the early 1800's. Dedicated to the war god Oro, Taputapuatea was the historical epicenter for the great canoe voyages that fanned out on their own voyages of discovery throughout the South Pacific. In the old days human sacrifice was popular so there was a downside to being a beautiful virgin. Although Claude was fascinated with the ancient islander religions, he was even more focused on the political situation.

Claude proclaimed that "…wealthy Frenchman do not come to French Polynesia. *Demis* control politics and the Chinese control business."

As our resident guide rambled on, we learned that Frenchmen who invest in French Polynesia bring home their money tax-free after five years. Claude proclaimed that Paris crime syndicates laundered drug money in the Society Islands but the influx of francs was a huge boost to the stagnant island economy. After seeing dozens of brand new 4-wheel drive trucks motoring about the Marquesas, I had been curious how the locals paid for the fancy wheels. Claude had the answer. The French government allows French citizens to deduct the cost of the trucks since they were theoretically driving on primitive coral paved roads. Our host wondered about the fate of the islanders since France had recently stopped its nuclear testing and was shrinking its massive subsidies to French Polynesia.

After all his ranting and raving, Claude lit up a cigarette and confessed that he would retire in Raiatea. He envisioned a languid existence of drinking wine, making love, and staring at the sea.

Enclosed in the same barrier reef as Raiatea, diminutive Tahaa is renowned as the Vanilla Island. The trick is navigating through the maze of nasty reefs. Barrier reefs are typically not solid walls of impregnable coral—there are usually chinks in the armor. The key is to locate the chinks since GPS technology is ineffective when mated to charts drawn in Captain Cook's day. PL was our spotter as I gingerly motored past sharp coral heads lurking in the dark turquoise water. With the high sun at our back, the telltale blacks and browns of shallow coral reefs contrasted vividly to the bottle green of deeper water and the aquamarine of a sandy bottom. After PL located the perfect patch of sand, our anchor splashed down and the pressure was off. The rich aroma of vanilla perfumed the air.

With our friends from *Promises*, we boarded a Land Rover for a tour of one of the island's sprawling vanilla plantations. As the owner demonstrated how to graft and harvest vanilla plants, he explained that the future of Tahaa is bright. The French planter pointed out that Polynesia is renowned for having the most equitable climate and least labor-intensive lifestyle in the world. The French perceive themselves as the worker bees in modern French Polynesian culture, leaving the native Polynesians to their indolent and lazy lifestyle.

An immense necklace of coral protects the exquisitely beautiful lagoon surrounding Bora Bora. Motu islets dot the serene anchorages. Most mornings brought golden sunshine and a sapphire sky dotted with billowing puffs of white clouds. Sunbeams captured the jutting spires of Archipels Croisieres. Memories of wet cloudy weather began to fade as we slowly turned a deep shade of brown to match the color of the coconut shells holding our evening cocktails. During our month in Bora Bora it seemed as if we were living inside an impressionist's painting.

As we snorkeled the crystal clear waters of the sprawling lagoon, majestic stingrays would streak by us in squadron formation. Sometimes in the afternoon we would gather our friends, lash our dinghies together, and drift across the placid anchorage as we sipped sundowners and applauded another day in paradise.

Riding our bikes around the six-mile circumference of the island was a reality check and a study in the real estate mantra of "location-location-location." The west side of Bora Bora featured luxury hotels and cabanas where the gorgeous aquamarine lagoon lapped the sandy beaches. As we pedaled around to the east side of Bora Bora, the contrived South Seas persona of the resorts disappeared. The native islanders lived in a collection of old Quonset huts, dumpy houses, and broken down hovels. Bora Bora's barrier reef has only one narrow entrance to the sea, yet effluent is dumped into the lagoon with no thought about the environmental consequences.

Once we sorted out our timing, PL and I could make the circuit in three hours, just in time for lunch at Bloody Mary's restaurant. The legendary Mary's, although a bit of a tourist trap, was the ultimate funky restaurant boasting sand floors, a stone washbasin fed from a waterfall, cascading tropical flowers, fish entrees fresh from the lagoon, and Jimmy Buffett memorabilia—my kind of place.

Bora Bora's major draw in July is the eagerly anticipated Bastille Day festivities in the main village of Vaitape. Dancers from throughout Polynesia compete for the coveted best of show prize during *Fete*. The staccato beat of the drums, the exotic headdresses, and the sensual dances of the contestants weave an exotic South Seas mood. As with the equally sensual Tango of South American fame, Tahitian dances celebrate sex. Authors have likened the intimate dance routines to the vertical celebration of horizontal desire.

Many of the locals disliked the paternalistic attitude of the French and reverted to their own Tahitina language. Behind the grandstand PL stumbled upon a group of huge Polynesian grandmothers, all decked out in flowing white dresses and flowery hats. The matronly ladies were exchanging puffs on a couple of shared cigarettes, like teenagers sneaking behind the barn.

The dancers wore down after a long day of competition and so did we. We hiked back to the quay where scores of bobbing rubber inflatables were tied together. Because our dinghy was no longer adjacent to the dock, I suggested to PL that perhaps a modest jump from the dock would land her in our inflatable unscathed. Unfortunately PL managed to crack a rib when she tripped on an errant dinghy line, fell into our inflatable, and crunched into the outboard motor. My mate was no longer a happy camper. I kept my own counsel as I helped her to her feet. The first aid of choice was a couple turns of ace bandage around her midriff, a few pain pills, profuse apologies, and a frosty gin & tonic—not necessarily in that order.

Arnold's Weather Net, one of our few sources of weather information, predicted 35-knot winds and twelve-foot seas for our upcoming 600-mile passage to the Cook Islands. I decided to hang around until the weather sorted itself out. Our friends Nick and Joan had just flown in to join us on the next passage so it was just a matter of waiting for the next weather window. *Pilgrim* had sailed for the Cook Islands a day prior, but got run over by the nasty weather system.

About 100 miles to the west, Sue cranked up *Pilgrim's* radio and called for help. Steve had severely lacerated his thumb while securing their wind generator and Sue was frantic. The only reasonable alternative was for the exhausted crew to turn *Pilgrim* around and bash back to Bora Bora so Steve could receive professional medical help.

A day later a very battered *Pilgrim* emerged from behind the breaking seas off Bora Bora's outer reef. After *Serenade's* fast inflatable dinghy delivered her skipper Kirk and myself to the wildly pitching sailboat, we sailed *Pilgrim* through the barrier reef and into our anchorage. Nick stabilized Steve's injured thumb and a tot of brandy was passed around. Since Brian of *Renaissance* was fluent in French, he pleaded Steve's case with a French physician ashore. Ultimately Steve hopped a flight to Papeete for a surgical repair of his thumb, but *Pilgrim* and her owners were safe.

Being a full-time live aboard does present a number of other challenges, laundry for one. PL likes to recall the time when she was walking with friends ashore and happened to glance out in the bay. Her friends assured her that those were indeed clothes draped over *Osprey's* lifelines. PL was flabbergasted since she never really considered laundry, a pink job in yachtie parlance, to be part of my typical blue job endeavors. All the ladies congratulated me on my major accomplishment, a tribute to my feminine side. I basked in the glory of my new, unencumbered persona.

Later PL noticed that none of the water jugs she used for laundry had been tapped. How did I manage to do all that laundry without using any water out of the jugs? No problem! My sure-fire express laundry technique involved taking a nice warm shower without pumping the water out of the shower stall drain. After I toweled off, I merely tossed the dirty clothes into the bottom of the slightly flooded shower stall. Next step, and part of my secret technique, was to stomp on them for a while—basically the same concept as crushing grapes for vino. Then I simply rinsed the churned up clothes under the showerhead and hung them on the lifelines to dry. Apparently my technique was not the breakthrough I had hoped since a scowling PL banned me from the laundry detail.

Although I flippantly note that command at sea can be lonely at times, the ongoing dynamics of world cruising was teaching me that I was not in command of much. It is extraordinarily difficult to reframe a life shaped by a controlling personality, but I was starting to explore my options.

9

The Coconut Milk Run

o o o o o o o o o o o o o o o o o o o o o o o o o o o o o o o o o

...an education in the world inside, an education in one's self, a chance to learn one's own self, to get on speaking terms with one's soul.

—*Jack London,* **Cruise of the Snark**

Since we had waited out the questionable weather, our passage to Rarotonga in the Cook Islands was relatively peaceful and much more enjoyable with good friends. Even the four-hour watches went more quickly with Nick and Joan to share the duty. I was becoming more at peace with myself as the ocean worked its magic.

During the passage to the Cooks, Joan and PL concocted great meals in the bobbing galley. Some of the entrees were recognizable, others were not, as the boat went through its downwind rock and roll routine. PL, a gifted chef on either land or sea, considers good balance and a sense of humor the keys to offshore cooking. But even *Osprey's* master chef seemed to get a bit testy whenever a surging wave crest would sluice through the galley's open porthole and splatter her with a surprise saltwater shower. It is tough to be upbeat when a culinary masterpiece is hurled across the galley by the corkscrew motion of a lurching boat.

Although many cruising guides make a big production out of provisioning for a long voyage, PL learned that there was no reason to get overwrought about the concept. We found stores even in far-flung locales and they usually stocked at least the basics. Everybody has to eat. Sometimes the fare was unfamiliar or maybe a tad exotic, but then again that is part of the adventure.

The Cook Islands are a collection of low-lying coral atolls and high volcanic peaks. Although the Cook Islands are self-governed by rather colorful politicians, the 21,000 residents are citizens of New Zealand. Rarotonga, one of the fifteen islands in the country, is home to over half the population. The islands chain lies 600 miles to the west of Tahiti. As we had seen at Fete in Bora Bora, the Cook Islanders know how to dance.

The Flame Tree Restaurant, nestled in a coconut grove within earshot of the pounding surf, is renowned in the cruising community. A special farewell dinner for Nick and Joan was in order and the Flame Tree fit the bill. I favored the pork loin with pawpaw and cumin coulis. As the menu noted, this creation brings together pork and tropical fruit in a combination that is exotic and very appealing. Scalloped breadfruit and green beans with coconut complemented the entrée. *Osprey's* Shooting Star Award was duly awarded to the Flame Tree and noted in the ship's logbook. PL's copy of Sue Carruthers's *Flame Tree Cookbook* is now dog-eared and scarred for good reason.

Rarotonga not only has charm, but it also features English as the official language—a welcome change after four months in French Polynesia. To stretch our sea legs and see what Rarotonga had to offer, PL and I rustled up the *Serenade* crew for a cross-island jungle hike. We spent the morning scrambling up to the summit of an exposed jagged rock known as the Needle and then gingerly picking our way down a steep jungle footpath towards a country road on windward side of the island. Our efforts were finally rewarded with double-scooped Hokey Pokey ice cream from a ramshackle roadside stand. After the ice cream hit, it was just a matter of thumbing a ride back to the harbor.

The next day an unannounced gale screamed through the narrow entrance of tiny Avatiu harbor and ambushed our small flotilla of unsuspecting, Med-moored cruising sailboats. We were sitting ducks, stacked two rows deep perpendicular to the concrete pier. Violent wind shifts and breaking waves tossed a number of vessels against the rough walls of the quay. PL and I were lucky to be aboard and even luckier to be Med-moored one row out from the unforgiving wall. I barely had enough time to fire up our engine and power away from the carnage. Although our anchor was hopelessly tangled in the ongoing melee, I slammed the throttle to the stops to take the strain of our bowstring tight anchor chain. A few of the boats suffered major damage as they smashed into the quay. Chunks of fiberglass and pieces of irreplaceable gear snapped off and sunk under the churning froth. After the gale blew itself out, I strapped on my scuba gear and helped salvage bits and pieces of our friends' broken equipment that littered the bottom. The seafloor looked like an underwater boat parts store.

Niue is not a big place. Located 600 miles west of Rarotonga, Niue is a massive, jungle topped volcanic rock in the middle of nowhere. The surrounding water is deep and the cliffs are exposed. Old time seafarers dubbed the place Savage Island. Niue is one of the world's smallest self-governing states. Although no longer a dependency of New Zealand, Niue still retains close ties with its neighbor to the south. Since Niue is not exactly action central, the citizens decided to hype their proximity to the International Date Line with the innovative slogan: "Watch the last of this day in the entire world—the end of yesterday. We've already seen the first of tomorrow."

Because Niue has no decent anchorages, the local diving club installed half a dozen mooring buoys in front of the town of Alofi. We snagged a buoy and then decided to take our dinghy ashore. With no dock and no beach and very few seaborne visitors, a do-it-your-self hand-operated crane perched on top of the town's concrete seawall—a clever device to chum in yachties. Once again I was on the backside of the learning curve as I stared at the contraption. As our dinghy surfed up to the steps on the seawall, we scrambled out of the inflatable. Fortunately we managed to control the wildly gyrating dinghy with rope as I latched a hook from the overhead crane onto the dinghy's lifting bridle. PL and I cranked and sweated to hoist the inflatable and by and by the dinghy was winched onto the high pier. It was sort of like lassoing a jumpy heifer.

After checking in at the very loose customs operation, PL and I decided to explore the island. Since we were now pros at operating the crane, a trip back and forth to the boat was doable so we brought our bikes ashore. The island's 1960 vintage concrete hurricane houses are not particularly beautiful, but the locals became believers when a 1959 cyclone tore through their community. As we pedaled along the narrow country roads, PL pointed out gravesites in front of the small homes. The personalized roadside graves featured pictures of the deceased and mementoes of their lives. Apparently a long tradition of self reliance and close family ties explained the residential grave concept, but it seemed there would be a rather limited resale possibilities if a local opted to sell a piece of land that featured a collection of buried ancestors.

Eventually we found the coral fringed tidal pools of Limu—a place renowned for its curious open roofed caverns. Since Niue had not been blasted by the latest South Pacific hurricane, the snorkeling was great.

Unlike the brusque attitude of French Polynesia, Niue's warm and generous welcome felt just right. The locals were friendly and accommodating and very anxious to interact with us. The Niue Yacht Club held regular meetings, published a newsletter, and even flew its own yacht club burgee. Interestingly enough, none of the local members owned a sailboat. Late one afternoon a few of us were socializing with several local businessmen who also served in assorted government posts. One of the ministers suggested that Niue should host a sailboat race. Since we were in the midst of comparing beers, in this case New Zealand's Steinlager vs. Niue's Fiafa, we got caught up in the spirit of the moment and volunteered our boats for a sailboat race—a first for Niue.

Between that evening and the next afternoon, the town rallied together and enlisted thirty residents who wanted to crew. The government ministry closed for the day. By noon, the local police boat had been transformed into a committee boat and hooky-playing officials crowded the seawall in anticipation. All five visiting sailboats, each jammed with a crew of Niue citizens, rallied to the starting line and the race was on. Our significant others watched from a nearby hill, along with the local TV station crew who filmed the entire event. The saga only lasted an hour and since there were no rules, none were broken—a five-way tie was announced at the end. Later that evening there was an awards banquet. The five skippers were presented with Niue Yacht Club T-shirts and all the beer we could drink.

The following evening the weather started to deteriorate, so we reluctantly said good-bye and sailed away with pleasant memories and happy hearts. About an hour out, the radio sprang to life. "*Osprey, Osprey, Osprey....* This is the Niue Yacht Club calling to say good-bye and wishing you a pleasant journey."

PL and I returned the sentiment and the next thing we heard was "God Bless America" being sung over our radio. The *Osprey* crew was a bit misty eyed as we sailed over the western horizon bound for Tonga, 240 miles away.

"Where did all the pigs come from?" It was the first question that came to mind as PL and I strolled down the streets of Neiafu. In Tonga there were pigs on the beaches and sidewalks and streets and in the stores. Everywhere we looked, there were pigs as well as assorted ducks and chickens—squalor personified. Tongans are famous for their feasts, and inevitably the feasts featured a succulent little porker as the main entree.

Tonga prides itself on being the first landmass on earth to be struck by the rising sun. It works for them because the International Dateline is only 180 miles to the east. Our introduction to Tonga was a shakedown at customs. The huge plodding officials wanted to be gifted with a selection of videos, porno preferred. PL countered that *Osprey* did not carry tapes, but if we did, the offerings would tend towards Disney flicks. Although Tongan officials seemed oblivious, the

United Nations has consistently vilified Tonga for indiscriminately selling passports and citizenships.

Osprey lingered in Tonga the best part of a month, but we only soaked up a smattering of what the country had to offer. The kingdom of Tonga consists of four major island groups, 170 some islands in all. Pick of the litter, and our favorite, is the Vava'u group. Vava'u is affectionately known as a Pocket Paradise because the fifty islands in the group are relatively close together. Sailing and exploring is done in the protected waters of an oblong thirteen by fifteen mile lagoon—a radical change from our previous months in the exposed reaches of the South Pacific. Bare-boat charter operations consider the Vava'u Island group a relatively benign place to cruise. In an apparent effort to make things easier for potential charter customers in Tonga, the local cruising guide listed each recommended anchorage by number—a rather industrial concept even adopted by the locals. We enjoyed the lyrical sounds of Polynesian names so the notion of treating each unique anchorage as a number on a checklist was a bit much for our crew.

The superb snorkeling and phenomenal sea life around the Tuamoto was our gold standard for diving. Tonga's snorkeling was…good. Unfortunately a 1993 cyclone wiped out many of the coral reefs, but schools of startling beautiful tropical fish were still about. The weather gods seem to have it in for Tonga. Cyclone Waka subsequently flattened Neiafu with 80-knot winds and ten-foot waves on New Year's Eve, 2001. Although a few cruising boats were lost, no deaths were reported.

In Tonga older men and women wear skirts, whereas the younger people tend to dress in westernized clothes. Most native Tongans go barefoot or shuffle around in sandals. For special occasions *ta'ovalas*, basically woven pandanus mats, are cinched around ample bellies and worn over their street clothes. *Ta'ovalas* are a carry over from the old square-rigger days when visiting sailors wrapped their torsos in bolts of sailcloth to be presentable to the very conservative Tongan officials. In those days the natives were not above a bit of cannibalism, so it paid to be respectful. A proper *ta'ovala* covers from knee to solar plexus and emphasizes girth—the perfect accessory for the huge Tongans.

In general the local folks are aloof and in no hurry, *fake Tonga* as they say. About mid-afternoon small groups of children livened things up a bit as they walked the streets on their way home from school. Each school fielded a different uniform but they are unanimously traditional. Tonga is less progressive than either the Cook Islands or French Polynesia. No short skirts or T-shirts are in sight. Girls dressed in longish *vala* skirts with sparkling white blouses and an occasional hair ribbon. The boys wear either long pants or a wrap around knee length *tupenu* skirts. Many of them also wear an attitude.

By far and away our favorite Tongan adventure was our dive of faith at Mariner's Cave. The dining room sized underwater cavern is hidden under a rocky cliff exposed to the long Pacific swells. The trick is to snorkel close to the jagged cliff wall, skin dive ten feet down, and then paddle furiously about twenty feet horizontally through a narrow underwater tunnel. Good karma was with us as we resurfaced inside a mysterious and surreal cavern. Only a few rays of filtered sunlight crept into the grotto's clear blue waters and clouds of vapor hung on the mossy domed ceiling.

A local legend tells the story of a beautiful princess who feared for her life because her family had many enemies. The princess was spirited away to Mariner's Cave by her lover, a chief from another tribe. He brought her daily gifts of food, water, and clothing, as well as fine oils in which to bathe. The young chief won her heart and she agreed to marry him. Together they devised a secret plan. The chief returned to his people and counseled them to leave the warring clans of Tonga and seek a new life in Fiji. When the tribe's elders asked him why he would attempt such a trip without a Tongan wife, the chief assured them that he would find a suitable wife along the way. True to his word, the handsome chief paddled his canoe to the rugged cliff above the secret cave, dived into the sparkling water, and emerged a few minutes later with the girl whom his companions surmised to be a goddess. Sailing on to Fiji the lovers married and lived happily ever after.

John and his extended family lived in a small beach community of grass and woven reed houses where they hosted a Tongan feast for us. The food was wrapped in banana leaves, then layered on top of hot rocks and covered with the freshly dug dirt. As our dinner cooked in the *umo*, we toured the property seeing banana, papaya, and coconut trees and a large garden that supplied the compound with assorted root vegetables. Several of the local women spread large pieces of tapa cloth along the pathway and displayed their intricately woven reed baskets, arguably Tonga's most prized export.

As feast time approached the carefully wrapped bundles were removed from the *umo* one layer at a time. The sweet aromas were tantalizing and exotic. Before long we were in the Tongan mode sitting on the floor and using a combination of a stiff leaf and our fingers to gorge ourselves. PL and I finally pushed ourselves off the floor after wolfing down embarrassingly huge quantities of fresh papaya filled with melted coconut cream, sliced onion served in a coconut shell, steamed clams wrapped in banana leaves, roasted pig and chicken and fish, corned beef, Chinese noodles, assorted salads, and watermelon. The local kids put on a dance routine for our benefit. Unlike the sensual hip rhythm of Tahitian dances, Tongan dances involve only the arms and hands—not much skin and not much rhythm. The aspiring dancers oiled their exposed limbs in the hopes of having a few dollars pasted on their arms.

The Methodist and Mormon missionaries definitely made their mark in Tonga. Church going is a main event. In the modest little community of Hunga, population 300 people, there were five churches. The service started at 10 am but the church bells and singing began at 5 am. The church itself was a simple structure—one room constructed with pandanus-leaf walls, a corrugated roof, and a floor covered with handmade grass mats. The altar was draped with old Christmas decorations, streamers, and tinsel. A huge velour beach towel was nailed on a wall next to a faded poster of the King of Tonga. Behind the altar a giant black velvet painting, adorned with tinsel and well-worn party streamers, depicted Jesus holding his dripping sacred heart. The congregation sat crossed legged on woven mats dressed in their Sunday best. The women wore long dresses and woven straw hats adorned with paper flowers and ribbons. Many of the men wore skirts topped with a vintage sports jacket, shirt, and tie. Some people tied the traditional *ta'ovalas* over their clothing. No one wore shoes. Three Hungan priests performed the service as children roamed freely from lap to lap. The singing was loud and boisterous, but even so we could hear the competing hymns being belted out from the church next door. I found the unconditional faith of the parishioners disarmingly appealing. Gradually, and quite surprisingly, I found that my former hard charging disposition was slowly being displaced by a more gentle and accepting character—bit by bit my new life was unfolding.

Rumors about a tree house-type lodge perched on a hillside overlooking one of the outer anchorages intrigued us. After anchoring on the lee side of the Vaca'eitu Island, I motored our dinghy to a frail dock. PL and I hiked 20 minutes up a steep dirt path to meet Hans, an expat from Austria. Hans built the entire facility himself from local materials without power tools.

The intimate bar overlooked the turquoise waters of beautiful Ava Pulepulekai Channel, a passage frequented by humpback whales. Since this early September day was also the first anniversary of Tyler and Ashley's death in India, PL and I toasted Tyler and Ashley and then planted a small aloe plant in their honor. The kids would have loved the view.

Further up the path Hans pointed out the rustic log restaurant and a simple home built on stilts. After our meal Han's provided a personal tour of the compound, where he lived with his Tongan wife and 9-year old son. A firm believer in self-sufficiency and rabid about environmental issues, Hans shared with us his outspoken views about higher education. Tired of seeing kids learning skills useless in Tonga's subsistence economy, Hans and his wife home schooled their son. In Hans's world living off the land and preserving the traditions of his son's Tongan forefathers was the consummate educational experience.

Our farewell evening in Tonga was celebrated at Pete's Hunga Beach Resort, otherwise known as anchorage #13. After a pint or two of the local Royal malt beer, we became mates with three New Zealand couples who were just finishing their bareboat charter. Bernie and Trish, Lindsay and Penny, as well as Ru and Geoff, were into sailing—naturally a few seafaring tales slipped out that night. While rallying to our dinghies in the wee hours, our new Kiwi friends invited us for a stay in their hometown of Christchurch should PL and I ever get down to New Zealand's South Island. We eventually did that very thing.

In early September we sailed for Fiji. Although the trip was a relatively short 400 miles, negotiating the treacherous Oneata Passage and the scores of offshore reefs got our attention. Fiji is not user-friendly for the charter crowd, but its 300 some islands scattered over hundreds of miles of ocean are renowned as the best cruising in the South Pacific.

These days only about fifty percent of the local population is native Fijian. East Indians comprise most of the competing cultural mix. Historically Fijians own the land and the East Indians provide the workforce. The volatile mix of old-time landowners favoring the status quo versus the enterprising newcomers clamoring for equality makes for a shaky economy and confrontational politics, but the country seemed to struggle along.

We found the bustling capital of Suva, on the main island of Viti Levu, to be a radical change from the slow lackadaisical lifestyle in Tonga. A huge dose of culture shock assaulted us as we strolled down paved streets, dodged whizzing cars, and encountered stores jammed with people. Fijian officials often wore a conservative skirt-like *sulu* with sports jackets, whereas the policemen seemed to favor more dapper, colorful *sulu* uniforms that featured a rakish arrow point hem. A new six-screen cinema, complete with air conditioning and popcorn, had just opened. Our last movie hit was in San Diego so PL and I became steady patrons of the new cinema during our five-day Suva stay. Even though the Royal Suva Yacht Club is a nice watering hole, the heavy rains got to us. We weighed anchor and sailed for the more remote islands of Fiji.

It is considered good form, civilized, and polite to pay your respects to the village chief when your boat anchors at one of the more traditional outer islands in

Fiji. The visitor is expected to present the chief with a gift of kava root. The gift is in exchange for permission to visit the chief's island and be under his, or her, protection. Other cruisers had prepped us about the fascinating tradition, so I had bought half a dozen bundles of the gaily wrapped, brown pepper plant twigs while I was wandering through the public market in Suva.

Since not many sailboats were about as we cruised the outlying islands of the Yasawa group, our first village encounter was a solitary affair. In traditional Fiji the head is considered sacred, so PL and I left our sunglasses and hats aboard. It is not good policy to be impolite in a society that boasts huge people with cannibal ancestors. Lucky for us the human entrees have been eliminated over the years in the interests of the tourist trade.

After landing our dinghy on the long sandy beach, I hesitantly presented our ribbon bedecked kava root bundle to the chief's intermediary. In due course the chief invited us into the community hut where PL and I sat down crossed-legged on a woven mat. Normally women are not allowed, but the chief must have known that my lady is a princess and not to be trifled with. The chief and several of the village elders joined us. After we were all seated in a circle, the *sevu sevu* ceremony began. The chief's assistant used a mortar and pestle to grind the tangy pepper plant with a bit of water. In the old days the saliva of a virgin was added to the concoction, but time marches on. The chief threw out a few indecipherable Fijian phrases apparently welcoming us to his village. Although neither of us could understand a word, we surmised that this was the critical juncture that determined the fate of early sailors—the natives debated whether to welcome them or eat them.

Mumbling *"bula bula,"* Fijian code for welcome, the headman then dipped a coconut shell into the unappetizing brown liquid as the elders clapped three times. The clapping was repeated as the coconut shell was passed from one person to the next. The villagers liked their yaqona (kava) drinking, so the chief called for a few more rounds. Kava is definitely an acquired taste that combines the hint of gritty dishwater with a lingering pepper tingle that assaults the lips and tongue.

Now that PL and I knew the system, we decided to visit a few more islands and perfect our newly acquired *sevu sevu* skills. A gift of kava and a friendly smile worked wonders everywhere we anchored. In the astonishingly clear, warm waters of Navini Island, my payoff was a dive on the submerged wreckage of a vintage WW II British Spitfire fighter. An endless parade of brilliantly colored tropical fish swam by the cockpit of the old fighter as if they were paying their respects.

On Wayasewa Island the *Osprey* crew joined the *Pilgrim* crew to celebrate National Teacher's Day with the locals. When we trudged ashore a huge Fijian mom by the name of Millie adopted us. Sixty students from Naboro town kept us entertained with their skits lampooning their teachers. Although PL and Sue packed food to share at the school's potluck, Millie was so enthralled with having white skin outsiders as her guests that she would not allow other students or parents to sample our picnic offerings. Millie apparently considered her immediate family very honored to have us as guests and she was not about to share the glory or the food.

Eventually we threaded our way through the maze of outlying coral reefs, and sailed to Malololailai Island—the gathering place for cruisers known as Musket Cove. Rather than the Pidgin English and the indecipherable Fijian of the outer islands, our crew was now in the midst of English speaking yachties. After being duly initiated as lifetime members of the Musket Cove Yacht Club, we heard some bad news from the cruiser grapevine.

Camelot, a 47-foot San Francisco based sailboat, had struck an offshore reef south of the Yasawas and sunk. Just prior to the accident, Jan and Bill had been skirting a jagged coral reef relying on their GPS navigation system. Regrettably an overcast sky filtered out the greenish brown colors warning of shallow water and their inaccurate chart did not jibe with their GPS position. The tide was on the ebb, as was their luck. Fortunately Bill and Jan were rescued by another cruising boat, but they lost everything.

A small commuter aircraft landed on Musket Cove's short dirt airstrip, and a husky Fijian customs officer stepped out of the plane nonchalantly toting a large box under his arm. After the replacement inverter for our electrical system was dutifully delivered to me, the *sulu*-clad official gave me a smart salute and then he stepped back aboard the plane. I was barely able to heft the package as I staggered back to our boat. Although the five-day delivery time from the States was impressive, watching how easily the huge Fijian handled the 100-pound inverter was even more amazing.

10

Gale Warnings

When the full displeasure of the elements falls upon a man, he is temporarily overwhelmed and permanently changed from within. After the trial he is either dead or forever afterwards humble and discreet.

—*Ernest K. Gann*

Osprey, along with our cruising sidekicks aboard *Promises, Serenade,* and *Renaissance* gathered at Vuda Point Marina in late October. There was no avoiding the inevitable—the South Pacific hurricane season was on its way and it was time for us to sail south. Our plan was to sit out the six-month hurricane season in New Zealand during the Southern Hemisphere's spring and summer. The high seas weather south of the Tropic of Capricorn is renowned for packing a punch as strong frontal systems blast through the area every week or so. Since it would take us longer than a week to reach our next port of call at the Bay of Islands, I assumed *Osprey* would be nailed at least once by a nasty weather system. The conventional wisdom is not to get popped twice.

With that thought in mind, it seemed prudent to have an extra hand aboard *Osprey* for the passage south. Friends back home had put us in touch with an enthusiastic young man who they deemed a fine sailor. Although I should have known better, I invited him aboard sight unseen. Unfortunately our new crewman suffered from bouts of melancholy, immaturity, and…seasickness.

Although the farewell party at First Landing Restaurant was a nice sendoff for our group, the officious Indian from Fijian Customs did not share our cheerful outlook. He would only check us out at his convenience, and then only if we sailed from Fiji immediately, regardless of the weather forecast.

Fiji's Nadi Radio and New Zealand's Met Service, both excellent sources for weather, predicted a decent weather window for our 1200-mile passage to the

North Island. Bob on *Rejoice*, the weather guy on the cruiser radio net, agreed that we were all good to go. Made sense to me.

I was well aware of the horrendous Queen's Birthday Storm of June 4, 1994 when a cold, extra-tropical cyclone devastated the cruising fleet sailing to Tonga from New Zealand. This catastrophic event occurred one month after the official hurricane season was declared over, so it is common knowledge that nasty weather can pop up quickly and unpredictably in that section of the Pacific Ocean.

Sustained wind speeds of 34 to 47 knots are recognized as a gale. A low-pressure system generating winds in excess of 48 knots is known as a storm. A very low-pressure violent rotary storm producing mountainous seas over forty-five feet, shrieking winds in excess of 64 knots, and torrential rains qualifies as a hurricane or tropical cyclone. These notorious designations relate to sustained winds, far more ominous than wind gusts. To put it in perspective: it is difficult to walk into 20 knots of wind; it is impossible to walk into 40 knots of wind; 80 knots of wind can transform you into a human hang glider.

The Beaufort scale is the accepted nautical yardstick to measure wind force. The scale goes from 0 to 12 with Beaufort number 0 being calm and 12 being a hurricane. A gale rates 8 on the scale. Beaufort 10 storms pack winds to 55 knots and generate thirty-foot waves with overhanging crests. Beaufort 11 means a ferocious assault of 63-knot winds and forty-five foot waves. Beaufort 12 is a hurricane. Surviving a full-blown storm at sea in a cruising sailboat is problematical at best.

Just as *Osprey* cleared the outer reefs of Fiji, the promised winds from a massive high-pressure ridge came our way. The strong breeze made for lumpy confused seas. Our young crewman took to his bunk and was never heard from again for a week. The slow pounding slog out of Fiji's coastal waters was just a primer in the ways of the Southern Ocean.

Four days later a severe weather front slammed into us. The system haunted us for thirty hours and easily rated as the worst weather we encountered during our entire circumnavigation. With sustained winds of 35 knots, gusts to 45 knots, and fifteen-foot breaking seas, this gale got our attention. Since the massive onslaught came from our stern quarter, I stowed the mainsail, hoisted a storm staysail, engaged the wind vane autopilot, and let *Osprey* sort things out. PL and I were securely tethered in *Osprey's* cockpit with safety harnesses and bundled up in our warmest clothes. With only two of us standing watches, sleep became a scarce commodity in our small damp world of violent winds and raging seas. Our sloop mimicked a rocket sled as she raced up the face of the ragged wave crests with the screaming winds tearing into her small staysail. Then *Osprey* would slide down the other side of the towering slopes into a watery crevasse, leaving the staysail flapping fitfully. Occasionally a breaking wave would engulf our cockpit and stagger the boat—it was scary as hell. As the cold water drained out of the cockpit scuppers, the boat seemed to just shake it off and then continued about her business of delivering her crew safely to the next landfall.

Eventually bad weather goes away. Our clothes were soaked and the cabin looked like a grenade had exploded below, but the three of us were ok. During a bout of nasty weather you just deal—the frightening moments and lingering doubts resurface later. If the purpose of life is to know yourself, our sailing passage to New Zealand was one of my defining moments.

11

Home of the Kiwis

It is with the heart that one sees rightly; what is essential is invisible to the eye.

—*Antoine de Saint Exupery,* **The Little Prince**

As *Osprey* sliced through the ridges of broken water just north of New Zealand's Bay of Islands, a spectacular sunrise embraced the sheer rock headlands and turned the cliffs a shimmering emerald green. The hillside was shrouded in mist and a slight chill was in the air. The ink blue and slate gray waters of the vast Pacific Ocean gave way to the sparkling bottle green of coastal bays.

New Zealand is at the top of our "we could be happy living there" hit parade. Although similar in size to Great Britain and Japan, New Zealand has a far more interesting climate. The northern tip of the North Island is a semitropical land renowned for Kauri pine forests. Most of the Kiwis live on the North Island—the home of the country's largest and most cosmopolitan city, Auckland.

In contrast the South Island is a more rugged place. The Southern Alps run the entire length of the South Island and boast 12,316-foot Mt. Cook as their alpine centerpiece. The crown jewel is Fiordland National Park, the sparsely settled wilderness located in the southwestern reaches of the island.

The Roaring Forties wind belt, an area between south latitudes forty degrees to fifty degrees, is dominated by horrendous westerly winds that sweep unimpeded thousands of miles across the southern oceans. The only landmasses that stand in the way of the howling winds are the Aussie island of Tasmania, the southern reaches of Argentina, Chili's Cape Horn, and New Zealand's South Island. Small wonder that the Kiwis are famous for their mountaineers and sailors.

To hear the Aussies tell it, New Zealand's population of mutton is "down to the last 45 million." Although New Zealand grazed 70 million sheep just twenty years ago, the world of synthetic fibers and a global economy have changed the economic model that initially spawned the sprawling Kiwi sheep stations.

The native people of New Zealand, the Maori, comprise about 15% of the population, but their language and customs permeate the culture of the *Pakeha,* NZ residents of European descent. Maori *wakas,* or war canoes, roamed the South Pacific long before Captain Cook came on the scene. *Kia Ora* is a wish for good health. The Kiwis are rabid about their All Blacks rugby team and the burly players keep the legend alive with their very intimidating pre-game *haka,* the Maori war dance.

Other than sand flies, the Kiwis do not have much to worry about in the way of annoying or dangerous animals. Sheep comprise the majority of four legged creatures and the fuzzy ones are the essence of mellow. There are no snakes and the only dangerous spider is the rare katipo. No dangerous sea creatures prowl beneath the coastal waters of New Zealand. New Zealand is a treasure trove for bird lovers. The symbol of New Zealand is the small and stout kiwi, a flightless nocturnal bird. The *Osprey* crew especially enjoyed the raucous kea—an inquisitive, fearless and amusing parrot renowned for pecking at almost anything in sight.

The Kiwis are an unpretentious, hospitable, and downright friendly lot, but they are also very protective of their agricultural tradition. A major concern for Kiwi officials is the accidental introduction of rabies to their small island country. Pets aboard yachts are quarantined, and most of the fresh food and vegetables aboard are burned in the incinerator at the custom's shed. But it is all done with a smile.

The Opua Cruising Club greeted us with a barbie in our honor. After rolling a few snarler*s* and downing a pint or two from the generously stocked chilly bin, PL and I not only knew we had come to the right place, but we had also learned the Kiwi translation for sausage and ice chest.

With a six-month stay in New Zealand on our horizon, a set of wheels was in order. Our solution was Old Blue, an '84 Toyota Corolla with a checkered history. Kiwi drivers seem to lack a survival gene in their genetic makeup. They drive with carefree abandon and horrible manners. In the British tradition the cars sport steering wheels on the right side and the traffic onslaught is from "the wrong side." If a Kiwi is headed for their "bach," or holiday cottage, get out of their way. Since many motorists reverted to a Third World taxi cab driver mentality when behind the wheel, defensive driving was the key to survival.

Kate flew in from Italy to celebrate the Christmas season with us. A long distance call from my brothers Mark and Peter shattered the homecoming. They gently told me of our mother's passing. I felt like I had been kicked in the teeth and I was extraordinarily sad. Mildred was healthy and lived well into her eighth decade before the sudden stroke ended her life. My mother passed away without regaining consciousness. My first inclination was to fly home but the decision had already been made to have the memorial service prior to the call. Since my dad Harley had died just prior to our sailing trip and we were still recovering from Tyler's death, my family and friends concluded that a Christmas spent with Kate far outweighed the familial duty of a memorial service. Intellectually I knew my brothers' decision had been the right call, but I was bombarded by a tangle of conflicting emotions. Within the short span of a few years, I had lost my dad, my son, and my mom—it seemed like the earth had shifted under my feet and there was not much left to cling to. I was blessed to have Kate and PL to share the load.

Mildred was a truly remarkable woman. She was an incredible mother, grandmother, and friend. Kate, PL, and I spent the next few days reliving the wonderful memories so much apart of our close-knit family. We grieved for my mom and toasted the life of a magnificent human being. My world, along with my five-year plans, was imploding around me. I needed time, space, and a new outlook.

Our small family decided that a holiday celebration was a must so I fired up Old Blue and drove south. We were all dazzled by the beautiful New Zealand landscape. The sprawling rural pastures were dotted with fuzzy white sheep. The North Island also has its share of cattle, as well as domesticated deer herds and an occasional ostrich farm.

Much to Kate's chagrin our trio also caught the Sheep Show at the Agridome. Sheepdogs expertly herded over a dozen varieties of sheep onto a multilevel stage. The star was a fluffy merino ram with spectacular curved horns. A shearer grabbed one of the oblivious sheep and whipped off its heavy wool coat in less than a minute. The process did not faze the sheep but it dazzled me. The ladies informed me that they preferred their wool in the form of soft downy merino wool sweaters.

The idea of an underground float trip, or black water rafting, had been on my agenda for quite awhile, but the concept was a surprise for Kate. Along with a dozen other unsuspecting souls, our trio got togged up in wet suits, caving helmets, and miner's lamps. The next step involved jamming our tail ends into the inner tube of our choice. After the inner tube fitting, the game plan became more interesting. Our assignment was to leap off a six-foot high riverbank, land butt–first on our inner tube, and then rocket down a modest sized creek leading into an underground cave that resembled a dark, dank elevator shaft. As we shot through the underground rapids past stalactites and stalagmites, our enthusiastic Kiwi guide called for "lights off." In the dark gurgling bowels of the 1.5 million year old Ruakuri Cave, thousands of twinkling glowworms lighted the ceiling of the winding cavern—the ultimate E-ticket ride.

Ed, a fellow dentist from Auckland, introduced PL and I to the sophisticated and cosmopolitan offerings of his city early on. When Kate subsequently flew into town, PL knew just where to go and what to see. Kate and her mom browsed the shops of Auckland while I checked out the action at the Royal New Zealand Yacht Squadron. As our trio traveled in New Zealand, our long thoughtful talks helped give my life a little more perspective. In early January Kate flew back to Florence to resume her job with Georgetown University.

Fish is not a major ingredient in the Kiwi diet, but the native green lipped mussels proved an exception to the otherwise uninspired seafood fare—the razor clam size mussels are inexpensive and delicious. Since the concept of zingy sauces, exotic preparations, and delicate pastas is foreign to most Kiwi palates, we became well acquainted with Kiwi classics such as meat pie and Pavlova, a cake that is NZ's national dessert. Beef and domestically raised red deer meat are popular with the locals, but New Zealand lamb gets our vote. So, despite the best intentions, our diet definitely took a turn toward the carnivore segment of the dining spectrum.

Hurricane seasons dictate the itinerary of cruising sailboats. During the South Pacific's six-month tropical cyclone season, many cruisers temporarily adopt New Zealand as their home. Not only is New Zealand a very hospitable port of call, it is also a great place to refit boats that have seen their fair share of wear and tear. Blue water cruising definitely chews up and spits out equipment—it is not a matter of if but rather when. Although the excellent boat yards and skilled craftsman can be had at reasonable prices, boat parts are quite "dear" in New Zealand. Gulf Harbor Marina, our hangout for the season, boasted a country club atmosphere with great boatyard services to boot.

During one of our jaunts into Auckland, PL and I wandered into a computer store. The dazzling display of electronics mesmerized us—we reacted like a couple of deer caught in the headlights of an onrushing car. A very gracious Kiwi salesman reined us in, endured our naive questions, and then guided us into the world of Windows 95. We walked out of the store with a shiny new Toshiba laptop and a fresh respect for technology. As our friend Sue helped us to unravel the mysteries of email, our life took a quantum leap forward into cyberspace. AOL was no longer just an indecipherable puzzle. Our days of pining away for snail mail to arrive at some far-flung American Express office were behind us.

The South Island of New Zealand, a world many North Island's rarely visit, is one of our favorite places. Many of the locals are farmers, ski-bums, fisherman, and tour guides. Our South Island mates scoffed at the big city ways of the North Island.

In Christchurch the Kiwi party animals, formerly of anchorage #13 in Tonga, invited the *Osprey* and *Renaissance* crews for a reunion at Rue and Geoff's home. Ample doses of mosquito repellent, better known as Steinlager beer, washed down our feast of spring lamb, fresh shrimp kabobs, and snarlers. Our gracious hosts then made it their mission to introduce us to Christchurch for a few days. Christchurch is very English in style, a picturesque city with its own River Avon winding through the center of town. We listened to the eccentric Wizard spout his philosophy from a ladder in Cathedral Square, strolled the luxuriant botanical gardens, and dined at inviting outdoor cafes. Christchurch is a find and well worth a return visit someday.

We hugged our new mates goodbye and then drove south for our Milford Trek rendezvous—sadly an 18-wheeler ruined our day. The oncoming tractor-trailer rig passed a disabled bus on a blind curve as we casually motored around the bend in the opposite direction. Our foursome had little warning as Smiley, Brian and Kathleen's beater car, bounced off the semi's huge wheels. After it was all over, Smiley was totaled but none of us was injured.

We left Smiley at the wrecking yard in Dunedin, slung on our backpacks, hopped a bus, and made our way to Queenstown. Armed with our YHA Youth Hostel cards and a new lease on life, PL and I dropped into the hostel mode. Enthusiastic travelers, from teenagers to very senior citizens, added color and charm to the hostel's communal kitchen. Sharing a bunkroom with a group of college kids was an education in itself.

Queenstown is a picturesque mountain resort on the shores of Lake Wakaktipu, a very casual Lake Tahoe type of place. Queenstown is also ground zero for adrenaline sports: jet boating, hang gliding, bungee jumping, river rafting, helicopter skiing—you name it, and when the season is right, they do it. Since it was too early for snow, I chose bungee jumping. I ended up with a T-shirt and video to prove I did indeed hurl myself headfirst off the 143-foot Kawarau Suspension

Bridge. Tyler had made the same leap a few years prior so I just followed my son's lead.

Now that PL and I had the Kiwi bus system scoped out, we caught a ride to TeAnau—the staging area for the Milford Trek. A vintage motor launch ferried our group of self-guided trampers up to the remote headwaters of Lake TeAnau. Besides a few fellow Americans, our trekking companions hailed from South Africa, Israel, Germany, Switzerland, England, Australia, and New Zealand.

Billed as "the finest walk in the world," the Milford Trek is a four-day, 35-mile tramp through luxuriant rainforest, meandering river valleys, and glaciated alpine tundra. The trek is booked months in advance. All the communal cabins featured bunk beds, toilets, and propane cook tops—a definite upgrade from tent camping. Each day a new group hikes into the river camp, the first in a series of three overnight lodges on the Milford Trek. After a relaxing overnight toes up, trekkers are required to move on to the next camp so their present digs are available for the next oncoming group. No dillydallying in the Kiwi park system.

The trail fronting the clear winding river eventually transformed into a steep zigzag path punching up to Mackinnon Pass. The morning drizzle turned into a snow shower as PL and I climbed to the summit. At the top, we ducked into a warming hut for a spot of tea and a bit of a thaw out. As we started our descent down the other side, the weather broke and the afternoon sun enveloped us in a warm glow. A series of first-rate switchback boardwalks bridged a couple of spectacular waterfalls and spiraled into the lush valley far below.

Our rather international assortment of trekkers rated the experience akin to tramping in their beloved Alps. As hardcore Pacific Northwest aficionados, we likened the place to the Cascade Mountains of Washington State. In the end our trekking group descended to the shores of Milford Sound, a stunning 10-mile long fjord carved from sheer granite cliffs. Mitre Peak, an imposing 5560-foot pinnacle, majestically towered above the surrounding snow capped peaks. After our launch ride across the impossibly beautiful Sound, everyone went his or her separate ways. The special bond of traveling companions was severed as each of us reentered our private worlds once again.

Since PL and I were feeling in a rather expansive mood after our trek, we opted to fly back to Auckland. The commuter flight made several stops along the way, so we hopped off for a few minutes at each airport to stretch our newly buffed out trekker legs. At our first stop I was reboarding the plane when a jabbering man behind me started pawing the back of my prized bungee jumping T-shirt. After I sat back down I discovered the mumbler was none other than David Helfgott, the Australian concert pianist who was the subject of the movie Shine.

David, his wife, and his therapist were being treated like royalty by the flight attendants in the first class cabin. I thought no more about the incident until the next stop. Once again we exited the plane to stretch a bit but Helfgott spotted me, grabbed my hands, and proceeded to chatter away. David's fast forward, rapid-fire nonsensical babble touched on a bit of everything from bungee jumping to piano concerts. Towards the end of this rather one-sided hyper conversation, David gave me a huge bear hug as he was led away by his wife and therapist.

We were introduced to the rather unique experience of sailing from New Zealand towards Australia twice, in one season. Actually our first trip was a bit short lived. *Osprey* was about twenty miles north of The Bay of Islands when our transmission decided to die—a bit of a bother.

Marita Shan, Skybird, and *Pilgrim*—the other boats in our small flotilla—graciously offered to stay with us, but nothing could be done so they cruised on to Brisbane. We unfurled the headsail, tacked *Osprey* towards shore, and caught the afternoon sea breeze back into the Bay of Islands. In true Kiwi spirit PL put on the kettle as we tried to sort it all out. As we finished our tea, it became very apparent we did not have many options. We sailed into Opua through a maze of moored boats and eventually picked up a mooring at Ashby's Boat Yard.

Next morning an obliging Kiwi mechanic emerged from the bowels of the boat and announced that the V-drive transmission had indeed packed it up. Since there was no such animal available in the South Pacific, I ordered the little beast from the manufacturer in New Jersey. We waited two long weeks for the new arrival to show.

Actually hanging around the Bay of Islands is not bad duty. PL and I soaked up the rural feel with hikes through the Norfolk pine forests and ferry rides to some of the outer islands. Small waterfront towns like colonial Russell were a step back in time to the rowdy whaling era. Although the local school kids wore conservative uniforms, their rugged heritage dictated bare feet

The North Island is renowned for its ancient Kuari pine forests. The trees boast magnificent cylindrical trunks measuring up to twenty feet in diameter and spiraling more than a hundred feet into the clear Kiwi sky. We tramped through an impressive stand of Kuari trees, and then suddenly broke out into a strikingly handsome hillside meadow covered with thick soft grass. Below us the quiet waters of a deserted cove bathed the foot of the rolling knoll. Our only company was a few seabirds perched on the remnants of a nineteenth century whaling station. The day was sunny and bright. We flopped down into the tall-sunburned grass and soaked up the incredible moment, one of our indelible memories of New Zealand. Rather than chase after meditation, it had come to us.

Eventually the V-drive was shipped to Auckland by way of the Seattle dealer. Allen, the affable customs guy in Opua, kept me updated just so I would not constantly haunt his office. After a mysterious delay in Auckland the fabled part finally arrived at the Allen's customs shed. My DHL delivery was big news in Opua that day.

After our crusty mechanic pronounced us "Good as gold," we were out of there bound for points west. The Tasman Sea is notorious for creating unpredictable and sometimes violent weather. Fortunately our crew only ran into a few squalls during our spirited nine-day, 1250-mile passage from New Zealand to Australia. We traded the cool damp fall weather of the North Island for the semitropical warmth of Australia's Queensland.

12

Down Under

Out of clutter, find simplicity; from discord, harmony; in the midst of difficulty lies opportunity.

—*Albert Einstein*

Few countries have national holidays celebrating a convict legacy. Australia Day commemorates the date of Jan 26, 1788 when 11 ships with 700 some convicts aboard sailed into present day Sydney. In Oz the local folk hero is Ned Kelly, an Irish convict who donned homemade body armor before battling the police. Aussies have come a long ways since a rather slow start out of the blocks. We loved the place. In Aussie speak, "Bob is your uncle."

Australia, thirty times the size of New Zealand, is for the most part a dry and harsh continent. Only about 10% of the land is cultivated and most of the population lives in the coastal regions. Most guidebooks would agree that Australia is a rugged hunk of the planet. It has more things that can kill you than anywhere else. Ten of the world's most poisonous snakes call this place home. Lethal stonefish, ticks, octopus, snakes, and jellyfish lurk about as well as man-eating sharks and crocodiles.

Oz definitely has variety and then some. Sydney and Melbourne, the crown jewels of New South Wales and Victoria, offer sophisticated ambiance, wonderful cultural events, and fine restaurants. The beer guzzlers favor the far outposts of the Northern Territory outback. Queensland, stretching from the Gold Coast of Brisbane to the remote Cape York Peninsula, conveniently bridges the gap between the city slickers and the crocodile wrestlers. One commonality that bonds all Aussies is Vegemite—they love the stuff. The British answer to peanut butter, Vegemite has the consistency and taste of sticky bouillon cubes.

Kate rejoined us in Brisbane for a two-month Australian stay. As the resident advisor at the Georgetown University villa in Florence, part of Kate's employment package was airfare home during school breaks. Since our home was aboard *Osprey*, Kate's passport acquired a number of exotic stamps as she continued to join us in far-flung ports.

Kate, by ten months the most senior of our Irish twins, was Tyler's mentor by aptitude, attitude, and sheer force of personality. Although I nicknamed our firstborn Bug because she was a premature baby, the vibrant and dynamic young woman who greeted us in Brisbane had come of age. Kate exuded poise, style, and charm. Her sophisticated persona was accentuated by her education, broadened by her international travels, and tempered by the fateful disaster in India.

The festivities began with ten days of big city life while *Osprey* was moored in the Brisbane River. Brisbane is a glittering, urbane city with an innovative marine transportation system. Catamarans and launches whisk passengers up and down the Brisbane River to residential areas, office complexes, parks, and shops.

Our trio celebrated Mother's Day by hopping aboard a ferry bound for a koala and kangaroo sanctuary upriver from Brisbane. Cuddling a koala was fun—the friendly little guys were fuzzy, docile, and surprisingly heavy. While Kate and I fed a baby kangaroo, a huge ostrich-like bird with a nasty disposition sneaked up behind PL. Suddenly the emu wrapped its beak around PL's ear and literally tore off her gold earring. PL's ear lobe fared okay but one of her best earrings was now making an unexpected detour through an ostrich sized gullet. Since the ladies were not willing to search through emu droppings dressed in their Sunday best, and I was a bit reluctant to slit the offending bird's throat with my Swiss Army knife, the emu unwittingly claimed PL's prize earring by default.

Our mate Terro Hammond called Brisbane home, so the former America Cup navigator took it upon himself to show us his town. Along with his lady Norma, Terro introduced us to the friendly folks at the Royal Queensland Yacht Squadron. As Norma wryly observed, many of the Yacht Squadron's ladies were enchanted when the snowy haired paragon of Australian sailing stopped at their tables to introduce us. It is a tough business being a legend, but Norma reluctantly conceded that she supposed someone had to do it.

Sailing the reinforced trade winds from Queensland's Brisbane to the Torres Straits was a barnburner ride, sort of like torching off the afterburners on a fighter. Along the way we sailed in the lee of The Great Barrier Reef, about 1200 miles of contiguous reefs that have created the largest living organism on earth. Since the constant barrage of blustery weather and large following seas left us with relatively few protected anchorages, the scattered resort islands and harbor towns along the Coral Coast were very welcome sights.

Unlike the placid lagoons of the South Pacific, The Great Barrier Reef was a wild and untamed region that pushed our limits. Wonderful tropical creatures greeted us from huge 80-pound mara wrasse to turquoise lipped giant clams the size of beer kegs. The water was a bit on the nippy side and the visibility varied, but there was always something interesting to see and nasty creatures to avoid.

One of our favorite haunts was Great Keppel Island. An ancient beachcomber became smitten with Kate. As we sampled his tea and freshly baked scones, the grizzled "mayor" of the island regaled us with great stories. The spunky old timer vainly tried to convince Kate to stay so they could celebrate his ninetieth birthday together. Obviously he did not subscribe to Clint Eastwood's adage that a man has got to know his limitations.

The Whitsunday Islands, 450 miles NNW of Queensland's Gold Coast, are billed as the yachting mecca of Australia. But the glossy tourist brochures failed to mention prolonged bouts of stiff breezes, choppy seas, and relatively chilly water. My two ladies made it abundantly clear that clinging to a rolling bunk in less than ideal conditions left a little something to be desired.

One squally afternoon *Osprey* was nestled inside a rather tight reef anchorage about the size of a tennis court. Suddenly a major wind shift pivoted us around our anchor and pushed the stern of our boat dangerously close to jagged teeth of the Hook Island's coral infested shoreline. The short steep seas relentlessly pounded into the narrow mouthed inlet and abruptly wrapped our anchor chain around a submerged coral head. The boat was violently jerked up short, like an errant horse being viciously reigned in by an unsympathetic rider. Horses have a flexible, muscular neck to absorb a sudden shock. *Osprey's* rigid anchor chain was not as forgiving—the result was a mangled anchor bow roller...and chaos.

With horrible visions of *Osprey* being splattered on a windswept reef or obliterating all her bow fittings, I barked orders while PL and Kate valiantly coped with the bow's erratic whipsaw gyrations. Over the howling wind I yelled at my hysterical wife and daughter, a breech of protocol and civility in the crew's view. Although my intent was to warn PL and Kate about the lethal consequences of being snagged by the heavy anchor chain, my crew already had the big picture. Kate hastily grabbed a pair of cooking mitts for a bit of protection and then tried to sort out the mess on the bow. PL fired up the engine and powered the boat forward to take a bit of the strain off the grinding anchor chain that was trashing the bow. I struggled into my scuba gear and then dove over the side to check out our limited options.

From my perspective thirty feet underwater I could watch the unfolding drama. An incoming wave would jerk *Osprey's* bow to the sky and wedge the wrapped chain even tighter around the huge bommie. Then the bow would dive into the next wave trough and the battered chain would go slack. I sucked up an entire tank of air in about ten minutes as I unwrapped bits of chain. Every time the boat bow dipped down, I gingerly grabbed a section and unwrapped it from the coral. After I got the chain unraveled, my harried crew dangled a rope down that I tied off to our newly freed up anchor. I flopped back into the cockpit, peeled off my diving gear, and regrouped. We retrieved the anchor by winching the rope aboard from the side of the boat and bypassing the pretzel-shaped bow fittings. As we got our wounded boat underway, I just stared glassy-eyed at the carnage on deck. Whenever I am asked of the most important piece of equipment on our trip, I always point to PL and Kate.

At least we faired better than Captain Cook when his ship hit a reef while charting the Great Barrier Reef in the vicinity of Lizard Island. The intrepid captain lucked out since the bommie in question broke off and plugged the gaping hole in *Endeavor's* wooden hull. Although it took Cook's party two months to repair the damage to their vessel, our repair took only two days. The Aussie engineer from Airlie Beach who designed and installed our new stainless steel anchor roller assured me the massive assembly was there for the duration. So far the bulletproof guarantee seems to have done the trick.

Hayman Island, one of seventy-four Whitsunday Islands, is an opulent world-class resort with a European ambiance. Visiting yachtsmen were free to stroll the elegant grounds, but the resort required overnight guests to book lodging ashore—most cruising budgets precluded a long visit. The architecture and artwork were extraordinary but, then again, so were the birds and animals.

The antics of the colorful lorikeets, the resident parrot of Australia, were wildly entertaining at first—a regular flying circus. Our relationship with the little parrots soured a bit after we discovered the pesky birds were into stealing our lunch as well as any bright, colorful trinkets they could wrap their beaks around.

Towards evening the brown fuzzy fruit hanging in the high branches of the palm trees started to unfurl…suddenly gossamer wings sprouted from the fuzz, then pointy ears and a small fox-like face emerged—upside down. As if a silent roll call had been broadcast, hundreds and hundreds of huge fruit bats dropped from their high perches and soared off in search of their evening meal.

It was off to Cairns, party central of Queensland, in early July. After helping settle *Osprey* in at Yorky's Nob Marina, PL and Kate hopped a flight to Melbourne for a pampered week at Robinson's By The Sea, a B & B near St. Kilda's. My crew felt sorry for me, so I was allowed to fly in a few days later after I put in my locker time on a few boat projects. The ladies reminisced about life in the big city as they pointed out civilized accoutrements such as a huge bed with fresh linens, a bathtub with an endless supply of water, a flush toilet, and a dining room table that did not roll or pitch. I took their point.

Since Melbourne is a thousand miles south of Cairns, the temperature is much cooler. For the first time in a long time our coats got a workout. The nip in the air actually felt good after spending so much time in the hot tropical climate along Australia's northeast coast. Melbourne is beautiful, modern, and definitely full of diversity. Kate and PL enjoyed the shops and museums as much as I enjoyed my reprieve from the never-ending blue jobs aboard *Osprey*.

When I mentioned Seattle to an eccentric trolley car conductor, the guy's eyes lit up as he made an unscheduled stop in the middle of a busy intersection. The enthusiastic driver launched into a long-winded history lesson extolling the virtues of the retired Melbourne trolleys that had been shipped to Seattle for the new waterfront rail line—definitely more information than I needed.

From Melbourne another flight took us north to Sydney for a five-day stay. Our guesthouse was located in the charming seaside village of Manly. A short ferry ride zipped us into Sydney's magnificent harbor with its soaring Harbour Bridge and renowned sail-shaped Opera House. We indulged ourselves with great dining and local wines from nearby Hunter Valley. Interestingly enough Australian wines are less expensive in Seattle than in Sydney. With PL and Kate pointing out the nuances and helping me through the rough spots, we attended a performance of Renaissance music at the Opera House and browsed through Sydney's museums and art galleries. The stunning sights of Sydney and the easy living was a very nice diversion, but then it was time to snap back to our personal reality show of voyaging west.

Back in Cairns PL and I found it hard to say goodbye to Kate, now a veteran crew after two months aboard. Our small family was carrying on and blossoming despite the lingering sadness over Tyler's death. After all the hugs and good wishes, Kate flew back to Italy, but she would be visiting us again for Christmas in Thailand.

Poignant words from one of Tyler's favorite "Grateful Dead" songs came to mind and set the mood of the moment: *Fare you well, fare you well, I love you more than words can tell.*

As *Osprey* sailed into the sparsely populated northeast coast of Oz, the prospect of encountering carnivorous saltwater crocodiles loomed. Since these man-eating salties inhabit the estuaries north of Cairns, swimming ceased to be on our agenda. Ominous looking signs warned, "Estuarine crocodiles inhabit this river system." The signs depicted a crocodile's open jaws adjacent to a swimmer. The universal red diagonal slash over the swimmer suggested that swimming could be hazardous to your health.

The Flinders Group is named in honor of Mathew Flinders who circumnavigated Australia in the early 1800's and gave the continent its name. Located off the coast of northern Queensland, the remote islands seemed like a perfect place to soak up a bit of solitude and check out the ancient Aboriginal caves we had heard about.

After PL and I had dragged our dinghy up on a deserted beach, we hiked across Stanley Island in hopes of learning more about the Aboriginals who had once occupied the island. We eventually spotted a few Aboriginal stick figure sketches etched in the face of a cliff. A few hours later we wandered back to the dinghy and discovered a new development on the beach—massive footprints on either side of an undulating furrow in the mud, a saltie on the prowl. It was time for a quick exit..

Australian Customs and Immigration aircraft patrol the relatively deserted waters of the Northern Territory and northern Queensland in order to spot boatloads of illegal immigrants from Indonesia and New Guinea. One of our few contacts with the outside world was our daily encounter with the patrol plane as it buzzed low over *Osprey*. The pilots greeted us on the radio and then with a friendly wag of the wings flew off—a welcome visit from an old friend in a desolate section of the continent.

The Torres Strait, separating Australia's northern Queensland from Papua New Guinea, is claimed to be one of the windiest areas in the world. Locals told us it blows like hell in July and August, and then backs off in September. After rounding Cape York, the infamous straits concoct an unnerving brew of nasty reefs, violent currents, and sunken ships. Fortunately for us the seas were placid, the wind was gentle, and the skies were clear. Darwin was 700 miles to the west as PL and I sailed over the top of Oz and into Crocodile Dundee country.

Darwin, our gateway to the outback, is a funky place perched on the top of the continent in the Northern Territory. The town was rebuilt after it was wiped out by a cyclone a few decades ago. *Osprey's* temporary home was the new marina at Cullen Bay, which is situated in a lagoon complete with condos and restaurants. Since Cullen Bay had its own set of locks, the water level at the marina never varied in a region renowned for twenty-foot tides.

As I strolled the docks, I noticed a battered fifty-foot sailboat that had just limped into port. The exhausted skipper explained that an unlighted freighter in the Java Sea had collided with his uninsured yacht. The hit and run freighter kept on going even though the stricken yacht's crew shot off distress flares and broadcast a Mayday message. One of the sailboat's three crewmen was washed overboard, but his mates rescued him. Although the crew and the boat survived, the skipper assured me that you are definitely on your own in Indonesia.

Exploring the Australian outback intrigued us so we booked a one-week 4x4 camping safari. The catch was getting to Alice Springs, where PL and I would theoretically hook up with our guide and new traveling companions.

Our introduction to the outback was a twenty-hour bus ride from Darwin to Alice Springs. The bus driver assured us that the massive crash bars welded to the grill would be sufficient to deflect wayward kangaroos and dingoes, but hitting a wild camel or wild horse might slow us up. Reflecting on this tidbit of news, we spent a fitful night trying to sleep as the mammoth bus rumbled along through the desolate desert landscape. Once every few hours the bus would pull into a ramshackle shack that seemed to double as petrol station and outhouse. Luckily there was usually a cool drink in the station's "esky" to parch a traveler's thirst.

An hour after our arrival in Alice Springs, a gracious Aussie waved us aboard his sturdy 4 x 4 lorry. After hooking a huge chuck wagon-type trailer to his rig, Allen introduced us to a dozen new mates—an international mix of travelers who joined us as our rig bounced across endless miles of untracked territory through the baking outback. Under a limitless night sky alive with thousands of twinkling stars, we ate damper around the campfire and listened to the haunting sounds of the didgeridoo. Sleep came easily as we bundled up under the warm covers of our swags.

Ayers Rock, the world's largest monolith, gleams in shades of crimson, orange, and gold at sunrise and sunset. The best show is at dusk when the setting sun paints the Rock in an awesome spectrum of progressively darker red hues. Uluru, the aboriginal name for the colossal rock, owes its unique color spectrum to heavy deposits of iron and subsequent burnishing by eons of sun and wind. Uluru seemed to mystically burst from the flat desert plains of the outback, which was reason enough for us to slog up the steep weathered flank to its 1142-foot summit. Since a few climbers have fatally pitched off the Rock, we had no issue with following the ranger's advice about using the preset climbing ropes

Aboriginals, whose lineage dates back 50,000 years, descend from a line of people striking out from Southeast Asia about the same time Cro-Magnons overshadowed the Neanderthals in Europe. One evening our bunch was sitting around the campfire, when suddenly a strange group of bobbing shadows startled us. We could hear a bit of harsh guttural clucking as the shadows materialized into a small band of wandering Aboriginals. Our guide invited these very shy folks to join us. The amateur magician in our group proceeded to put on show that startled the newcomers. As the appreciative audience applauded, our magician magically pulled a quarter from behind the ear of an ancient Aboriginal woman. The venerable lady was astounded by the simple trick and her traveling band broke into hysterical laughter—their stone-age countenances assumed the guileless wonderment usually reserved for children

At an Aboriginal encampment one of the residents schooled us in the subtleties of the primitive and uniquely beautiful native artwork. Aboriginal artists paint Dreamtime stories to depict their Aboriginal heritage and the folklore that goes along with it.

A drug and alcohol rehabilitation outpost was a graphic demonstration of the Aborigine's plight. The center attempted to offer the resident Aborigines the impetus to live like their ancestors instead of cowering on the edge of the white man's world. Scores of Aboriginals lived along the riverbank close to the rehab center. Many of these forlorn souls were abandoned children addicted to petrol sniffing. Assimilation of the Aboriginals, about 2% of the Australian population, into mainstream Australia has been a difficult affair and it was not until 1966 that the government's all white Australia policy was abandoned.

It seemed that all the native people we encountered in the South Pacific shared a common plight. Whether the islanders are Polynesian, Tongan, Fijian, Maori, or Aboriginals their encounters with the early European explorers in the twilight of the eighteenth century decimated their cultures. Oceania was changed forever as colonialism and missionaries inadvertently gutted the cultures—disease finished the job. Not a proud legacy. It made me wonder just who was uncivilized.

13

More than just Bali

Indonesia is a sprawling 13,000-island archipelago extending more than 3000 miles along the equator. It is the world's fourth most populous nation and the biggest Muslim country on earth.

PL and I sailed into Kupang, Indonesia in late August after a pleasant four-day passage from Darwin. Kupang is busy, noisy and quite dirty, but also exotic and mysterious. As *Osprey* dropped the hook in the colorful harbor, the Muslim call to prayer reverberated from a Mosque overlooking our anchorage. The chanting began before 5 am and was repeated five times a day as the worshippers bowed to Mecca—a ritual that would become quite familiar over the next two years. Once ashore, we began our exploration of the city and immediately went into sensory overload. Everything looked strange and sounded foreign. Ditches lining the streets were piled with an assortment of rotten food and garbage. The accompanying vile aroma challenged even the hardiest of noses. Colorful bemos, basically tricked out minivans, clogged the streets and blasted us with rock music from their stereo systems. A constant barrage of chatter came our way as the taxi drivers tried to lure us into their vehicles.

Our bewildered looks seemed to attract every con man and hustler in town, but then Jimmy the Fixer latched on to us. Jimmy offered to act as our guide and as his name implied, The Fixer also smoothed things over with the local government bureaucrats who seem to prey on us yachtie types. For a $50 fee the Fixer secured our entry papers, served as our interpreter, arranged for diesel delivery, and organized a tour of the countryside.

Jimmy's van rumbled through the hinterlands and into a few small villages during our road trip. It was a humbling experience to view the subsistence culture of the locals, but the friendly shouts of "Hi Meester" and "Hi Meeses" was certainly a welcome break from the aggressive yelling of the Kupang taxi drivers. Unlike New Zealand and Australia where we enjoyed the comfort and security of a modern westernized existence, Indonesia was intimidating. PL and I were definitely entangled in the Third World where people struggle to survive and poverty is just an accepted part of life.

The conveniences taken for granted back home became just a cherished memory. A trip to the post office turned into a 45-minute mime act as my mate tried to buy six postcards and stamps. With no ATM's, exchanging cash for local currency was a two-hour study in frustration. Since 3,000 rupiah only equaled one dollar, the wads of rupiah seemed like stocking stuffers for our pockets. Communication was always a challenge. After waiting in line for an hour, a fellow yachtie was refused service because his money was deemed too dirty. Another friend was refused a cash advance because the local bank telexed a request for one million dollars instead of one million rupiah.

North American style toilets are almost non-existent in rural Indonesia, as in much of the Third World. Instead of a familiar porcelain throne, the standard toilet fixture consists of two molded foot patterns straddling a strategic center hole that plunges into the abyss. Next to the hole sits a large tub of water with a ladle. The person using the facility squats down, straddles the intimidating gap, and does his or her thing. When the job is done, water is ladled into the hole and apparently some sort of flushing occurs. Toilet paper is nonexistent. The left hand is judiciously dipped into a tub of water and then used to wash one's privates. Drip-drying completes the call to nature. *The Lonely Planet Guide Book* mentions that it is indeed bad form to offer your left hand for a handshake greeting. It always pays to carry your own toilet paper.

The villagers lugged tremendously heavy water jugs two kilometers from a reservoir to provide their community with drinking water. The reservoir water supply was also used for bathing and washing clothes. The concept was simple and effective, but not even close to hygienic. Three tiers of pools provided a first level for drinking, a second level for bathing, and a third level for laundry.

PL and I visited a family who lived in a stick shack with a fire pit in the center to cook the food. The cornhusks hanging from the ceiling would eventually seed next season's crop. In fact the only food they had was corn since rice was not in their budget. Life is not easy for these peasants. A young mother of four small children wove *ikat* cloth, the famous textile unique to Indonesia, on a loom in the back of her hut. After two weeks of labor, she produced one small bolt of *ikat* that sold to a merchant for $10—a fraction of its retail value. Her four children huddled silently together on a rough wooden bench and stared at us in bewilderment. We saw no toys, books, or even paper. Poverty took on a whole new meaning after that visit.

PL went for a stroll with her friends Carol and Sue. Since kamikaze bemo drivers hurtled down the streets of town with carefree abandon, the ladies quickly switched to a defensive pedestrian mode. After cheating death they walked towards a quieter area of town armed with their smiles and a few pertinent Indonesian phrases. Such simple courtesies never failed to surprise and delight the locals, no matter what the country. The Indonesian people are very small and quiet, but they could not resist peeking at the three foreign women in their midst. Carol, being close to six feet tall, must have seemed like a giantess. PL's light hair and Sue's bright colored dress gleamed like exotic Christmas ornaments in the sedate Indonesian world of jet black hair and conservative clothes. Aware that they were drawing a curious crowd, the threesome continued their walk exchanging nods and bidding the Indonesians, "*Selamat pagi,*" or good morning. Women greeted them with big smiles as the trio strolled through the alleyway. The children trailed behind them as though these foreigners were a new version of the Pied Piper.

Eventually PL and company chanced upon a group of women talking and cooking over several open fires in a cemetery. Piles of feathers, bones, and chicken feet surrounded the chattering cooks. Another group of women was skinning animals, presumably goats. With only a pile of heads and horns and assorted body parts scattered about, the main entrée was difficult to identify. However, the swarms of flies enveloping the carcasses graphically demonstrated the hazards of dining locally. PL smiled and continued on her way trying not to look overwhelmed. Although the accommodating cooks motioned that the intrepid ladies would be welcome to stay and eat, the culturally challenged yachties shook their heads no thanks. PL and her two sidekicks murmured "*Selamat tinggal,*" waved goodbye, and beat a hasty exit.

On the outskirts of a fishing village, PL and I approached a group of men hustling local products. After buying a silver belt and a small basket it was about time to leave, but then a scruffy young merchant with the bright red teeth of a hardcore beetle nut chewer offered me a great deal on a homemade wooden comb. I pantomimed no thanks and doffed my straw hat displaying a very tan and very bald head. The surprised vendor got the joke and soon he and his curious friends were all bent over from belly laughing at the spectacle.

During the next five weeks our travels took us from West Timor to Lombok through Indonesia's southeast island chain of Nusa Tenggara. As we sailed from east to west the parched, arid environment morphed into a more lush, tropical landscape. Although many of the people we encountered were poor economically, their cultures were rich in diversity.

An overnight sail from Kupang to the island of Flores brought us to the home of Hery, The Fixer's little brother. Because the Fixer had given his bro a heads up call, Hery was there for us when our flotilla of five boats sailed into town. Hery schmoozed the local cops so our check-in was painless. Although the Keli Matu volcano and its famous three colored lakes were new to us, Hery assured us they were not to be missed. We arranged to meet Hery and his van the next morning at 5 am on the beach. Unfortunately no one in our cruising party considered the implications of surf landing in the dark with only Hery's headlights as our guide. When morning arrived a loud bell rousted us awake. The bell not only called the local Muslims to prayer, but also doubled as a tidal wave warning system.

Since it is considered poor taste for women to wear shorts or sleeveless tops in Indonesia, PL selected a pair of long pants and a shirt with sleeves. Suitably attired she hopped in our dinghy and we headed for the beach. Although a dim pair of headlights was the only thing visible in that predawn hour, I suddenly heard a roar and realized that the surf was up. After assessing the situation I came up with a plan. I locked down the dinghy wheels and proceeded to surf our small rubber boat towards the beach. The first mate's task is to hop out of the dinghy at the right instant and pull the wallowing inflatable toward the beach while I yank up the outboard motor. The drill then calls for both of us to drag the dinghy out of the raging surf and wheel it up on the beach in a triumphant manner. When PL heard the skipper's order to jump into the supposedly shallow water, she jumped. Sadly the water was a bit deeper than I had figured.

From this point on accounts of the story differ, but the frothing surf did engulf a very surprised first mate. Needless to say, PL was drenched from head to foot, but she valiantly tried to drag the dinghy onto the beach while the surf tried to yank both she and the wayward inflatable back into the bay. She was tumbled around like a rag doll going through a spin dry cycle in a dryer. With sand and grit covering her body and filling every orifice, PL staggered out of the breaking waves and crawled to shore. It has been reported that she also harbored a few ill thoughts about the skipper.

It was still totally dark outside and the whole incident might have passed unnoticed except for a group of Hery's friends who were there to meet us. A very kind man took pity on PL and quietly suggested she go with him to his nearby cousin's house. My very damp first mate sloshed alongside the good-hearted guy and she stood quietly while he explained to his sleepy eyed cousin why a soaking wet foreign woman was standing outside the cousin's doorstep so early in the morning. Soon PL found herself being led through a long dark hallway into a small room that apparently served as the bathroom. In the center of the bathroom stood a concrete well. On top of the well hung a bucket connected to a pulley system. As the empty bucket was lowered into the well, another full bucket of water emerged. She rinsed her salt soaked clothes and tried to wash the sand off her body as best she could. Stark naked and alone inside a strange dark room, PL found a battered cooking pot—now she had the makings of a shower. I was banned from the room but I could hear her pouring water over her head. Soon my disgruntled companion was at least semi-clean but still without a stitch of clothing to wear. I guiltily offered a dry sweatshirt and her friend Sue loaned her a pair of extra shorts. At that stage dress code ceased to be a priority.

After PL was spiffed up, our group boarded the waiting vans and joined Hery to see the famous colored mountain lakes of Keli Mutu. The fabled deep lakes, which change color from time to time, are carved into the flank of Keli Mutu volcano just shy of the summit. We trudged up to about the 5000-foot level of the mountain on a clear sunny morning. Just below us the lakes were spectacularly beautiful in their full livery of blood red, ink black, and robin egg blue. A few years back the three lakes were reportedly turquoise, green, and black. Our guide suggested that perhaps the changing colors were the result of the different minerals that leached into the lakes. We were told the legend about how the souls of the dead inhabit the three lakes. Young people's souls go to the warmth of the red lake, old people's spirits travel to the cold of the blue lake, and the demented ghosts of thieves and murderers are plunged into the black lake. We have no word on how a soul would react when the lake changes color.

Osprey sailed from Endes and eventually anchored at Lehok Uwanda Desami, a pristine marine park on Rinca Island. The parched hills framed the warm, clear blue waters of our lagoon anchorage—a gorgeous place. The main attractions are the Komodo dragons, or *ora*. Dragons grow into ten-foot, 220-pound monsters that are capable of incapacitating and devouring water buffalo or the occasional tourist. Our guide reassured us that typically their daily fare leaned more towards goats, deer, and monkeys. After spying several of the large carnivorous monitor lizards our diminutive local guide, armed only with his forked anti-dragon stick, warned us not to provoke them. We deemed the park ranger's words very sound advice indeed. Although it was a sweltering morning, being on the lookout for rogue dragons kept us from daydreaming about tall frosty tropical drinks.

Moyo, a small island off the coast of Sumbawa, boasts the small and very exclusive Amanwana Resort. The canvas-roofed, teak floored bungalows are situated next to a secluded cove on the edge of the lush jungle. A fashionably attired young man greeted us. He explained the visiting rules for cruiserss and graciously conducted a private tour of the luxury nature camp. The 1997 cost per night was $670 and according to our guide, the late Princess Diana had stayed there on occasion—a bit out of our budget. As we were leaving our escort suggested that we visit the nearby village and greet the chief. He also mentioned that any donations of food or clothing would be very much appreciated by the locals. PL took his advice and put some things together to donate to the villagers before going to visit.

Although the isolated anchorage was fairly untenable, meeting the folks from the small community turned out to be the highlight of our stay on Moyo. After presenting our gifts to a contingent of villagers who met us on the beach, we were invited into the chief's hut. PL and I felt quite honored when the chief offered us seats at his table, adjacent to himself and his father. The headman's wife and a collection of curious neighbors sat on the floor next to us. Although we could only muster a few Indonesian phrases to explain our visit, the serenely calm elders listened very graciously and pretended to understand everything. A woman appeared carrying a tray of very sweet tea. After our tea was poured a plate of elaborate rice cookies were placed on the table. Later on a jackfruit was cut open and passed around. PL and I were encouraged to dip our fingers into the soft flesh and extract bite size pieces. It was delicious! Soon everyone in the room was participating in the process and the huge jackfruit disappeared. It was hard to accept anything from those fine people since they obviously had so little, but the villagers were determined to be hospitable and we did not wish to offend. It is instructive to consider that the cost of one night at the Amanwana Resort would feed and clothe their entire village for months.

PL and I became rather spoiled with our daily regimen of anchoring in beautiful secluded coves and snorkeling in gin-clear, eighty plus degree water. As much as we loved skin diving in the coral reefs around Fiji and Tonga, the coral formations in Indonesia were even more vibrant and spectacular. The immense coral gardens are energized by the brilliant tropical sun and glow in radiant hues of pink, blue, orange, yellow, and green. Exquisitely colorful tropical fish added to the rainbow of dazzling colors. It is a fine thing to swim with giant grouper, black tipped reef sharks, and hawk billed turtles. Unfortunately preservation of the reefs and fish is not a priority in Indonesia where corruption and poverty is rampant. Native fishermen often used dynamite to harvest their catches. Many Indonesians, not unlike the citizens of other developing countries, treat their part of the planet like a garbage dump. In a pristine anchorage I watched a neighboring boat pass a bag of garbage and a few rupiah to a couple of locals in a wooden dugout. My friend's plan was to hire the native guys to take his garbage ashore and burn it. The reality was a bit different. The unconcerned paddlers pocketed the money and then with a shrug dumped the garbage into the crystal clear bay just behind the environmentally conscious, and now incredulous, yachtie.

Selat Lombok, a turbulent strait renowned for raging currents and colorful lateen rigged fishing canoes, separates Lombok from Bali. The gulf is not just geographic. Whereas swinging Bali has enthusiastically embraced tourism, Lombok only tolerates it. Many of Lombok's Muslim residents cling to their agricultural heritage and conservative views. Liberal minded backpackers may flock to the white sandy beaches and hedonistic fun in the sun lifestyle of the Gilis Islands on Lombok's northwest coast, but traditional island prohibitions still forbid menstruating women from visiting Lombok's temples.

PL and I figured the local taxi service to be the ultimate low budget operation. The Lombok translation of taxi is a single sway backed horse, only one step removed from the glue factory, valiantly pulling a wooden cart. The drivers jam their clunky wagons with as many paying customers as possible, but the tired horses have a tough go dragging lead butted tourists up Lombok's hilly back roads. Although no discounts were offered on our horse wagon ride, we hopped out of the cart on the uphill sections in hopes the horse would not expire and leave us stranded.

Religion is an integral part of the Indonesian experience. Hinduism, Buddhism, and animism tinge this dominantly Islamic country with diverse perspectives concerning humanities place in the overall scheme of things. Since *Pilgrim's* crew promised to look after *Osprey*, we left our baby snuggly anchored in Lombok and hopped a local flight to Yogyakarta, Java. As the cultural heart of Java, Yogyakarta is a fascinating place renowned for exquisite batik and traditional performing arts. It is also the gateway to imposing edifices that glorify the diverse religions of the Indonesian archipelago.

Borobudur, one of the greatest Buddhist relics in SE Asia and the primo tourist attraction in Indonesia, highlighted our trip to Java. The mammoth stone monument depicts a seekers flight through the cosmos from the trials of the everyday world to a spiraling ascension to nirvana, the Buddhist heaven. I envisioned myself stumbling along after losing my son—hardly a spiraling ascension. My pain was still very real and my soul had been laid wide-open, but I too was now exploring the possibilities of change and transformation.

In order to give equal due to both the Buddhists and Hindus, PL and I also attended the Ramayana Ballet in Prambanan as more than a hundred dancers and gamelan musicians retold the story of Rama Wijaya and princess Dewi Shinta. A local expat explained that the acrobatic spectacle was a fable about monkey armies, giants, and clashing battles. The ninth century story is carved into the base of the soaring spires of the Hindu temple Shiva Mahadeva that shimmered in the distance.

After our return from Java, *Osprey* and crew sailed to the legendary island of Bali. The relatively new Bali International Marina is a crumbling affair with bad wiring and dilapidated piers. Balinese culture is alive and well but you have to look for it. We rented a car and hightailed it for the countryside, away from the huge resorts and masses of foreign tourists. Although careening through the horrific traffic in the tourist areas was mind numbing, the payoff was an escape into a serene countryside of terraced rice paddies, wild jungle gorges, and volcanic mountains.

Our guesthouse in the art colony at Ubud overlooked acres of glistening rice paddies where backbreaking labor is a way of life. It seemed to us that work in an art studio or woodworking shop would be more appealing, but the laborers probably did not have much choice. Even though English fluency is one of the fastest tracks to upward mobility in tourist areas throughout the world, children of the field hands are usually put to work rather than sent to school. Unfortunately schooling in Indonesia, while inexpensive to a tourist, is not free. It was shades of India all over again when PL and I stumbled across an elaborate and colorful ceremony. Actually the smell gave it away—a cremation ceremony. At least the Balinese version involved a bit of festivity whereas the Indian version featured circling vultures.

The charming seaside town of Candi Dasa was a welcome retreat from the constant strains of international cruising. Wendy, our genial B&B hostess from Melbourne, spent many of her holidays at Ida Beach Village, so she graciously booked a cottage for us months earlier. Lolling about in our beach chairs and enjoying the luxury of a well run, intimate resort revitalized our outlook. PL was so revitalized she did not even flinch (well, maybe a little) when the ancient male masseuse blithely peeled down the top of her one-piece swimming suit during her massage on the bar's veranda. The European guests just continued sipping their sundowners. PL not only received an excellent full body massage, but both of us discarded a bit of North American conservatism that day—of course PL's discard was much more personalized.

In the fall of 1997 we celebrated PL's fiftieth birthday and our twenty-seventh wedding anniversary. The season also commemorated the second anniversary of losing Tyler and Ashley in India. Although we were excited about cruising up the Red Sea and entering the Mediterranean by spring, it was difficult to part with good friends who lingered in SE Asia and others who sailed south around the Cape of Good Hope. Conflicted emotions graphically reminded me that life is a dynamic, challenging affair—I was just along for the ride.

Osprey's resident Shellbacks crossed back into the Northern Hemisphere as we journeyed north through the Java Sea. After eighteen months in the Southern Hemisphere, PL and I had a few adjustments to make from an atmospheric science point of view. The Southern Cross was out and the North Star was in. October was again part of the northern autumn instead of the Southern Hemisphere's spring. High pressure now spun clockwise, the polar opposite of the southern version.

Most of our energy was focused on avoiding huge cargo ships, rusty fishing trawlers, and hundreds of tiny wooden sailing sampans. Although our radar could pick up large vessels chugging our way through the haze and smoke, wooden sampans and canoes were usually a surprise until we were eyeball to eyeball. Typically we sailed alone so any decisions and schedule changes were our baby, but occasionally an incident would make us rethink the wisdom of being a lone sailboat in notoriously hostile waters.

An unflagged, grimy fishing trawler steamed towards us and then veered away at the last possible second. The scraggly crew wore ski masks. Since a pirate intercept of *Osprey* on the high seas seemed like a distinct possibility at the time, we made a frantic radio call in hopes of contacting other yachts. A veteran cruiser in the South China Sea answered our call and noted that our situation was neither dire nor life threatening. He explained that the ski masks protected the fishermen from the intense sun and the intimidating approaches were merely to encourage the trawler's evil spirits to jump from their boat to ours. After scaring hell out of us, the grungy boat circled back around in hopes of scoring on some cigarettes. Our trading stash of Marlboros dwindled and our collection of vaulting evil spirits skyrocketed as we pacified superstitious fishermen from the Java Sea to the Indian Ocean.

Because of the El Nino weather pattern, the heavy monsoon rains were late and the devastating forest fires in Sumatra and Kalimantan were uncontrolled. Our 900-mile dash across the Java Sea to Singapore was plagued with fickle breezes, searing equatorial sun, and heavy acrid smoke from the forest fires hundreds of miles away. Damp bandanas over our noses warded off the choking smoke and gave us that certain outlaw look.

About five days out of Singapore *Osprey* was motoring along in calm water, with not even a puff of breeze to be found, when our transmission decided to quit…not a good situation in that area of the world. I spouted a few assorted profanities while I tore open the engine access hatch. After flailing around in the roasting hot engine compartment, I located the culprit—a rusted out transmission oil cooler. The silky smooth red transmission oil had been transformed into a puddle of turgid brown salt-water goop. Since we were alone and in the middle of an area renowned for pirates and such, our options were rather limited. In one of her keen flashes of insight, PL suggested that perhaps it was possible to suck out the offending water with our Shop Vac…a great idea, and it worked! Fortunately I was able to rustle up a replacement oil cooler from my stash of spares. We installed the new oil cooler, refilled the transmission with oil, and *Osprey* was under way again.

PL proved once again that there are two key elements to cruising as a couple: *Choose a good woman and listen to her.*

14

Strait of Malacca

○ ○

To have lost the taste for marvels and adventures is no more a matter for congratulation than losing our teeth, our hair, our palate and finally, our hopes.

—*C.S. Lewis*

Singapore is a classic example of work in progress. Our navigation charts promised navigation buoys and open waterways, but we stared at landfills and high rises. The local authorities simply borrowed dirt from Malaysia and Indonesia to expand their thriving island kingdom.

As PL and I sailed into Singapore, one of the world's largest shipping ports, our radar screen lit up like a pinball machine—a target rich environment. The massive harbor was chock full of shipping. Huge cargo vessels and mammoth oil tankers dwarfed the scores of weathered coastal freighters and rusting fishing trawlers. Since many of these rather substantial vessels jockeyed for position in the anchorages, we steered clear out of sheer self-preservation. *Osprey* eventually found a home at Nongsa Point Marina, a rather upscale complex on the Indonesian side of Singapore Strait. A swift passenger ferry ran from the marina, across the strait, and into downtown Singapore—our transportation problem was solved.

Singapore is sort of the Switzerland of Asia. Strolling past towering office buildings spilling over with elegant shops and cosmopolitan restaurants was a huge dose of culture shock after cruising Indonesia for three months. Throngs of people paraded along pristine sidewalks passing one huge shopping center after another. It was quickly apparent that buying and selling make Singapore tick. Money is the key ingredient—you need plenty and there is no end of places to spend it. Singapore, with its free port status and exotic location, has long been renowned as a shopping paradise. Although the locale is fascinating, there are not as many bargains to be had these days because of the competitive global economy. Since the bustling metropolis is only sixty miles from the equator, the sun rises and sets about the same time each day of the year. The climate is typically hot and humid. For a touch of variety, the NW monsoon brings heavy rainfall and thunderstorms from November to January.

The government of Singapore is into mandates: fines for tossing gum on the sidewalk, caning for civil disobedience, and death for illicit drug possession. The crime rate is understandably low. Access to the center of the city by private vehicles is limited since a car's license number determines which day of the week city driving is legal. Although this approach to law enforcement appeared a bit heavy-handed, the city sparkled with clean sidewalks and uncluttered streets. Raffles Hotel, an elegant century old vestige of the British Empire, invented the Singapore Sling so the *Osprey* crew felt duty bound to visit the famous bar and enjoy a sip of history.

A cluster of elderly gentlemen in Chinatown etched an enduring portrait of Singapore in my memory, as they hung a number of beautifully gilded birdcages on a teahouse wall. The wizened old men serenely sipped tea and contentedly listened to their pet songbirds sing. The bird that continues to warble its own song and pays no heed to interlopers is a bird with panache. Both the beautiful birds and their proud owners seemed oblivious to the commercial chaos around them. I learned that if I was to find such serenity, I must also loosen my grip.

A three-week trip back home was on our agenda. PL and I left *Osprey* tucked away at Nongsa Point, made our way to the stunning Changi Airport, and hopped a flight back to Seattle. Our first homecoming since San Diego was nice as far as reunions go, but the cruising lifestyle was ingrained in our souls. We now defined ourselves much differently. Our detachment was interesting to us but distressing to many of our friends. It was painfully obvious that we were much less invested in rehashes of our former life. It was time to move on and turn the page.

Our reintroduction to life in the tropics was an assault of stifling humidity and violent thunderstorms as we cruised into Malaysian waters. The quick dose of reality therapy jolted our jet-lagged minds. Heptavax inoculations and weekly Larium medication insulated us from the endemic problems of hepatitis and malaria, but there was no silver bullet to protect *Osprey* as we sailed through the infamous Strait of Malacca. The South China Sea is notorious for vicious pirate attacks. Although most of the incidents involve large ships, small cruising sailboats are not exempt. The most dangerous regions are purported to be the southern Philippines and northern Indonesia. The narrow Strait of Malacca separates Indonesia from Malaysia and is inordinately targeted by renegade bands of pirates. Our plan was to run the 500-mile gauntlet quickly.

We threaded *Osprey* between scores and scores of small fishing boats as horrendous electrical storms blasted the coastline. Caution was the operative word at this stage—PL and I were more than a little edgy. After a long day of dodging thunderstorms and small fishing boats, we anchored *Osprey* behind a small bight of Malaysian coastline. The night was pitch black and the anchorage was deathly quiet. Suddenly I was wide-awake. Strange voices filtered down our companionway and a bright light flooded our cockpit. Disoriented, nervous, and scared I crept out of the cabin and saw a small fishing boat pulling alongside. I began to rethink our rationale for not carrying a gun aboard. I stumbled below to grab a flare gun and a can of pepper spray, but the intruder inexplicably slipped away into the inky night.

At first light my gut instinct was to make tracks fast. As I fired up the engine, PL powered up *Osprey's* electric anchor windless and hauled the anchor aboard. Unfortunately when I shifted the transmission into gear, the engine died. As we unceremoniously drifted out of our protected anchorage, I was absolutely dumbfounded that my faithful diesel refused to start. Now we faced a shallow shoreline, questionable locals, unpredictable currents, and a sick motor. Fresh out of choices and not willing to stick around in an area I figured was about to swarm with pirates, I strapped on my scuba gear and jumped into the murky tepid water. The racing ebb almost ripped my hand away from our dive ladder as I worked my way towards the propeller. My dive light barely cut through the muddy outflow but then I found the answer—a ragged fishing net was wrapped around our rudder and propeller. After I hacked off the net and crawled back into the cockpit, PL casually motored us out into the strait. As we reconstructed the saga of our nighttime intruders, it became pretty evident that our uninvited visitors were just a couple of fishermen trying to retrieve their hopelessly tangled net.

The Royal Selangor Yacht Club sounded like an interesting place so we decided to stop. As *Osprey* sailed into Port Klang bound for the yacht club, the stench of raw sewage and decaying garbage assaulted us. Like many of the Malaysian harbors, the waterways in Port Klang are filthy and ecological awareness was a pipe dream. Amazingly enough the clubhouse was nicely appointed, the staff was professional, and the food was quite good.

After our huge meal, we decided to walk it off with a stroll around the harbor. Sheets of heavy rain and massive lightning strikes set the tone for our evening. Suddenly I stepped into a deep, narrow trench that served as the local sewer. Fortunately the tall brush concealing the slimy drain padded my fall. Rather than a fractured leg, I escaped with just a bruised shin. Rumors about nasty infections and suppurating lesions abound in the tropics—I considered myself mighty lucky. The primitive sanitation and drainage systems outside the major cities speak volumes about the government's priorities in Malaysia. The authoritarian regime bragged that one of the tallest buildings in the world was situated in nearby Kuala Lumpur, but the bureaucrats seemed unconcerned about the impending ecological nightmare in the countryside.

After PL helped me hobble back to the yacht club for a medicinal cognac, our friends from *Topaz* stopped by the bar. John and Lois had signed up for the Raja Muda International Regatta that was sponsored by the Malaysian raja, an avid yachtsman. The action was to start soon when the assembled yachts raced out of Port Klang. Although the race from Port Klang to Langkawi did not appeal to us, we all agreed that a trek through the hill country in Thailand was a fine idea. *Topaz's* Lois, a no-nonsense can do lady, told us she would make it happen.

Reading the hype from the Malaysian tourist bureau we assumed Penang would be our chance to relive a bit of the grand colonial era of the nineteenth century. Rudyard Kipling and Somerset Maugham whiled away the hours at the venerable Eastern & Oriental Hotel, whereas we were stuck at the decrepit Penang Yacht Club dock. R & R was on our minds, but repairing our diesel's sputtering starter took center stage. Although Penang is billed as a colorful, multiethnic community and a cultural crossroads, I was mainly interested in a starter solenoid. We spent the better part of a day scrounging through dusty auto parts stores and grubby shops, but it was an exercise in futility. Marine supply stores are nonexistent. After exhausting all our resources and ourselves, PL finally spied a junk dealer squatting in a grungy back alley surrounded by a mountain of used engine parts. He glanced at our sick part, mumbled something in Malaysian, shook his head, and handed it back to us. Discouraged PL and I started to wander off, but then the junk guy motioned for us to sit. Babbling a few more indecipherable phrases our hero scooted off on his motorcycle. Making ourselves as comfortable as possible on a three-foot pile of dirty metal pipe and greasy fittings, we began our vigil. Twenty minutes later the enterprising local reappeared with a grimy cardboard box. Even though the worn package looked as if it had spent a good deal of time waiting to be discovered, the reconditioned part turned out to be exactly what our starter needed. The mechanics and technicians in developing countries seemed to have a knack for reconditioning or fixing gear that our culture would give up for dead.

Although I was getting a bit cynical about the Malaysian take on sightseeing, we decided to give it one more try. As *Osprey* sailed into Malaysia's northwestern region, the waters suddenly turned miraculously clean. The polluted harbors in the Strait of Malacca were happily in our wake and now a fabulous landscape and clean cruising grounds emerged. The southern reaches of the Andaman Sea lapped the beautiful coastline and the pristine waters stretched north to Thailand. We decided to go with the flow and anchored in a small cove adjacent to the Lake of the Pregnant Maiden. While the legendary 95-degree waters of *Tasik Dayang Bunting* promised aspiring parents fertility, PL and I were strictly interested in a casual swim with no strings attached.

As we pushed further north, Rebak Island got our nod. The island lies just off-shore from the duty free port of Langkawi and featured a state-of-the-art marina. The adjacent resort complex is the pet project of the then prime minister, Dr. Mahathir. The entire operation was very well done and beautifully rendered. Things were starting to go our way since the place also boasted a swimming pool and duty free liquor. Captain Ahmed, a dapper looking Malaysian in a crisp white uniform, took our lines as we pulled into the Rebak Marina. Not only was Ahmed the man in charge, he was a consummate PR guy who made us feel very welcome. Soon PL and I were introduced to new friends from Britain, New Zealand, and the USA. It also happened to be Thanksgiving. Even though the cruisers comprised a dozen nationalities, the unique American holiday prompted the management to organize a huge dinner and everyone was invited.

Tony Farrington, author of *Rescue in the Pacific* and a long-time marina tenant, graciously hosted our table. Tony's book recounts the true story of disaster and survival in a Force 12 Storm midway between Tonga and New Zealand. The Queen's Birthday Storm in June 1994 precipitated the biggest search-and-rescue operation of modern times in the South Pacific. One sailboat lost three people, but twenty-one other sailors on assorted boats were rescued. The cruisers involved were prepared and sailed after the hurricane season was over. They were simply in the wrong place at the wrong time when the totally unexpected, savage weather "bomb" devastated the cruising fleet.

Most experienced cruisers realize that you can only cover so many of your bases. At times events spin out of control and the unthinkable can happen. We knew the feeling firsthand after the awful tragedy in India. Ever since that time, PL and I became a lot less concerned with the fates. We would live large.

15

Thai Takeout

○ ○
Our life is frittered away by detail...simplify, simplify.
—*Henry David Thoreau*

Thailand's Phi Phi Islands were love at first sight. As we cruised through the clean warm waters of southwestern Thailand, our world changed for the better. Everything from the deliciously spicy food to the gentle Buddhist inspired Thai massages lured us into the magical atmosphere. Soaring limestone cliffs, bleached white beaches, and fine anchorages offer incredible scenery and outstanding cruising. Phi Phi Don is considered one of the three most beautiful islands in the world despite the tourist hordes that have discovered the charms of Thailand's outer islands. We could look at the mass of humanity more philosophically from the private world of an anchored cruising yacht.

In mid-December Kate flew to the island of Phuket to spend the holidays with us. Together our little trio cruised the tropical waters around Phuket and soaked up the enticing Thai culture. Travel agents dub Phuket the Pearl of the Andaman Sea, whereas more cynical locals consider Phuket the playground of the rich. To yachtsman Phuket is synonymous with interesting harbors, good provisioning, and lots of action. While the Thai political regime and the police were not above a bit of corruption, the local people were hospitable and kind.

Just to the north of Phuket lies Phanga Nga Bay, which is famous for James Bond Island. Bond immortalized the place when he zoomed in between the jagged cliffs of the stunning karst mountains in his micro-sized aircraft. *The Man with the Golden Gun* was long gone, but vendors still hawked 007 memorabilia to gaping sightseers. A colorful assortment of long tails—canoes powered by weed eater/propeller contraptions—delivered the hotel crowd into the clutches of the resident hustlers.

We sailed away from the throngs and into the far reaches of the bay. The sheer sided limestone islands punched up vertically from the placid aqua marine waters leaving gnawed, hollowed out bases that looked like the work of a gigantic beaver. The *Osprey* crew hopped aboard our ship's dinghy to check out the catacombs that perforated the gigantic monoliths. The maze of narrow waterways teemed with bats and monkeys and weaved through an obstacle course of stalagmites and stalactites. Suddenly a constricted passage exploded into a sun-drenched hong, literally our own personal grotto buried inside the mountain yet open to the sky. I convinced the ladies to peel down to their bikinis since the small lagoon was so private. Just then a swarthy German photographer aboard a chartered long tail motored on in. The guy insisted that PL and Kate pose for him, but they screamed no way as they scrambled for cover. Even though I took a lot of abuse for that incident, I still saw a smile or two from my two models.

Bangkok is a study in chaos. The harried traffic cops wear facemasks to protect themselves from smog and pollution, as seemingly deranged drivers blow through intersections with absolute abandon. Our crew favored defensive walking for short distance jaunts. For the traveler who is feeling lucky or bullet proof, there is the tuk-tuk—a three-wheeled motorized rickshaw. When I had to visit the US Embassy to add more pages to our bulging passports, my tuk-tuk guy promised a quick trip. Apparently the concepts of safety and comfort did not compute. The tiny 2-cycle tuk-tuk engine sounded like a chainsaw in heat as the unflustered driver tore along assorted sidewalks and careened across park lawns just to prove that he did indeed enjoy a better on time record than the plodding taxis and busses.

The Chao Phraga River is a major thoroughfare through the city and its fleet of long tails considers the murky waters a ready-made grand prix racecourse. Although the hair-raising river ride is a fast way to get around, the filthy spray from the polluted, oily river is tough on clothes. As a consequence, the locals cover up with newspapers.

If Kate had not been with us, PL and I would have missed the number one attraction in Bangkok, the Grand Palace. As the three of us strolled down the street, a well-dressed young man identifying himself as a Thai medical student got into lock step with us. After he sucked me in with his friendly demeanor, the potential doctor explained that the palace was closed. Our anonymous benefactor offered to take us on a tour of a far more interesting building he knew about just around the corner. Kate takes no prisoners and calls it as she sees it. She explained to her mom and dad, her own little country mice, that the guy was a con man hustling us into his shop. The deflated flimflam man split and Kate took over the tour.

The Chakri dynasty of the Kingdom of Siam created the monumental edifice of the Grand Palace over 200 years ago. Kate, our art history authority, termed the architecture nothing short of stunning. The gilded artwork is unique to Southeast Asia. Over a hundred extremely colorful temples and buildings occupy the grounds, but *Wat Phra Kae,* or Temple of the Emerald Buddha, is the star attraction. The mysterious Emerald Buddha, about two feet tall and said to be carved from a solid block of jade, dominates the temple and stared serenely at me from its 10 meter high throne. It seemed the statue was encouraging me to still my body, calm my mind, and relax.

Chiang Mai is the second largest city in Thailand. Much more laid back and livable than Bangkok, Chiang Mai is also the jumping off place for adventuresome trips through the infamous Golden Triangle of Myanmar, Laos, and Thailand. Our master plan was to trek through some of the mountainous northern area and mingle with the hill tribes. Kate, PL, and I flew into town for a rendezvous with the *Topaz* crew, our compatriots for the upcoming jaunt. Between the seven of us, we had done a lot of research and we knew the trek was physically demanding. Fortunately all of us were compatible sorts. Our outfitting company spun tales of glorious scenery and fascinating, primitive people. Interestingly enough warnings about opium-smoking guides and occasional robberies were not part of our trek briefing. Since we were only taking backpacks on the trek, I asked the manager of Suriwongse Zenith Hotel to stow our extra luggage under lock and key. The accommodating hotelier peered at our bags stacked in the hotel lobby, draped a nylon mesh net over our gear, and assured me that our bags would be properly stored and protected.

We gathered up our packs and hopped into the back of a battle-scarred pickup. After bouncing along dusty pot-holed mountain roads for five very long hours, the beat up 4x4 finally wheezed its way into a small village. After our crowd staggered out of the cramped pickup bed, the truck hightailed it back down the mountain and then our real adventure began. Joey, our spaced-out guide, muttered a few words about the upcoming saga. Our trek would involve negotiating a couple of steep mountain trails, visiting three different hill tribe villages, floating down a river, and hopefully reuniting with our pickup later in the week.

Kom, a diminutive local kid whom Joey dubbed Egg Boy, was hired to carry four-dozen eggs and a bit of flour. The spirited little guy subsequently pattered up the steep mountain trails in flip-flops while he toted two precariously balanced trays of very fresh and very fragile eggs without mishap. Our entourage was off to visit the Karen people, a hill tribe that have lived in the region since ancient times.

Our initiation began with an elephant ride. Kate and PL rode in a seat strapped to the elephant's back, while I straddled the big guy's neck and dangled my boots behind its massive gray ears. Our noble beast spent the next three hours browsing along the river and plodding through streambeds. Periodically the footloose pachyderm would rip a papaya tree out of the ground and whirl the huge tree around with his trunk. Rather than argue with our elephant, Kate and PL figured the best approach was to let him eat whatever his heart desired. My job was to duck whenever the tree came my way. After a long morning of lurching about on the elephant, our trio clamored off the beast to rest our sore bums. Now it was the matter of stretching out my bow legged elephant driver legs and launching into the hiking mode.

Since more than a fair share of the world's opium poppies are grown in this region, it was a bit intimidating to walk through meadows brimming with the thigh high, bright pink flowers. We did not spot any suspicious pickers or DEA types, although our guide probably was not above smoking the stuff. Just before nightfall seven very bushed trekkers staggered up a steep hillside and spread out into a small village, which consisted of a dozen ramshackle huts built on stilts. Joey directed us to a disintegrating shack that would be our bunkhouse. Our overnight accommodation would make a Spartan proud—a crumbling bare wood floor with that certain gamey smell accented by boarded up windows. Despite our efforts to cozy up the place, the bunkroom looked an awful lot like the community stable. In the room next to us, Joey squatted with several other village people around an open fire. Amazingly enough a tasty meal of rice and vegetables materialized, served by candlelight no less. Things started looking up.

Every now and then small children peeked at us through the gaping cracks in our hut. Before long the sparse little room was full of villagers, children and adults alike. With a bit of sign language, a lot of smiles, and Joey's assurances the villagers became more at ease. The *Topaz* and *Osprey* ladies dug around in their packs and miraculously produced balloons, candy, pencils, and paper. While the small items are a staple of teachers throughout the world, the unexpected gifts were an unheard of luxury for the villagers. The Thai version of Pictionary was born that very evening. When it was time to say goodnight, there were a lot of grinning brown faces lighting up our primitive digs.

The village had no electricity, kerosene, or propane. Other than small cooking fires, candles were about it. The twinkling lights that danced about the ink black field far below were the Karen hill tribe version of fireflies—sputtering torches carried by the village boys as they played a night game of soccer. Since our overnight stay was high in the mountains, the temperature plummeted during the wee hours and our bunkroom became mighty chilly. Each of us emptied our packs and dressed in every stitch of clothing we could rustle up. We huddled inside our sleeping bags and glommed together in a futile attempt to stay warm, but seeing our breath was tough on morale. At 3:30 am the resident rooster, who lived under the floor of our shed, decided to crow. Any hopes of a mellow morning went the way of the buffalo as pigs, goats, and dogs joined the impromptu reveille.

Our trek had entered the river rafting stage when Kate pointed out that the lashings tying together our bamboo raft were disintegrating. As the shallow rock strewn rapids tore into our fragile raft, PL grabbed a paddle and started to yelp. I thought my mate was perhaps getting into command at sea. Truth be told PL could care less about her own command, but she was more than a little protective of her swollen finger since a wasp had just zapped her favorite digit.

"Oh yeah," Joey intoned in his nasal slur, "watch out for the wasps."

Our exit strategy depended on an overdue pickup truck. Fortunately the clunky Toyota eventually showed. After the downhill, bone-crunching return trip to Chiang Mai, I hobbled from the truck and back into our hotel. I noticed a familiar lumpy cargo net in the middle of the lobby. Not only had our gear not been locked away, it had not even been moved.

PL and I have not seen the *Topaz* crew recently, but we have kept up with their exploits by email. Although Lois and John are about fifteen years further down the AARP trail than PL and I, their sailing misadventures make our exploits pale in comparison. After our trek John was hospitalized after a fall from his dry docked sailboat in Thailand, then Lois was medically evacuated from *Topaz* in Sri Lanka. Subsequently *Topaz* lost a transmission driveline in Oman. As Lois and John sailed up the Red Sea, *Topaz* struck a sandbar off the coast of Eritrea. The spunky couple was actually featured in the *Wall Street Journal* because a fellow cruiser broadcast their plight on an Iridium satellite phone. Although Iridium's article in the WSJ was a bit self-serving, it did detail how the *Topaz* crew was rescued by helicopter and their sailboat salvaged. Subsequently Lois and John beat the system. While we spent weeks hammering up the Red Sea, the undaunted couple cleverly made the same journey aboard an Italian freighter, which carried them and *Topaz* to the Mediterranean.

For New Years Eve, Patong Bay hosts a spectacular fireworks display that rivals any Fourth of July show on the planet. As if the pyrotechnics are not enough, the beachfront clubs feature another Thai specialty, transvestites. The gorgeous girls who dance in the lavish productions are the products of very skilled plastic surgeons. One could say that from a frontal perspective, their dancing assets are uplifting, firm, and perky. Since the flesh business at Phuket's assortment of clinics is thriving and competition for patients cutthroat, it is a case of buyer beware.

The anchorage at Au Surin was our last stop before sailing west. We were anchored off the gorgeous shores of Pansea Beach in the lee of the very upscale Amanpuri Hotel. As we helped Jeremy and Sandrene haul water out to their small cruising boat, a charming woman asked me where we were headed. After hearing my brief rundown of our adventures, Mary decided that her entire family would love to hear our story. She invited us to dinner. A chauffeur driven golf cart picked us up at the foot of a meandering switch back trail which led to Mary's private family compound, a foursome of open sided teak pavilion suites in the Zen tradition of understated elegance. Our generous hosts listened attentively to our stories while we feasted on fabulous Thai food prepared by two excellent chefs. Before PL and I returned to *Osprey*, our benefactors insisted that we accept a gift box brimming with excellent food, fine wine, and good books. Now it was time to move down the line.

Prior to Kate's flight back to Italy, the three of us reminisced about our travels and philosophized about our future. Tyler was still very much in our thoughts, but our world now seemed to encompass a wider view. After months of international travels, we were quite aware that our personal tragedy was not a unique event. We became aware of our own pain—now we had the chance to expand our concept of suffering and become more compassionate of others. Our worst nightmare had happened and although the scars were fresh, our spirits were emerging from the wreckage and climbing back towards the sun.

16

The Indian Ocean

o o o o o o o o o o o o o o o o o o o o o o o o o o o o o o o o o o o o o

Only those who will risk going too far can possibly find out how far one can go.

—T.S. Eliot

The horizon was as thin and hard as polished bronze, but something had changed. After an uneventful 1100-mile sail from Thailand, PL and I now had company. Huge supertankers started to materialize out of glistening sunrise as *Osprey* closed on Sri Lanka. All that shipping was bound for an island that is only 270 miles long and 145 miles wide. Known as Ceylon during the British heyday, the small island of Sri Lanka is home to 18 million people—roughly the same population as Australia. It is also known as the teardrop of India.

Our destination was Galle, a crowded but secure anchorage that visiting yachts shared with the unimposing Sri Lankan Navy. For security reasons, the navy drags a net across the harbor entrance every evening to discourage the Tamil Tiger suicide frogmen from swimming in and raising havoc with their motley collection of small ships. Each night the military tosses dozens of stun grenades into the water just in case the bad guys are stupid enough to be swimming about. Although the unexpected blasts caught us unawares the first night, we became relatively callused to the frequent rattle in our rigging as the grenades exploded around us.

Although the Tamil Tigers did not hassle us, the customs and immigration people did. The local bureaucrats specialized in shaking down unsuspecting yachtsmen for bribes. Marlboros, booze, *Playboy* magazines, and videos were at the top of their extortion list. To save myself a lot of aggravation, I hired the Windsor Brothers Yacht Agency and they in turn dealt with the corrupt officials.

The brothers were embarrassed by the graft and went to great lengths to make our stay enjoyable.

Due to the unstable political situation, it seemed prudent to cut our stay short in Sri Lanka—just long enough to take a quick peek and then continue on our way. Sarah, a local guide and driver, admitted his van was not much to look at but "...safe, *Sahib.*" With the *Skybird* crew in tow, PL and I scrambled into the island sled and then Sarah did his thing. The trip inland featured a tooth rattling van ride along a twisting coastal road followed by a harrowing journey through the mountains. The mountains of Sri Lanka are an achingly beautiful backdrop to tiered rice paddies and colonial era tea plantations. At a weathered tea factory PL purchased a stash of fragrant orange pekoe tea since the former British colony was not into coffee.

The volatile mix of oblivious drivers on disintegrating roads merged taxis, busses, and overloaded trucks with ox carts, tuk-tuks, and bicycles—a case study in continual pandemonium. The nine-hour driving marathon to our hotel left us totally exhausted, but it certainly was an ultimate 150-mile education in the chaos theory. Amazingly enough our team rumbled into the mountain retreat of Kandy unscathed. Traffic was horrific but Sarah, our unperturbed Sikh driver, thought nothing of it.

In Kandy we recuperated at the Suisse Hotel, a classic lakeside retreat that overlooks *Daladan Maligawa*, the Temple of the Tooth. The temple's principle icon is an enshrined incisor retrieved from the funeral pyre of Buddha, Lord Sidarttha, in 543 BC. The tooth was smuggled into Sri Lanka in 301 AD. Since that time a visit to the temple is one of the most revered Buddhist pilgrimages. Due to the violent ethnic clashes between the Buddhist Singhalese in the south and the Hindu Tamils in the north, security at the temple was very strict. Before entering the temple visitors were searched—one line for women, another for men. After passing through security, PL and I left our shoes at the temple's entrance. Our flashy jogging shoes stood out like beacons in the huge pile of dusty sandals left by the pilgrims.

Within the enormous gilded halls of the temple, shrines and murals depicted the story of the tooth relic. Several burly Buddhist monks guarded the carved golden tomb that holds the relic, while others monks reverently prayed. The atmosphere was strikingly peaceful with subdued chanting in synch with muffled drumbeats. PL and I left fragrant lotus blossoms as offerings, as did many of the pilgrims and visitors. Sadly, five days after our visit a bomb exploded outside the temple killing fourteen people, including three suicide bombers from the Tamil

Tigers. Loss is the great equalizer. In the end each of us is just a frail human and any sense of control is an illusion.

Sarah assured us that he had a surprise in store for us as he careened down the mountain road. Eventually our eager guide stopped the van and invited us to stroll down a long winding path. Around the bend was a muddy riverbank and a bit further up, the Pinnewala Elephant Orphanage. There were scores of baby elephants just doing their thing and looking mighty cute in the process. We helped bathe a couple of the friendly youngsters and they returned the favor. Each small orphan drank about forty liters of milk a day so the overworked attendants were more than happy to give us a crack at bottle-feeding the little fellows.

Back in Galle, PL and I began provisioning *Osprey* for the next leg of our trip. Since our prospective itinerary included dozens of countries and each country required its own courtesy flag, PL scored when she found custom made flags for $2 apiece. Water and basic staples were relatively easy to come by and of acceptable quality. The murky diesel pumped from rusty fifty-gallon drums was bad stuff that subsequently clogged my entire supply of fuel filters.

Although I had ordered a case of the locally brewed Singh beer, it never showed. Experienced cruisers constantly reiterated that the best way to handle the vagaries of the Third World is to not get overwrought. PL and I decided to just clear out of Dodge and shoved off for the Maldives, a chain of small islands about 450 miles west of Sri Lanka. This passage marked our halfway point around the globe.

The Maldives are a collection of about 1200 small coral islands that are grouped into clusters of atolls and located off the southwest tip of India. We sailed for Ihavandifulu Atoll, which is the most northern island in the chain. As *Osprey* cleared Eight Degree Channel and sailed into the placid lagoon, the warm humid breeze wafted the fragrance of frangipani trees across our deck. Six hours after we dropped the hook, a ragtag government crew showed up to inspect our boat. The customs guys were delayed because their elderly patrol boat had been stranded on the reef at low tide, but then again they were in no hurry.

A contingent of friendly local men met us on the beach and proceeded to show off their island. Following our guides across a white sandy beach and through a forest of spindly coconut palms, PL and I were escorted to a courtyard behind a small white cinderblock house. Bright pink bougainvillea cascaded over the walls of the sandy little oasis. Our host, a rather formidable islander named Ahmed, flashed a huge smile and welcomed us into his home. Ahmed and the village chief ran competing businesses that specialized in selling jugs of diesel to visiting yachtsmen. The chief was visiting another island so the golden sales opportunity came to Ahmed.

PL and I relaxed in the shade of a coconut palm while Ahmed's assistant offered us small green coconuts as refreshment. A shy young islander skillfully punched a hole into the top of each coconut then motioned for us to drink the refreshing clear liquid hidden inside the tough husk. Ahmed, otherwise known as the Judge, animatedly discussed life on Uleguma Island while the *Osprey* crew sipped the cool coconut milk. Ahmed reveled in his role as roving goodwill ambassador and promised us warm island hospitality during our stay.

The village of Fahivaa is an island blend of coral stone dwellings, a mosque, a store, and an open-air school. The 400 Muslim residents subsist on aid from Singapore, Malaysia, India, and Australia. In 1993 the island received a grant from "Save The Children" that funded a new grade school. The modest community is immaculate and the people neatly dressed. A tuna factory located on a neighboring island is the sole industry in the area.

Coconut, rice, fish, potatoes, eggs, papaya, pumpkin, and bananas are homegrown. If the islanders yearn for variety, additional foods can be imported but at great expense. The only store in town offered a few brands of soap, a couple bottles of catsup, several bags of white rice, and a limited assortment of canned fruit—all displayed on sagging wood shelves inside a dark cinder block hut.

The villagers' small stone homes were sparsely furnished and tidy, despite the dirt floors. Coconut palms, breadfruit trees, and sprays of tropical flowers brightened the streets so even the most austere homes appeared warm and inviting. Women patiently swept the sand surrounding their homes to clear away the fallen leaves and debris. The locals seldom travel since there is no public transportation. The few sailing yachts that stop each year constitute the mainstay of foreign visitors. Cruisers are the focal point of the islanders. As guests of these generous people, we found ourselves with a full social calendar including dinners, community games, and dancing.

We were humbled as the locals opened their hearts and their homes to us without the slightest qualm. Children merrily flocked around us and they delighted in reciting over and over their two or three English words. One afternoon PL took dozens of balloons and a ball of yarn to shore. Each child in the village sported a balloon that day—lots of twinkling eyes and brilliant white smiles.

Our visit to the Maldives coincided with the end of Ramadan. Ramadan is considered the fourth of Islam's five fundamental pillars of faith, a month of fasting and reflection. The locals were in the mood to celebrate and all the yachties were invited. A tug of war pitted the island's women against the men, a rather lopsided contest. The yachties threw in their lot with the local ladies, the men of Uleguma were routed, and the startled women prevailed. Pandemonium broke out from the ranks of the normally staid females. Judging from the expressions on the faces of the losers such behavior from the womenfolk was unexpected and…well, a bit unwelcome.

A cruiser from a small French sloop was slouched under a palm on the periphery of the happy crowd. Whether it was a sudden synapse of sympathetic neurons or a glimpse into another man's heart, I knew I had to speak to the disconsolate man. As I approached, Philippe looked up and mumbled a half-hearted French accented greeting. Normally I would have called it good and walked away, but I was inexplicably drawn to him. As if a cosmic switch had been tripped, Philippe tearfully poured out his story.

Philippe and his wife were bound for the Maldives when they tuned in their ham radio for the daily BBC news broadcast. A raspy voice, fading in and out of the static, announced that a bomb had exploded in a small African town and two European aid workers had been killed. Philippe's daughter was one of the victims. The mind-numbing news bulletin blindsided the stunned couple. Their carefree cruising days were over and their lives were in shambles. Philippe's wife chose to fly home so the Frenchman was left on his own. Philippe had basically checked out of the world and had been sailing aimlessly for weeks. Eventually he ended up on Ihavandifulu Atoll with me. I grieved for his loss and told him I understood. As we became more comfortable with one another, I shared my agony about Tyler's death. I never found out what became of the French single hander, but I hope our shared stories helped to quench some of the fires of hell raging in his soul.

Towards the end of our stay PL and I were spending a rainy afternoon aboard *Osprey* when I recalled that a villager had casually invited us ashore that evening. Although the weather was nasty and surfing the dinghy ashore was a chore, I recruited a few of our friends for an evening visit to the island. A young villager greeted us at the crumbling dock and proceeded to lead us through the poorly lit village. Our curiosity was piqued, but none of us had any idea what lay in store. Just as we approached the darkened school, a sudden blaze of gaily-colored lights illuminated the whole place. Unbeknownst to us the small community had banded together to host a banquet in our honor. We were surprised and flattered, but more than anything else, awed by the outpouring of kindness. As the honored guests we were served first as the villagers graciously looked on. It is one of our most treasured moments.

Next evening Ahmed invited Yasir, the customs guy, and me to go night fishing aboard his boat. The huge islander was very proud of his old leaky wooden skiff even though an extra crewman was required to constantly pump the bilge. Eventually we managed to putt out to the edge of a coral reef. Ahmed sagely advised me about his secret techniques for night fishing. Although the lesson was longwinded, the bottom line was to bait up with a fish head and then dangle my fishing line over the reef. After dispensing his bit of native lore, my fishing mentor fired up a cigarette, perched himself on a threadbare cushion, and gazed out to sea. Patience personified.

17

The Arabian Peninsula

o o o o o o o o o o o o o o o o o o o o o o o o o o o o o o o o o o

What is the only thing that passes across the face of the sun yet leaves no shadow? The Wind.

—*Arabic riddle*

Osprey punched into the fresh breeze of the NE monsoon as she sliced through the Arabian Sea on a powerful beam reach, bound for Oman. After 1200 miles of glorious sailing in concert with the pleasant dry wind blowing across *Osprey's* starboard side, we cruised into the anchorage at Mina Raysut—we were not alone. Whereas only 6 cruising boats had visited the previous year, now thirty long-range sailboats were anchored in the snug harbor. The influx of foreign sailboats was a testament to the sultan's improved public relations program.

Qabus ibn Sa'id, the sultan of Oman, became head of the government after usurping his father in a bloodless coup about three decades ago. The sultan's father shot himself in the foot to save face and prove that blood had been shed prior to his exile. After the take over, the new sultan made drastic moves aimed at revitalizing the country. The regime instituted democratic reforms understanding full well that Oman's oil would eventually be gone. New hospitals, parks and schools, including a university, were built—a testament to a farsighted public works program. Modern thoroughfares replaced the ancient dirt roads.

When the reigning sultan's father ruled the country, he owned a Rolls Royce that eventually sputtered to a stop. Rather than import infidel mechanics, the old guy hitched the ailing limousine to a team of donkeys. The old sultan personified the conservative heritage of the Arabian Peninsula, while the present sultan embraces modernization and diversification. Unlike many countries in the Middle East, westerners are welcome in Oman.

According to our guide, Oman is basically a vast desert of sand dunes and jagged hills. Parched trees and spindly bushes offer little shade in the arid countryside where Bedouins tend their flocks of goats. Not many horses or cattle, but scores of camels meander back and forth across the roads. Drivers tend to stay alert since there is a $2000 fine for hitting a camel, not to mention the cost of repairing the vehicle.

In ancient times the Queen of Sheba lived high on a cliff by the sea and surveyed a busy port city that was the key to her kingdom. Her vista was the Indian Ocean that stretched to the Horn of Africa. Grain was stored in underground caves and shipped up the Red Sea and into the Persian Gulf. The lucrative sea trade stretched between Zanzibar, India, and China. Today the former imperial port is nothing but a brackish estuary. Under a blistering sun our group wandered through the ruins of the Queen's former glory where we met a group of Italian archeologists who were searching for evidence of the ancient granaries. As the sweating Italians unearthed shards of broken pottery, the requisite Omani consultant sipped a cool beverage and lounged in the shade of a Land Rover. The Middle East is a treasure trove of antiquities and the governments tightly control outside access to any hidden treasures.

Scruffy little frankincense trees grow wild along the riverbeds. In biblical times frankincense was more valuable than gold, making Oman the wealthiest country in the world. Now a kilogram of the pale sand colored crystals can be bought for pocket change. Compared to the densely populated countries in Southeast Asia, Oman is sparsely settled. Fortunately for us the westernization of Oman combined with the vast oil wealth has produced a population who actually like Americans.

True to the conservative Ibadi Islamic tradition of Oman, local Muslim women are seldom seen in public. When the shy ladies do venture out into the sweltering heat, they are covered from head to toe in *burqas*—basically heavy black choir robes. A black veil covers their faces so only their hands and feet were visible. Hands and feet are decorated with ornate designs painted with henna and accentuated with an abundance of glittering gold jewelry. In Oman it is illegal for a Muslim women to even look out an open window with her face uncovered. Pictures published in foreign magazines suffer a censor's black magic marker if a woman is depicted sans black robes. Although most visiting Western women make an effort to dress modestly by wearing garments that cover legs and shoulders, they are still conspicuous. It was obvious from the curious stares that the rich heritage of a very traditional society still flourishes in Oman.

The culture is a study in contrast. In Salalah, the city near our anchorage, local men were extremely polite and gracious. Omani men did not hesitate to stop and visit when they encountered us on the street or in a store. In town men strolled the streets dressed in light colored choir robes, or *dishdashas,* with their heads wrapped in brightly colored turbans, or *schmogs.* The exotic threads are reportedly comfy and they definitely protect the locals from the scalding Arabian sun. Frequently we saw men holding hands as they walked, obviously far more comfortable with touching than their Western counterparts. Oman is a country run by men. Banks, government buildings, restaurants, cafes, and most shops are staffed entirely with males. Men work behind the cosmetics counters selling lipstick and fragrances. The male citizens of Oman are not worker bees. They import laborers for that sort of thing. The local guys have time on their hands and lots of expendable income to buy large luxury automobiles. I gleaned all this information from various gentlemen who were kind enough to give us rides from Salalah's western style markets back and forth to *Osprey,* anchored twenty miles down the coast.

A fellow cruiser who doubled as a computer guru offered to tear apart our sick Toshiba laptop computer. Since onboard email was a huge deal for us, the ailing keyboard was replaced. Unfortunately only an Arabic keyboard was available in Salalah, so sending emails became a challenge more suited to Lawrence of Arabia than the *Osprey* crew.

The endless sky over the Arabian Sea was bursting with stars as *Osprey* caught the evening breeze and Oman faded from view. We were bound for Yemen, a few hundred miles away geographically but light years away economically.

In 1990 Yemen made the strategic miscalculation of backing Iraq in the first Gulf War. 850,000 Yemeni workers were subsequently deported from Saudi Arabia, in theory a US ally. The rampant unemployment fueled the fires of discontent. The Republic of Yemen burst into violent civil war in May 1994. After two months of fighting and thousands of casualties, the economy was in ruins and the country was in chaos. The devastating missile attacks launched from both sides obliterated sections of Aden and Al Mukalla. After northern forces captured the southern capital of Aden in July 1990, the southern secessionists capitulated.

The war torn shambles of Al Mukalla is a stark contrast to the cleanliness and orderliness of Oman's cities. We motored into a scruffy harbor fronted by bombed out buildings, a legacy of fighting a few years earlier. This was our first experience viewing a city that was literally blown to pieces during a civil war. Reconstruction would be a long time coming. Our passports were surrendered in exchange for gate passes. The stench of rotting garbage and failing sewers assaulted us as I negotiated our entry fee with a surly customs official. Because the proposed visa fee would be $85 if we stayed over twelve hours, PL and I decided a few hours poking around town would be more than enough. The harried port captain agreed that such government edicts were ruining their almost non-existent tourist industry.

The local citizens squatted amidst the rubble selling their wares, smoking, and socializing. The hesitant smiles of the few merchants made us feel welcome, sort of. Our goal was to ignore the mud and filth and concentrate instead on the colorful displays of tomatoes, onions, eggplants, and potatoes. The telltale whiff of a bakery led us to a rickety outdoor shop. Resident bakers busily kneaded individual balls of dough and then popped them into a wood fired oven. Unable to resist the fresh baked pita bread, PL made our purchase and then we munched our way back to the boat.

As PL started to raise the anchor with our electric windless, our alternator decided to pack it up—no alternator spells no battery charging in any language. Coping with discharged batteries in an exposed and uncomfortable anchorage is not my idea of fun. A long hour later I unraveled myself from around the engine and pronounced the replacement alternator good to go. Feeling a bit rummy after mucking around in the bowels of our rolling boat, I was more than happy to be underway again.

As we sailed into Aden our radio crackled to life as the harbormaster warmly welcomed us to his country. No mention was made of the harbor's perpetual oil slick that blackened the hulls of the unwitting foreign sailboats. Apparently the harbormaster's public relations program did not filter down to customs and immigration, since the conniving bureaucrats seemed to employ a never-ending series of hurdles to extract hard currency from us.

Omar, a *qat* chewing taxi driver, latched on to us with a promise to show us around. Omar told us all about *qat*, a woody narcotic shrub that constitutes the largest cash crop in Yemen. Omar cheerfully demonstrated proper technique. He started by chewing up a small mouthful of green leaves and then added to the mulch throughout the day. Eventually a golf ball size wad was stashed inside his cheek. Like a mumps epidemic, swollen cheeks were everywhere. Even the cops and soldiers preferred the hazy focus of a *qat* high to the harsh reality of everyday life. Since alcohol is taboo in this Muslim country, Omar maintained that *qat* filled the void. He proudly showed us a bag of his fresh stash that he was saving for an evening with his girlfriend.

Unlike Al Mukallah, Aden showed signs of repair and rejuvenation. New roads connected post war ruins with modern apartments and businesses. The market place bustled with activity in the late afternoon as the residents gossiped and shopped. Omar left us to naively wander up and down the crowded streets and alleys and peek inside the intriguing shops. We subsequently learned that Yemen is notorious for kidnapping westerners in exchange for ransom, a cash business second only to *qat* production.

After our market tour PL and I enjoyed a good dinner with Victoria and Kevin Hall, a young Canadian couple who taught for the International Schools. They had lived in Aden for three years and together they taught ten pupils ranging in age from seven to twelve. The children all had parents who worked in Yemen. Although the students represented a number of foreign countries, each child spoke fluent English and had traveled extensively. PL and her friend Viviane, both inveterate teachers, could not resist Kevin and Victoria's invitation to spend part of the next day in the classroom. They loved sharing their sailing experiences with the inquisitive and enthusiastic students.

Kevin offered us a telephone line to download email messages. It had been almost a month since our last opportunity to access AOL, so there was no shortage of messages. Kevin and Victoria have since left Yemen, but they told us tales of having their letters, phones, and email intercepted by the government. PL and I wondered how much of our email wound up in the hands of the local authorities. Since the culture is so insular, expat life was rather harsh for Kevin and Victoria. Locals do not socialize with outsiders. Videos were censored, alcohol was unavailable, and local entertainment was almost nonexistent.

18

Red Sea Flashbacks

o o o o o o o o o o o o o o o o o o o o o o o o o o o o o o o o o o

Nothing is too high for the daring of mortals:
We storm heaven itself in our folly.

—Horace

Osprey rode on the shoulders of a favorable southerly through the narrow Bab el Mendeb, the Straits of Sorrow. The Red Sea is capricious and challenging, but also compelling and magical. I spent hours reading and rereading everything I could lay my hands on to prepare us for the bash from Eritrea to Port Suez. PL and I steeled ourselves for strong head winds, choppy seas, and sand storms—not to mention unexpected visits from unmarked patrol boats. The beaches on the western shores of the Red Sea are reportedly littered with hidden land mines. The 1200-mile gauntlet demands respect.

Although some days proved a bit dicey, other days surprised us with calm beautiful weather and favorable winds. PL and I came through the experience relatively unscathed and perhaps a little wiser. To us the Middle East projects an aura of uncertainty and intrigue. The food tastes exotic and strange. Even within the same country, competing cultures and religions fan tribal warfare. America with her super power status and consumer driven culture is not winning any popularity contests with the conservative regimes in the area. The lush tropical forests of Southeast Asia are a stark contrast to the scorching deserts and vast sand dunes of North Africa. Camels and donkeys replace the water buffalo and elephants so ubiquitous to Asia. It has been said that the essence of cruising is carrying heavy objects long distances while walking along hot dusty roads in Third World countries. Both SE Asia and the Middle East are prime examples.

The first thing to be learned about the Red Sea is to savor the infrequent southerlies. Relaxed downwind sailing in a southerly usually lasts for only a day or so before the wind abruptly switches back to blow from the north for days or weeks at a time. Although favorable winds are more common in the southern third of the Red Sea, there are no guarantees. During our six-week slog up the Red Sea, *Osprey* and her tired crew were treated to three rounds of user-friendly southerlies. The standard Red Sea weather recipe consisted of a 15-25 knot northerly delivered on our snout and served with short, steep choppy seas.

In theory the prevailing northwest wind usually backs to the west at night and veers north during the day. The systems move through every three or four days with a brief lull in between. Arabic lore suggests thin wispy high clouds and a rising barometer precede strong winds. We tacked to windward inside reefs during the day, then tacked offshore just shy of the shipping lanes at night. It was much easier to make northerly progress by sailing close to the wind as opposed to punching through the sloppy seas under power.

The people of Eritrea were celebrating their independence from Ethiopia when *Osprey* sailed into town. Eritrea, a coastal country on the Horn of Africa, is a former Italian colony with Christian roots. After our seven-month immersion in the Islamic world, Eritrea was a respite with no Muslim call to prayer and no Muslim holidays to observe. Locals who could speak a bit of English were always interested in our views about their country. They were immensely proud of their newly minted freedom. Although we found most of the people friendly and welcoming, a few of the beggars were relentless in their pursuit of a handout. In developing countries there are always needy people, but the outstretched palms far outnumber any token gifts we could provide.

First stop was the port city of Assab. Our overly optimistic and slightly out of date *Lonely Planet* promised a charming town and quaint sidewalk cafés filled with contented locals eating pasta and sipping espresso under the shady trees. Lusting for a taste of fresh java and an Italian meal, PL and I along with the *Seabird* crew set out to find just the right place. The harsh reality of a war torn, ravaged economy became all too clear during our stroll about town. No freighters or tankers were anchored in the harbor and the huge loading docks were empty. Stores were poorly stocked and the dining possibilities were quite limited.

The Aurora Café seemed to be one of only a few places in town where a visitor could probably eat without getting sick. Our Starbuck trained taste buds rebelled against the local cappuccinos that featured an evaporated milk/Sanka concoction—the ultra sweet blend could curl the lips of a camel. Fortunately for our parched foursome, I spotted a familiar bull elephant logo. On a photo safari in Kenya in the late '80's, PL and I were introduced to Tusker beer. Now the quintessential beer of East Africa has even made it to the North African outpost of Assab.

Although there is little demand for Eritrean visas, the officious bureaucrats spent the best part of a day sifting through our applications. The immigration officer prided himself on his calligraphy skills and his hand rendered visas were indeed a work of art. His self-imposed mission was to grade our penmanship on the applications as PL and I dutifully filled out a pile of useless forms. My mate, an excellent calligrapher herself, aced the picky official's test but I flunked. Happily PL came to my rescue.

With visas in hand and a 25-knot southerly to greet us, we sailed from Assab. By the time Beraisole Bahir Selate hove into view that evening, the wind was gusting to 45 knots. Although our anchor was well set, the boat jerked and bucked violently in the very exposed anchorage. The sickening motion literally sheared *Osprey's* heavy nylon shock absorber from the anchor chain. Our sailboat was instantly transformed into an endangered species as the unforgiving anchor chain brutally tore into the bow fittings. Rigging a new shock absorber was essential in order to avoid major damage to our bow—a lesson I learned the hard way in Australia. PL and I strapped on our safety harnesses and gingerly crawled forward on the weaving, slippery deck. By the time we got the replacement snubber in place, PL and I were completely exhausted by the sickening motion of the boat. We dropped back into the cockpit and celebrated our deliverance with hugs and a round of brandy. The next morning *Osprey* motored out of the anchorage from hell in a flat calm, but by midday the prevailing northwest wind was blowing uncomfortably right smack on our nose—a mere taste of things to come.

Three days after leaving Assab the harbor of Massawa unfolded before us. The sunken ships, bombed out buildings, and heavy military presence definitely left a little bit to be desired in the way of ambiance. But a nice surprise awaited us. A cruising boat fresh out of Sri Lanka arrived with a case of Singha beer earmarked for *Osprey*. Our benefactor told us the beer I ordered in Sri Lanka finally showed up at the dock two weeks after we had sailed. We tipped a couple of the coveted brews in their honor. After scoping out the place, PL and I anchored *Osprey* next to the gracious folks on the beer delivery sailboat, prayed for the best, and then hopped the overland bus bound for the mountain capital of Asmara.

The frail bus was not fast so there was lots of time to rub elbows with the locals. Unfortunately the locals were not used to bouncing up a steep mountain road and consequently a number of those folks hung their heads out of the open windows and vomited in, on, and outside of the forlorn old bus. About half way up the plateau to Asmara, the bus pulled over for a rest stop. As we watched our fellow passengers disembark and wander out into the surrounding desert, it became quite evident that privacy was a not an issue in the toilet department. Trees were sparse so people were relieving themselves at every scraggly little bush in sight. Lack of toilet paper was not an issue since well-practiced left hands were apparently much more handy. Small wonder why the locals reserved their right hands for eating. In the name of subtlety and decorum, we averted our eyes and gazed at the birds flying overhead until our necks hurt.

After our cultural lesson concerning Eritrean rest stops, our bus lurched on. By now the occasional burned out tank just struck us as another piece of roadside litter. Camels are highly regarded in Eritrea as transportation and judging by the sputtering antics of our bus, probably a more reliable way to go from here to there. Whereas the bald eagle is the symbol of America, Eritreans favor the camel. The versatile beast serves the masses under the guise of a pickup truck, Humvee, milking machine…or main entrée. As our bus lurched around a bend, a herd of baboons hurtled across the road in front of us—the animal pulse of Africa.

Asmara's 1930 art deco architecture was relatively unscathed from the decades old war with Ethiopia. At the local coffee shop our Eritrean barrista proudly displayed his collection of patriotic victory posters as he animatedly rehashed his country's victory in the 30-year war for independence. Compared to the poor struggling inhabitants of the coastal towns and desert plains, the residents of Asmara are quite content with their lot. Cappuccinos were tasty and Italian fare hit the spot. A major highlight of the trip was our overnight stay at the Ambassador Hotel. The huge bed, luxurious bathtub, and CNN were nice touches and a bit of a departure from the modest offerings aboard *Osprey*.

As the only foreigners on the bus back to Masawa, our fellow passengers were very much aware of our presence. At our first rest stop the locals hopped off the bus and chowed down on *bani*—a large thin pancake served with a salad of humus, goat, chicken, and beef (hopefully). Regrettably the offerings at the bus stop did not look that appetizing, and I was a little skitterish about eating unidentifiable meat that could well be camel. Contemplating the makings of a good meal back on the boat, I bought a couple ears of corn at a roadside stand. One of the passengers mumbled something about animal feed, so I nonchalantly left the corn under some brush. Thinking the incident was over, I settled back in my seat. About that time the bus door opened, a young man hopped aboard, and proudly presented me with the lost corn. Our crew was neither alone nor forgotten.

Further north Tala Tala Saghir provided a protected anchorage and remarkable skin diving in clear, warm water. Swim call, our first since the Maldives, was the order of the day as our snorkeling deprived crew happily paddled above spectacular coral gardens. The vivid tints of the coral and vibrant colors of the tropical fish massaged the tangled emotions that still haunted us. Our exploration of the Red Sea became a passion that overshadowed our occasional bouts of melancholy. As if to sign off on the deal, a couple of pilot whales cruised through our anchorage while PL and I sipped a sundowner in the cockpit.

We enjoyed an ideal weather window as *Osprey* sailed north for Sudan—we ghosted along the coast on the shoulders of the gentle evening breeze. The orange glow of the moon highlighted the stark silhouettes of the coastal sand dunes and the Big Dipper beckoned us northward. At sunrise we threaded our way into the inner harbor of Sawakin, past the ruins of the old city built over ten centuries ago by the Queen of Sheba. The slave trade was a major industry in Sawakin until the end of WW I. In the early 1900's Port Sudan became the primary port in the country leaving Suwakin to succumb to the harsh, unforgiving desert. A probing shaft of sunlight framed the crumbling walls inside our standing rigging as our anchor splashed down in the ancient seabed.

Sudan is the largest country in Africa, but definitely not a poster child for stability or safety. The Arab government of Sudan is still fighting a long-standing war with the Christian SPLA rebel movement in southern Sudan. Menacing machine gun nests lined the shoreline as we picked our way through the choke point of the entrance channel. The harsh Sharia law of Islamic fundamentalism pervades the country. Locals are prohibited from owning seagoing craft in order to prevent the guerilla forces from launching amphibious attacks. The shores of Sudan are renowned for harboring terrorist camps, so poking into unfamiliar anchorages at night is not recommended. The US State Department and my copy of *The World's Most Dangerous Places* pointed out that the USA has no embassy in Sudan—you are on your own if something goes wrong.

After our brief exposure to the Christian influence in Eritrea, it was back to Muslim country. One of the tenets of Islam is to make a *haj*, a pilgrimage to Mecca in Saudi Arabia. The *haj* is made at least once in the believer's life if finances allow. At the outer entrance to the ancient harbor of Sawakin, a modern pier accommodates a huge ferry that hauls Muslim pilgrims across the Red Sea to the sacred city of Mecca in Saudi Arabia.

Abu Mohammed Hedabb from Sawakin Tourism Village is the man to see. There are other agents and other Mohammeds but he was the tall one with a briefcase. He delivered diesel, changed money, handled our paperwork, and insisted that Americans were welcome. Although meningitis and malaria are endemic and the political situation is volatile, Mohammed assured us all was well in Sawakin.

Camel caravans still called on Sawakin, a throwback to yesteryear. In the desperately poor village, only a small market and a couple of shops border the dusty streets. Most of the trade is with nomadic tribes from the coastal plains and the foothills. Rundown tents scattered in the nearby desert are a testimony to their rugged, transient lifestyles. The North African tribesmen favor bold tattooed slashes across their dark faces to distinguish their particular clan. The tribes still war with each other and the tough nomads carry ancient weapons for self-defense. The men are a surly lot who dress in white desert robes and sport long swords swaying loosely from their waists. The swords and daggers are not ceremonial. Caught up in the moment, I purchased a sword with, "…a history and lots of character" according to agent Mohammed, our self-appointed interpreter and bargain hunter.

Our early morning wakeup call featured buzzing mosquitoes, braying donkeys, crowing roosters, and the Muslim call to prayer. Mohammad just happened to arrange an early morning road trip to Port Sudan, so PL and I staggered aboard a sagging van as Mohammed began his spiel about Port Sudan, the Sudanese version of the Big Apple. Mohammad let it slip that the last group of cruisers he escorted on the questionable tour ended up in jail. Apparently Mohammed warned the cruisers not to take pictures of the soldiers or police, but a few of the yachties had a yen to photograph the derelict jeeps, obsolete armored cars, and grungy soldiers who man the roadblocks along the highway. Since the military establishment in Sudan does not care to be photographed, the impromptu photographic session could best be described as inopportune. The irate soldiers pulled over the van, confiscated the cameras, and hauled everybody off to jail for a few very scary hours of interrogation, harassment, and intimidation. Fortunately for the cruisers they were eventually released with a stern warning. The Sudan military, like their corrupt counterparts in Yemen, babble on about how the outside world just does not understand them. Our excursion was comparatively tame. Assorted urchins, vagabonds, and scheming vendors kept us on our toes but we had no run-ins with the military. The local market featured a few vegetables and some fresh pita bread, but PL passed on the baskets of rice and dried beans after she noticed several goats sampling the wares.

Next day the cruiser radio net buzzed with the tale of a British sailor who was shot at when he sailed too close to Hanish al Ka, a Yemeni island close to Bab el Mandab. Had the hapless Brit done his homework, he would realize that the island caters to rich Middle Eastern men temporarily escaping the strict Islamic prohibitions against wine, women, and song. The well-healed turbaned party animals like their privacy.

19

Egyptian Lessons

After our Sawakin adventure the wind gods briefly favored us with a southerly. *Osprey* surged downwind under her full spread of canvas bound for Safaga. Our optimism faded quickly as a howling thirty-knot northerly developed the following day. The dream of a four-day downwind jaunt was transformed into a two-week bash into steep, nasty seas. Each day PL and I punched northward twenty to thirty miles. After a rugged day of sailing, our battered boat and exhausted crew would either anchor behind an island or inside a *marsa*. A *marsa* is nothing more than a niche carved into the desolate desert coastline by eons of assault from the wind and seas. The small snug anchorages provided welcome shelter from the choppy seas, but the roaring wind still whistled through our rigging at full throttle. From *Osprey's* cockpit an endless vista of sand dunes stretched to the western horizon—spectacular sunsets are the norm. The desert is starkly beautiful and wonderfully serene. Even though the Red Sea is renowned for its clarity, the water cooled off as we sailed north so we were less apt to leap into the water for snorkeling expeditions. Beach walking was out because unmarked land mines littered the entire coast. Lots of reading and planning occupied our time. Our battered TV and VCR were completely destroyed when a bungee cord tie-down frayed and the whole lash up was hurled across the salon by a spiteful wave. The stereo also died.

Suddenly the persistent northerly veered to the east and then transformed into a fresh southerly. *Osprey* was back in her downwind element. By early afternoon our fresh southerly had kicked up to a very spirited forty knots with blockbuster seas to match. The plan was to broad reach for Ras Banyas, 120 miles away. Bypassing the anchorage at Khor Shinab, in retrospect a mistake, we charged into Egyptian waters with only a few spinner porpoise for company. Then another stiff northerly developed and the upwind slog began again.

Late on St. Patrick's Day the *Osprey* crew left the tropics behind, crossed the Tropic of Cancer, and encountered our first sandstorm at sea. Our barometer registered a phenomenal nineteen-millibar pressure differential during the course of that brutal day. Sand blotted out the horizon and filled every uncovered crevice on the boat. Our teeth felt gritty and the seas were rough as hell. Neither of us was very happy with our lot in life at that particular moment. Because we were exhausted, a dicey night approach into the anchorage at Ras Banyas seemed a better alternative than beating ourselves up offshore. Meyer aboard *Lady Kathryn* vectored us through the twisting channel with his radar as we homed in on his strobe light. In the driving wind and blowing sand, our anchor chain peeled out of the chain locker and suddenly it was over. *Osprey* was safely anchored. PL and I were numb with relief as we collapsed into our bunks.

The awful conditions had trapped scores of cruising boat in Ras Banyas, including a number of long lost cruising friends not sighted since Sri Lanka. The severe weather front that battered us brought a crippling sandstorm to the Suez Canal and a massive snowstorm to Jerusalem. Not much ashore but a rather dreary Egyptian military outpost—hunkering down was the operative word for us.

After we recovered from our sleep deprivation and sorted things out, the siren call of the Med lured us out of the crowded anchorage to points north. *Osprey,* in company with *Lady Kathryn,* pounded north to Fury Shoals, a reef in the middle of the Red Sea. The anchorage on the lee side of Fury Shoals was snug as could be so Meyer, Kathryn, PL, and I spent two days playing Bridge, reading, and kicking back as the wild weather raged outside the reef. On the third day the weather broke. Both boats set sail in clear skies and a fresh northerly breeze.

After the long stretch of miserable weather, PL and I thoroughly enjoyed our first decent day of sailing weather since our battering on St. Patrick's Day. The air was clean and clear, the warm breeze was gusting across our starboard quarter, and life was good. I was wound up and thoroughly jazzed about our fine weather window. I may have appreciated the moment, but I failed to appreciate the strong surface current that was setting us much further south than I had planned. My GPS was doing its thing and I assumed my chart plot was accurately portraying our position—a bad assumption. My inattention exacted a toll. *Osprey* hit one of the small, submerged reefs on the periphery of Fury Shoals. The jarring collision was short and sweet, but it sure as hell got our attention.

"*Lady Kathryn—Lady Kathryn—Lady Kathryn. Osprey* just hit a reef. Our position is 24 degrees 18.56 N and 35 degrees 26.98 E. We are a bit shaken up but otherwise ok. *Osprey* is intact and we are not taking on water. Standby."

With cool practiced detachment, PL flashed the radio distress call that every voyager dreads. A cruiser's worst nightmare unfolded as our keel pounded across the hidden reef. Fortunately *Osprey* was heeled over on a powerful beam reach and driving fast through cresting six-foot swells when the unexpected jolt shook the boat. Fate was not a hunter that day. Our keel merely glanced off the edge of the jagged coral and then *Osprey* plunged back into deep water. The boat was still in one piece, the rig was still standing, and the reef was nowhere to be seen.

Choking back a taste of bile, I headed our bruised boat into the wind to bleed off our speed so we could evaluate our situation. PL and I were stunned. We were completely alone and the desolate coastline of Egypt was still over the horizon. Luckily the bilges were dry and all the mechanical systems still operated normally. *Lady Kathryn* was 20 miles north of us when they heard our distress call—nevertheless they turned back to help. As we got our act back together, PL radioed Meyer that we had the situation under control and we would meet them in Safaga.

Towards evening *Osprey's* beleaguered crew sailed her into the lee of Mahalis Island and we picked our through the coral reefs into a relatively protected bay. I strapped on my well-used scuba gear, grabbed a couple tubes of underwater epoxy, and then jumped over the side to repair the grapefruit size ding on the forward edge of the keel. The only real damage was to the skipper's pride. A hot shower and a couple fingers of single malt put me back in the hunt. PL and I had been very, very lucky. At that particular moment, I did not feel especially philosophical. But as the time passed, I realized that the mishap had tested our mettle. The difficulties and problems we had encountered since the catastrophe in India had coincidentally armed us with an inner strength that was now serving us very well.

Three days later another gale smashed into us. Trying to make headway against 35 knots of wind and coping with the spindrift blown off the 10-foot wave crests was useless—we cranked *Osprey* about and raced downwind in huge lumpy seas with just a storm staysail flying. The *marsa* of Ras Toronbi was our fall back plan so I consulted *The Admiralty Pilot, US Coast Pilot,* and *Red Sea Pilot* for the navigational coordinates. My guidebooks agreed with one another on the waypoint location of the narrow reef strewn entrance to Ras Toronbi, but the *marsa* painted on our radar screen was a bit removed from the supposedly correct GPS coordinates. Cursing the assorted publications, PL and I braced for a wild ride and then surfed into the swimming pool sized *marsa*.

A couple of grungy Egyptian soldiers, the only inhabitants of the misplaced *marsa*, paddled a derelict rowboat out to meet us. The courteous young men checked our visas and then gave us a "thumbs up" as we presented them with their Marlboro gift pack. The soldiers kept to themselves at their small outpost, so PL and I were stuck watching the resident flamingoes. Over the next few days the molten orange desert sun baked the parched land and brought us to par broil. Dusk was a welcome relief as the intense heat dissipated and the flanks of the western foothills came alive in vibrant shades of ginger.

I picked up a weather report on our long-range radio that described a severe storm centered in the Aegean. Although the resultant low-pressure system brought snow to Florence, the lowered pressure gradient also decreased the strong northerly wind flow down the Red Sea—that was our clue to leave. Soon the conditions changed drastically for the better. We enjoyed a light WNW breeze and very modest swells all the way to Safaga.

Despite consular warnings discouraging travel to Luxor, the crews of *Osprey* and *Lady Kathryn* decided to live on the edge and tour the area anyway. The opportunity to see remnants of a civilization over 5000 years old and travel back in time to the days of Ramses II, the Son of Light was too much to resist. We anchored our sailboats just outside the surf line in front of the town of Safaga. By this time all of us needed a break. Our continued mental health was more of a concern than the chancy proposition of leaving our bobbing vessels unattended.

After the November 1997 massacre of 58 Swiss and Japanese tourists at Hutschepsut's Temple in Luxor, Egypt's tourist industry was severely depressed. Enter Abu Nageeb, Safaga's resident taxi driver and gofer, who introduced our quartet to Dr. Budaui, alias Dr. Helicopter. Dr. Helicopter freewheels on the fringes of many non-government sanctioned enterprises, but his forte is getting the job done and his motto says it all—"Insha'Allah" or "If God wills it." Since the good doctor promised to treat his new American friends right, he provided an excellent guide and coordinated an armed escort for our van from the port of Safaga to Luxor. In Luxor the heavily armed tourist police outnumbered the visitors.

Jimmy, our dapper multilingual guide, was a university graduate who majored in Egyptian history with a specialty in Luxor. Because mastering 5000 years of recorded history can challenge any scholar, Jimmy would need additional school-ing if he decided to guide in another region of Egypt.

Luxor is 450 miles south of Cairo and is built on the 4000 year-old sight of ancient Thebes, the residence for most of the New Kingdom Pharaohs. The awe-some temples of Luxor, Karnak, Ramses II, and Hatshepsut have captivated and intrigued visitors for centuries. The site of the Karnak Temple complex houses a magnificent collection of temples and pylons and columns in an area said to be large enough to accommodate ten cathedrals. Hutschepsut's Temple, renowned as a work of architectural genius, is a vast memorial built by the only female Pha-raoh and dedicated to her father.

The Valley of the Kings and Valley of the Queens are basically two box can-yons straddled between the Arabian Desert and the Nile. Known as the City of the Dead, the canyons constitute ancient Egypt's most imposing necropolis. These obscure arid canyons hid King Tut's treasures, the only undisturbed Phar-aonic treasures ever discovered, until the early twentieth century. Just prior to our visit, the Getty Foundation finished restoration work on the tomb of Queen Nefertari, the favorite wife of Ramses II. Jimmy led us through the steep, dimly lighted entrance into a magnificently decorated seven-chambered regal crypt. The spectacular murals depict Nefertari's life. The fantastically vivid colors glisten as though painted just weeks before, not thousands of years ago. PL wondered how Ramses II, who had forty wives, dealt with the other regal ladies who were not issued their own special tombs.

A battered wooden felucca, an ancient lateen-rigged sailing design dating back to Pharaonic times, was our passport into the ancient wonders of the Nile. Our very adept Egyptian skipper finessed the huge single sail rig as he skimmed past huge patches of bull rushes and papyrus reeds—perhaps the same foliage that hid baby Moses from the enemy millenniums ago. The timeless Nile, the longest river in the world, was just as inspirational to us as it was to the likes of Alexander the Great and Napoleon.

After our road trip it was time to get serious about reaching Port Suez in good order. Unlighted buoys, underwater pipelines, nasty reefs, abandoned hulks, rust-ing oil derricks, and all manner of unidentifiable lights contribute to the cruiser dictum of not sailing overnighters in the constricted Gulf of Suez. The Gulf of Suez is only sixteen miles wide at this point and we could make out the moun-tains of the Sinai to the east. Tremendous methane flames danced from the top gantry of towering oil drilling platforms and painted jagged orange brush strokes across the black canvas of the North African sky.

Four days later the Red Sea surprised us…again, with a horrendous sandstorm and its accompanying violent wind shifts. It was April Fools Day. Naturally the autopilot decided to pack it up about that time. The joke was on me as I hung upside down in a locker, bleeding the hydraulic autopilot system as *Osprey* flopped about in the churning seas.

At Port Suez PL and I motored past scores of huge anchored ships waiting to enter the Suez Canal. Soon we were following long rows of lighted channel markers that eventually led to the Suez Yacht Club anchorage. Even with GPS and radar, the night entry is a bit on the challenging side since the navigational markers blend with a sea of lights from assorted tugs, ships, and shore side buildings. Late that night we located a mooring buoy in the SYC anchorage. After securing our battle hardened sloop, PL and I fell into our bunks for a full dose of delicious, uninterrupted sleep. The six-week slog up the Red Sea was behind us.

Early next morning a blaring horn startled us awake. As we groggily peered out our hatch, our cohorts from *Lady Kathryn* waved to us from shore. They were standing next to another Dr. Helicopter tour van and they invited us to join them on a trip to Cairo. Opportunity called so PL and I slipped into some traveling clothes, grabbed our backpacks, and away we went.

The Pyramids are every bit as imposing as they appear in pictures. The Great Pyramid of Cheops, dating back 45 centuries, is built with over two million limestone blocks that weigh about three tons each. Although I expected to stroll inside a pyramid and glimpse a gigantic empty arena, the pyramid is actually a solid mountain of huge stone blocks penetrated by a series of long claustrophobic shafts leading to the tomb chambers. Our very conservative Egyptian guide insisted that the pyramids were constructed with the voluntary services of people who were dedicated to their Pharaoh. My reading suggested that the 100,000 slaves who labored on the massive project did not have much choice.

In Cairo PL and I stayed at the nineteenth century Mena House Oberoi, one of the exotic locations made famous in Agatha Christie's novel *Death on the Nile*. A former hunting lodge, the opulent old hotel is set on forty acres of park-like grounds on the edge of the Sahara just across from the Great Pyramids. No mysterious murders or blood stained table linens caught our eye as we strolled through the historic lobby of the hotel, but the ambiance of being within walking distance of the Great Pyramids on the Giza plateau is strange and exotic. The evening laser light show illuminate the huge pyramids with ancient Pharaonic images and clever graphics, a presentation that casts magical shadows on the surrounding desert.

Cairo, home to 15 million Muslims, is a huge sprawling mass of humanity. We were focused and bee-lined for the Egyptian Museum. The King Tutankhamen Galleries surpass everything else in the place. The astounding, untouched treasures were discovered in 1922 by English archaeologist Howard Carter. King Tut is a relatively insignificant Pharaoh who only ruled nine years, but his tomb held phenomenal riches. It boggled our minds to estimate how much unaccounted wealth grave robbers had carted off from the tombs of Pharaohs much higher up the food chain. Myer, PL, and I opted not to visit the Royal Mummy Room since we thought the entrance fee was a rip-off. Kathryn coughed up her money and was later pleased to report that Ramses II has red hair. Unfortunately, the huge museum lacks the funds to properly display their incredible collection of ancient artifacts. Dusty treasures seem to be haphazardly scattered about. It is like wandering around the set of an *Indiana Jones* movie.

Hookah pipes are synonymous with the Middle East—consequently I decided to sample the wares. Whereas some major world hotels feature cigar smoking rooms, the Cairo Hilton offers hookah pipes in their lounge. Now my fancy turned to flying carpets and lounging sultans as I puffed the mild apple tobacco through the burbling water jar and hose contraption.

When we returned from Cairo, our jaded Egyptian agent offhandedly mentioned that our Suez Canal transit day was moved up. Ibrahim categorically decided that *Osprey's* departure time was to be early the next morning—good thing I asked.

Each day a convoy of ships sails north from Port Suez to Port Said as another procession of ships sails south from Port Said to Port Suez. Large ships only require one day to make the passage. The two opposing convoys pass each other midday in the middle of the Suez. Smaller vessels require two days for the transit. Slower cruising boats like us anchor overnight at the halfway point of Lake Timsah, next to the town of Ismailia.

A Suez Canal pilot is assigned to every vessel transiting the canal. Most of the traffic consists of large ships on a tight schedule and the pilots all seem to have a need for speed. Antsy pilots aboard slow moving sailboats are notorious for surprising the skipper by jamming the throttle to the stops—not a good thing for either the skipper's mental health or the engines longevity. Since negotiating an 80-mile long ditch is relatively simplistic from a circumnavigation point of view, the pilot requirement for cruising boats seems to be more of a full employment program for the Egyptians than a safety issue.

The locals at Port Suez told us that late March to late April is the windy time of year. High winds, as well as sandstorms, can cause unexpected shutdowns of the Suez Canal. Egyptian army maneuvers can also wreak havoc on scheduled transit times through the canal. The land on either side of the canal is bleak desert with sparse vegetation and demolished buildings dating back to the Six Day War with Israel. The pilots have no kind words for the winning side.

After studying the raw, barren landscape, I would have to agree with Mark Twain's observation: *Who would want it?*

The pilot's responsibility is to safely steer his assigned vessel through the Suez at a designated speed and course. The first of our three pilots had little interest in steering *Osprey*, but he displayed a great deal of interest in getting to know PL. Although Mohammad claimed to be a devout Muslim, he fell far short of the ideal as he trailed my mate around the inside of our boat trying to make bodily contact at every opportunity. The chubby pilot left me to steer the boat as he continued his campaign to woo PL by mouthing, in broken English, "I Love You." While this saga unfolded inside the cabin, I was blissfully unaware and continued to steer *Osprey* north. Eventually PL handled the situation by hiding in the forward stateroom behind a locked door until it was time to say good-bye. Poor Mohammed was sad when his Madonna disappeared. Mohammad suggested spending the night with us at Ismailia, then continuing on with us the next morning. That suggestion was vetoed by a muffled "No way" coming from the forward compartment.

After thwarting Mohammad's advances and listening to his pleas for *bakeesh*, we finally arrived at Ismailia in late afternoon. *Bakeesh,* or a bribe, in this case a carton of Marlboro cigarettes and $10, was a small price to pay to be rid of a lovesick pilot. I refused his requests for whiskey and a *Playboy* magazine. According to yachties in the know, having to endure the antics of at least one corrupt pilot is about par for the course.

I hurriedly dumped Mohammad off at the pilot's dock, and then PL and I dropped the hook for the evening. As we debriefed each other about Mohammad's exploits, ice cold G & T's encouraged a more philosophical take on the bizarre day. Ismailia's inviting shoreline glistened with the sparkling lights of beautiful villas and handsome parks—a refreshing departure from the typical Red Sea offerings of scrub brush and sand dunes.

The next two pilots were complete gentlemen and very competent. I offered these men *bakeesh* as a tip for good service, a welcome change from the extortion I paid to the first pilot. Egyptian tourism ceased to be on our agenda after our third and last pilot transferred back to his pilot boat at Port Said. We were in the Mediterranean mode and it showed.

If nothing else, our six-week stint in the Red Sea put our lives in perspective. The experience encourages introspection and breeds humility. A perverse sense of triumph enveloped the *Osprey* crew as we cleared out of Port Said and sailed into the Mediterranean. I left a lot of my preconceived notions about control back in the Red Sea—everything passes and nothing remains the same.

20

The Contested Lands

Under brilliant blue clear skies, *Osprey* swept along the North African coast in a fine northerly breeze—Israel was our next landfall. PL and I were excited about our upcoming visit. Although physically Israel can handily fit inside the island of Sicily, on the Middle Eastern stage Israel is a 500-pound gorilla. The Jewish state, a patch of desert on the shores of the Mediterranean, was formed in 1948 by UN mandate. The kicker is that it was carved out of the historic region of Palestine. Israel's relatively small population of six million was suddenly surrounded by Arab states not particularly concerned about the longevity of the interlopers.

Sea temperature was 20 degrees cooler than the warm 85-degree waters of the southern Red Sea. Our reintroduction to warm seas would have to wait until August when we would be cruising the Turquoise Coast of Turkey. With just a few fishing boats here and there, our overnight sail from Port Said to Ashkelon was peaceful and serene. A waxing moon carpeted the Mediterranean in an amber glow as the gentle winds and calm seas seemed to beckon us eastward.

Suddenly we were blasted back to reality by a strident female voice on the VHF radio: "Unidentified vessel approaching Israeli territorial waters, identify yourself. This is the Israeli Navy."

I hurriedly keyed the microphone and informed the voice that *Osprey* and her American crew respectfully requested permission to moor at the Israeli port of Ashkelon. No radio response came my way. As *Osprey* closed on Israel's twelve-mile territorial limit, an ominous looking black patrol boat roared over the eastern horizon and rocketed towards us. I was excited about all the action so I convinced PL to stand on deck and wave—a seemingly great photo op featuring the gunboat's Star of David snapping jauntily from the vessel's flagstaff. The lethal looking craft quickly intercepted us. We suddenly felt very intimidated as the Israeli crew aimed their deck-mounted machine guns directly at us. PL has never let me forget that the sailors did not wave, but they had the audacity to point a gun in her direction. The Israeli Navy is not into huggy-feely type welcomes. The patrol boat never acknowledged us by radio, but they quickly decelerated to dead slow, approached within fifty meters of our vessel, and then slowly circled around us like a tiger sniffing out prey. It was rather unsettling to have grim looking, heavily armed sailors training large caliber weapons our way. Eventually Israel's version of a floating welcome wagon apparently concluded that PL and I were not terrorists because they fired up their turbines and sped off without ever exchanging a word with us. After being slammed around by the navy vessel's nasty wake, we regrouped and then continued sailing towards the land of milk and honey. My mate just rolled her eyes and awarded "thumbs down" to my impromptu photo session.

That incident was our introduction to Israel and its heavy military presence. As we came to learn, heavy security and military preparedness is a dominant part of Israeli society. It is a common sight to see young men and women of the Israeli military packing their weapons into movie theaters, stores, and restaurants. Since Israel is incredibly security conscious, the police and customs officials boarded us immediately after our arrival in Ashkelon. Our boat was thoroughly searched and we were extensively questioned about the variety of visas in our passports. Many of our stamps represented Middle Eastern countries that consider Israel a sworn enemy. If we had been journeying south towards the Arab states in the Red Sea, the Israeli immigration officials would not have stamped our passports—an Israeli stamp would brand us as unwelcome in many of the surrounding Arab countries.

After the formalities were completed, the staff of Ashkelon Marina warmly welcomed us. When PL and I arrived there were very few cruising boats at the new marina. The majority of our brethren were still battling their way up the Red Sea. In recent years Ashkelon has become very popular because it is just an overnight sail from Port Said, moorage is relatively inexpensive, the facilities are good, and the marina staff is accommodating. After a few days I discovered the downside to our marina. Ashkelon is located just north of the Gaza strip, and if tensions in the area boil over, the high-pitched scream of Israeli jet fighters blasts away the tranquility of the Mediterranean digs.

Although a few of the Mediterranean bound cruising boats sail directly from Port Said to Cyprus or Crete, the weather is still rather unsettled in early April and there is always a chance of getting popped. During the cruising season from May to September, Mediterranean weather is more predictable. Accepted weather wisdom suggests a reoccurring cycle that usually produces about a week of calm weather followed by a gale—a fairly accurate portrayal in our view.

Ashkelon was our first encounter with unlimited fresh water since Australia. PL and I devoted hours and hours to thoroughly scrubbing *Osprey* inside and out. From the tip of the mast to the bowels of the bilge, sand was everywhere. The Red Sea sandstorms blasted us with red grit that gummed up the winches, stained the sail covers, and sandblasted the deck. Our cockpit resembled a pig's mud wallow as the layers of caked-on grime slowly peeled away.

Because Ashkelon boasts a new marine haul out facility, I decided to paint the bottom and do a bit of mechanical work. Our previous haul out had been in New Zealand, a favorable but not cheap experience. But the "dear" marine hardware prices in New Zealand hardly prepared us for the "super dear" prices in Israel. Importing US manufactured marine products into Israel is an extremely pricey proposition.

I could chat with Eran, the boat yard manager, but most of the population in Ashkelon speak only Hebrew. Trying to decipher Hebrew is a difficult task for the uninitiated and our crew was sociologically challenged as we shopped in the stores, read the marquee at the cinema, or simply asked directions. From a language perspective, Israel is not a user-friendly country outside the larger metropolitan areas. Fortunately English is spoken in the cities and tourist areas, but in a small town like Ashkelon, communication is a constant challenge.

The political prospective of the *Lonely Planet* guidebook does not sit too well with the Israeli political establishment, so the book is unavailable in Israel. Depending on your political persuasion and cultural heritage, Israel may represent the lone outpost of democracy in the Middle East, or you might consider Israel to be an intruder. The people of Israel may share different visions for the future, but they all must deal with an issue that is on the front page of Israeli newspapers everyday—the Palestinian question. In the tribal Middle East memories are long and passions are hot.

Although some of Israel's established borders are subject to debate, it is a relatively small country—our six-week visit gave us ample time for the grand tour. Decent rental cars are modestly priced and consequently road trips became part of our lifestyle once again. Israel maintains one of the largest bus fleets in the world because the coaches double as military transports if a national emergency arises. It is a simple matter to hop aboard a bus in sleepy Ashkelon and be whisked to the sophisticated environs of Tel Aviv.

While we cruised the Indian Ocean a few months prior, Kate emailed us regularly from Florence. Although PL is much more perceptive, even I concluded that our daughter was smitten with Andrea, her Italian boyfriend. Kate described her man as kind, gentle, smart, and handsome…and a gourmet chef. When Andrea fired off an email assuring us that his friend Nadi would take care of us when we arrived in Tel Aviv, I was even more impressed.

Sure enough, Nadi met us in Tel Aviv and gave us an in-depth look at his city. Tel Aviv has a lot going for it—modern shops, sophisticated restaurants, and a sunny Mediterranean waterfront. Delicious Middle Eastern food served at Michel's Aladdin bistro in picturesque Jaffa bore little resemblance to the questionable fare we encountered during our Red Sea bash.

Nadi whisked us off to see the new and very modern marina at Herzilya and the upscale suburbs of Tel Aviv. The good life is alive and well if you know where to look. Strict antiterrorism measures, military checkpoints, and armed teenage soldiers were commonplace in Israel long before 9/11 brought the threat of terror to America's doorstep. Nadi was frustrated with the Palestinian issue and he felt that the majority of Israelis are much more concerned with peace and consensus than occupation and confrontation.

As Nadi squired us about, he chatted with a few of his business associates on his cell phone. When the phone was handed to us a lyrical, Italian accented voice came on the line. The surprise call was our first conversation with Nadi's good friend, Andrea. Little did we know that a few years, dozens of countries, and thousands of miles later the personable young man was destined to become our son-in-law. Tyler would definitely have approved

After saying goodbye to our gracious host, PL and I drove to the northern boundary of Israel and into Old Akko (Acre), an Ottoman-era walled city. Omar, a resident archeologist, is the man to see. As an Israeli Arab and as a dominant figure in the large Arab community in Acre, Omar offered us another insight into the diversity of Middle Eastern cultures. On our own PL and I would have ended up stumbling through a gaggle of slack jawed tourists—we would have missed the essence of the place. With Omar as our guide, we were squired through the exotic winding labyrinth of Old Akko, where we were introduced to local merchants who plied their trades in tiny shops. Instead of catering to the souvenir crowd, Acre cares for the needs of its residents.

Salah, a good friend from back home, told about a street in Acre named after his family, Yashruti Street. Sure enough we found the street and a large mosque.

Omar explained that mausoleums inside the mosque held the remains of Salah's father, grandfather, and great grandfather. These revered men were sheiks in a unique sect of Shiite Muslims who provide hospitality and lodgings to itinerant believers in Islam. Salah's brother, who resides in Jordan, is the present sheik. Because of Salah, Omar and the resident caretakers treated us with unexpected deference and kindness. Omar opened his home to us and we shared a meal with his huge extended family. Once again we were humbled by the unbounded hospitality of our hosts.

Just down the road a high wire fence, capped with razor sharp concertina wire, divides the northern border of Israel from the disputed land of Lebanon—not a happy place. A long history of warring factions has scarred the landscape and the people as well. In former times Beirut was the Paris of the Middle East, but a US State Department traveler warning convinced us to take the war torn capital off our list of places to see.

"Danger—Land Mines"…now that sign got our attention! Our small rental car chugged up the steep switchback road and past a minefield that had been a war zone when Israel battled Syria for control of the strategic Golan Heights decades ago. A rusty barbwire fence and an occasional warning sign graphically reminded us that unmarked landmines continued to be one of the dismal legacies of modern warfare. The military dictum of controlling the highest ground compelled Israel to annex the hills so any recurrent battles would force Syrian forces to approach the mountain fortress across the exposed, arid lands to the east.

A young Israeli soldier hitched a ride with us back to his guard post on the mountainside. The battle-scarred countryside gave way to rolling fruit orchards and crisp, clean air. Since conversing in Hebrew is not my forte, our adopted soldier resorted to sign language as he guided us to our overnight accommodations. Our short, muscular guide must have been a skier because PL and I ended up in a kibbutz ski village on the slopes of Mt. Hermon. English speaking hosts, excellent wholesome food, and a good French burgundy made our stay at Chez Stephanie an impressive event. As we strolled the chilly streets of the Jewish settlement, the remarkable vista of The Sea of Galilee, shimmering in the cold clear moonlight, unfolded in the distant valley far below.

Shrines and churches on the shoreline of the Sea of Galilee trace their ancestry back more than two millenniums, when St. Peter preached to the crowds and Jesus walked on those very waters. Although the rich histories of Christianity, Judaism, and Islam glorify the region, the bleak story of the Palestinian refugee camps blights the Holy Land. Our road trip wound south to the West Bank, a rich agricultural zone geographically west of the Jordan River. Jewish settlements,

Israeli military installations, Palestinian refugee camps, and frequent military checkpoints are volatile ingredients in a very explosive mix. It is unsettling to see chain link fences encircling squalid refugee camps and the mandated security roadblock inspections of Palestinian registered vehicles. Not much has changed since our visit to the biblical Judea and Samaria. The explosive mixture of frustration and resentment is a potential catastrophe for all the people of the Promised Land.

The mud baths in the Dead Sea were too tempting to resist. The Dead Sea, at 1305 feet below sea level, is the lowest point on earth…and the saltiest. PL and I slathered each other in warm mud for that sensual full-body wallow. After a shower, it was time for the effortless float in, actually almost on, the briny slimy waters of the Dead Sea. The sensation cannot be duplicated anywhere else in the world. I did not really believe the hype until I personally read a newspaper while floating on my back.

Just down the way was the sheer-sided 1440-foot mesa of Masada, one of the most popular attractions in Israel. Over two millenniums ago 967 Jewish defenders, many of them women and children, decided that the 15,000 Roman soldiers on the plains below would never take them alive. The enduring legacy of Masada's lesson is epitomized by the oath taken by each Israeli military recruit, "Masada shall not fall again." During the cable car to the stronghold at the top of the high plateau, we could see the remnants of the Roman encampments that surrounded the ancient Jewish community and precipitated their eventual mass suicide. The hardened zealots created an enduring mystique that eclipsed even the most treasured archeological artifacts of the era.

Jerusalem is surely one of the most striking and captivating cities in the world. Known by the Hebrew name *Yerushalayayim,* or City of Peace, this holy city is also known by the Arabic name *Al-Quad,* or the Holy. Not surprisingly the Israeli's 1950 notion of Jerusalem as the capital of Israel does not sit well with the Arabic population. Today most countries still maintain their embassies in Tel Aviv. The El-Aska Mosque, the Dome of the Rock, the Christian Church of the Holy Sepulcher, and the Jewish Western Wall characterize the diversity of beliefs within Old City walls. Our goal was to seek the elusive commonality that makes Jerusalem the holiest city in the world.

Strolling through the maze of narrow, twisted alleys inside the walls of the Old City, PL and I encountered not only vendors and tourists, but also believers and nonbelievers of every stripe. The diverse collection of souls had but one thing in common—everyone seemed to share the same hope that perhaps the ancient city was a portal into God's realm.

Our visit coincided with Passover. Hundreds of Hasidic Jews wandered around in their long black coats and large fur hats seemingly oblivious to the sweltering heat. The Western Wall was jammed with worshippers, but PL managed to squeeze in and leave our own personal note to God amidst the thousands of messages already stuffed between the tightly packed stones. Although our hearts grieved for what we had lost, our spirits rejoiced over what remained.

With Laurie, Carol, and Ryan of *Dolphin Spirit,* we rented a van in Ashkelon and then headed south across the Negev Desert to the port city of Eilat. After we checked in at the local hotel, a bus took us across the recently opened Jordanian frontier and then it was on to Petra, the Rose City. Since the blockbuster movie *Indiana Jones and the Temple of Doom* featured spectacular shots of Petra's carved sandstone temples, I was fired up to see the real thing. Scrambling past donkeys packing chunky tourists, PL and I tramped through the mile long Siq Gorge—a winding narrow claustrophobic pathway coursing between imposing sandstone cliffs. Suddenly the gorge was no more and we found ourselves face to face with the huge red hued temple of Indiana Jones fame, the Khaznah. Also known as the Treasury, the façade of the Greek-style temple was carved into the face of a thirteen-story sandstone cliff over two thousand years ago.

Petra's secluded valley housed thousands of cave-dwelling Arabs in earlier centuries, but today the uniquely carved caves are vacant. The Jordanian government relocated the cave dwellers so the mystique of the valley would be preserved for the burgeoning tourist industry. The architecture is imposing and clever. Homes, tombs, and temples are carved into the hillsides of a meandering valley that measures over two square miles. Some of the intricate sandstone entryways proved to be elaborate facades rather than the promised temples. Petra stonemasons of ancient times had little room for error. One slip of the chisel and an entire stone facade would be ruined. It was a pretty steep learning curve, especially for those of us who like to erase.

The recently signed peace accords permitted us to reenter Israel and to cross yet another frontier into Egypt's Sinai. Our destination was Mount Sinai and the monastery of Santa Katerina, of biblical burning bush fame. The resident Greek Orthodox monk pointed out his favorite icons, but the bush was what we came to see. The shrub is a bit of a disappointment—just a fenced clump of nondescript, hearty desert scrub.

The approach to Mt. Sinai is a modest hike past vendors hawking water and local guides offering camel rides up the incline. We hoofed it on our own. Eventually the walking trail became a steep rock scramble, but the payoff is the stunning view. As the shadow of rugged peak crept across the Sinai desert, the molten globe of the setting sun bathed the distant Red Sea in crimson. Each of us was profoundly touched to be standing on the 7800-foot summit where God is said to have delivered the Ten Commandments to Moses so long ago.

The low point of our adventure was the flash flood. Our mechanically challenged Egyptian van bucked and snorted through the muddy goo of a flooded stream bed as our chain smoking driver belligerently cursed the fates that had ganged up on his beater rig. After the waters in the *wadi* receded a few hours later, the mud splattered van delivered us back to the Israeli frontier.

Cyprus, the third largest island in the Mediterranean, gained its independence from Britain in 1960. In 1974 forces led by Greek officers decided to overthrow the Cypriot government. Since Greeks and Turks historically shared the island, the Turks invaded. As any local will quickly tell you, Cyprus is now carved into a southern Greek side and a northern Turkish side.

A pleasant two-day sail brought us to southern city of Larnaca, a favorite winter haunt for yachties cruising the Med. British friends Kathryn and David and his mom and dad, Jeremy and Bridget of *Halcyon,* livened up our stay with their British slant on how the game was played in Europe. Much of the politics eluded us, but Larnaca's excellent restaurants, quality stores, and well-stocked chandleries speak for themselves. *Osprey* was treated to a new starting battery and our crew gorged on assorted lamb specialties at the local bistros.

"Looks like a washing machine and refrigerator perched on the stern of that rusty sailboat." Turned out that it was.

As PL and I strolled over to check out the curious setup, a sturdy Russian sailor poked his head up from the contraption. In halting English the young voyager introduced us to his wife and daughter. Tasty Russian cookies were offered and the story unfolded. With little money and a bleak future, this adventurous family bought the old sloop, sewed their own sails, and then sailed from a small port on the Black Sea bound for the West. After passing through the Bosphorus, they slowly sailed from port to port along the Turkish coastline and eventually ended up in Cyprus. The used washer and refrigerator were their first major appliance purchases and they were ecstatic. We were happy for them and a little ashamed at our initial take on the situation. The cross-section of humanity that visits the transient moorages at Larnaca each cruising season definitely gives the place character.

With the requisite duffle bag of spare parts, our friends Salah and Liljana came aboard. Although they are powerboat folks in actuality, Salah and Liljana fit right into the blue water sailboat crowd. Like us, their bohemian lifestyle involves shuttling around the globe—now our crew had acquired an even bigger dose of wandering sea gypsy persona. As we waited for a decent weather window prior to sailing for the Turquoise Coast of Turkey, PL and Liljana strolled the waterfront and upscale streets.

Salah and I chose the lower road as we wandered through a few back alleys, but eventually we located the guru of anchor retrieval who I had heard so much about. Dr. Ironsides is a very clever welder who found his niche by catering to the cruising community and, more notably, manufacturing *The Finger of the gods.* After Salah and I tracked down the doc's digs, we were ushered into his cluttered machine shop. As I salivated at the prospect of acquiring *The Finger,* Ironsides spun the combination on his office safe, reached inside, and extracted his stainless steel masterpiece. Money was gladly exchanged and now I owned the ultimate anchor retrieval system. Salah could not resist the siren call so he too became a devotee of *The Finger.*

Although Dr. Ironsides does not include an operations manual with *The Finger,* I have since spread the gospel back in the USA. *The Finger* is the cruising boat's ticket to salvation. The five-inch counterbalanced trip hook is the discerning yachtsman's great equalizer against haphazardly anchored boats and junk laden harbors. Legend has it that *The Finger* originated in the Mediterranean, the ancient birthplace of Neptune and many other mythological gods. Honed to perfection over the years, *The Finger* is renowned among long-range cruisers and world-class voyagers.

The concept behind *The Finger* is elegant but simple. The top shackle of *The Finger* is attached to a sturdy line, which in turn is run to the bow of the boat. The line is then lowered until *The Finger* is deftly slipped under any assorted bits and pieces that have been dredged up by the anchor. At this juncture, the topside line is tied off and the newly unencumbered anchor lowered. *The Finger,* rather than the anchor, now supports the superfluous pile of rubbish that was dangling from the anchor. With a simple tug on *The Finger's* trip line, the offending flora and fauna is jettisoned and the boat good to go. No more dangling over the bow or straining my back as I tried to unravel an anchor fur ball—deliverance was at hand.

What did we like about Cyprus? It was clean and modern and full of interesting world cruisers. When a friend posed the question to a well traveled five year old, the little girl answered immediately: "I like Cyprus the best because they have kittens."

21

The Carpet Guys

Pure logic is the ruin of the spirit.

—*Antoine de Saint-Exupery*

The first day of our passage to Turkey was sort of like being on spin cycle in a huge saltwater washing machine. Actually PL considers it "my passage" since I had picked the weather window, and I obviously must have crossed the weather gods. By and by the seas mellowed out and so did the *Osprey* crew. As we closed on the coastal waters of Turkey after our 200-mile jaunt, a conglomeration of freighters, tankers, tugs, fishing boats, and yachts haphazardly zipped across our radar screen. This was our first encounter with *gulets,* large wooden Turkish charter boats that feature macho skippers charging around the coast at great speed oblivious to any nautical rules or decorum. My crew was at their best as we weaved and dodged our way through the Eastern Mediterranean's formidable obstacle course.

Turkey is bigger than Texas and commands 5000 miles of coastline stretching along the Aegean, Mediterranean, and Black Sea. The Turquoise Coast of southern Turkey is renowned not only for its warm, luminous blue water, but also for its pine-scented hillsides and secluded coves. Much of the 230-mile coastline is inaccessible by road so a cruising boat is just the ticket. The resort town of Marmaris is ideally situated in the center of the huge cruising area. Depending on the mood, *Osprey* could cruise east to visit the more ancient sites, or sail west towards the Aegean's less classical offerings. We leased a berth until spring.

"*Merhaba.*" Whether the hello is phrased in Turkish or English, the social aspect of cruising is alive and well in Marmaris. Ninety boats from a dozen different countries joined us for the winter at Netsel Marina. The marina features marble showers, an outdoor swimming pool, and a resort atmosphere. Resident yachties enjoy first run movies at the marina's outdoor amphitheatre. A full service boatyard adjacent to the marina handles just about any boat related project at reasonable prices. When our hometown friends Denny and Andrea joined us for their authentic Turkish experience, they were braced for an Eastern Mediterranean cultural immersion rather than the civilized offerings of the marina. More exotic experiences came our way as we traveled into the countryside.

Turkey always comes to mind when listing our favorite countries. Unlike the stereotypical portrayal of a burly mustached soldier with blood in his eye, we find the Turks to be friendly and hospitable. The country is huge with a variety of climates and topography to match. Food is inexpensive, delicious, and unusual. Extensive bus lines allow travel around the country with a minimum of hassle. Antiquities are among the best in Europe. The rapidly modernizing democracy is a bridge between the liberal mindset of Western Europe and the conservative cultures of the Middle East. Although the population is 95% Muslim, a dramatic contrast exists between the secular lifestyle in the big cities and resort towns and the conservative existence favored by the village people further inland. Whereas the beaches of the resort towns feature topless European women, the rural areas of the country expect a woman to display no more than her henna dyed hands and smiling face.

In 324 AD Emperor Constantine moved the capital of Rome to Istanbul and named the dynamic city after himself. Constantinople was the kingpin of the Roman Empire for 1000 years. In 1451 Mehemet II took exception to Roman dominance and took control in the name of the Ottomans. The dramatic shift towards modernization started in 1923 when Mustafa Kemal, a national hero of the Turkish War of Independence, decreed that times were changing and so would the Turks. Historically Turks had only one given name but Ataturk, as he became known, decreed that all Turks should choose a family name. Ataturk, or Father Turk, became Kemal Ataturk. Turkey was a cultural tinderbox at the time, so he demanded that all ethnic Greeks return to Greece and all ethnic Turks return to their homeland. The insightful maneuvering separated the Catholics from the Muslims, as well as the Greeks from the Turks. A modified Latin alphabet eclipsed the Arabic version. The fez, a tasseled Turkish box hat now favored by Shriners, was banned because Ataturk felt it was the badge of a backward people. Women were granted suffrage, civil marriages replaced religious marriages, and polygamy was abolished. Ataturk died in 1938 and was renowned for almost single-handedly turning the plodding traditional country into a dynamic nation.

I have never claimed to be a linguist, but usually I can wing it with Romance languages. The Turkish language is much more challenging. Although the guttural language did not exactly flow easily off my tongue, I managed enough words to get by. As always PL's command of the local language insured that our crew could communicate with the locals with a more personalized touch.

A language that did flow easily off my tongue was the string of uncharitable epitaphs I hurled at a French charter boat that ripped loose our anchor in the windswept harbor of Bozuk Buku. My demeanor was less than kind since PL and I happened to be exploring an ancient acropolis on a headland high above the anchorage. That is when I happened to notice that *Osprey* was underway. The rogue charter boat crew apparently could not get their anchor set so they sailed off, but so did *Osprey*—inconveniently our sailboat was minus her crew. Although we had carefully picked our way up the steep boulder strewn hillside, my adrenaline charged downhill sprint was a study in flying flip-flops. I leaped into our dinghy and fired up the outboard. Normally our potent 15 hp engine is bolted on our inflatable, but on this fateful day our anemic 3 hp outboard was in service. Even at full throttle, I just putt-putted along. I barely managed to intercept our wandering sloop before she drifted out of the football stadium sized harbor.

To many westerners Turkey conjures up visions of sultans and palaces complete with decadent harems filled with mystery and intrigue—outdated stereotypes that quickly evaporate after a foreigner arrives. Although Turkey boasts a vigorous economy, the threat of Islamic fundamentalists seizing control of the government and Kurdish separatists menacing the eastern provinces strains Turkey's economy and international reputation. Ultra modern sections of Istanbul, Ankara, and Izmir control the pulse of the country. Major Turkish cities were home to modern grocery stores, efficient transit systems, computerized banking, sophisticated electronic centers, and state of the art cinemas. Turkey's economy is on a roller coaster ride to modernization. The banking system favors European ATM cards. Our American ATM cards worked only sporadically. By limiting Americans to withdrawals of 20,000,000 Turkish lire, about $67, the Turkish banking establishment scores on lucrative transaction fees as we primed the blinking machine again and again for a bit of cash.

Even in modern cities we could wander down an unimposing alley and find ourselves back in another century, gingerly stepping on wobbly cobblestones fronting antique stone dwellings. Devout Muslims pray inside their domed mosques, while the pulsating local market place buzzes with chattering vendors. Depending on your persuasion there is lots to choose from. Wooden carts

stacked with freshly baked loaves of bread, baskets of assorted fruits and vegetables, and vats of green and black olives are always tempting. Freshly skinned goats
and sheep hang from the rafters. When it comes to purchasing a squawking
chicken struggling against its bound feet or fresh goat cheese stuffed inside a
goat's head, PL became a bit more standoffish. The scenes are chaotic but the
food is fresh.

The countryside is filled with scores of hot houses, where delicious tomatoes,
peppers, and cucumbers are grown year-round. Massive wheat farms and huge
hydroelectric dams pack muscle into the economic clout of the nation. Turkey
enjoys an incredible wealth of natural resources that will eventually make her a
major player in Europe. Old and not so old animosity from Greece and France
has effectively blocked Turkey's entry into the economic dynamo of the EU in
recent years. As tensions cool, perhaps Turkey's time will come.

Istanbul is one of the world's great cities, an exotic crossroads blending the
modern secularism of Western Europe and the rich Islamic traditions of the Middle East. Over the course of our ten-month stay in Turkey, PL and I made
repeated visits to Istanbul and the offerings were never dull.

In early June we were getting excited. Not only was it our first visit to Istanbul, but it was also a chance to spend time with Kate and her beloved Andrea. PL
and I definitely clicked with Andrea—we know a good match when we see one.
The Blue Mosque, Hagia Sophia, Grand Bazaar, and Topaki Palace are Istanbul's
"must see" attractions and all were within walking distance of our homey pension
at Empress Zoe. Our windows rattled as loudspeakers from the Blue Mosque's
graceful minarets blasted out the Muslim call to prayer. Just down the way the
Hagia Sophia (Church of Holy Wisdom) was much quieter. Although the massive dome started life as a church in the sixth century, the Ottoman Turks con-
verted the four-acre site into a mosque. During the Ataturk era the ancient
Byzantium legacy was retired as a religious forum, but the Hagia Sophia still
remains one of the largest enclosed spaces on the planet.

At Kate's insistence the four of us agreed to experience the same communal
bathing experience enjoyed through the millennia by Greeks, Romans, and
Turks. Since this particular bathhouse segregated the men from the women, we
parted at the classic stone entrance and agreed to meet an hour and a half later on
the street. I was shown to a cubicle where I undressed and stored my valuables.
After Andrea and I wrapped towels around our waists, we were led into a steam
room where each of us sprawled out on our own personal marble slab to sweat for
half an hour. Eventually a huge masseuse/wrestler type lumbered in to begin the

ritual cleaning. The stocky Turk resembled a loincloth-clad NFL linebacker. A huge drooping black mustache and a malevolent expression completed the look. According to the ladies, his female counterpart was clad in black string bikini panties—the chunky, topless rendition of a Middle Eastern peasant with a spiteful persona.

When the massive masseuse doused me with warm water and scrubbed me with a rough cloth, I flashed back to my mom scouring the unwilling faces of her three sons. Of course my mom was much more gentle and she lacked the bulk to flip me bodily from back to front. Besides sandpapering my brutalized skin to a dull sheen, the onslaught flushed grime out of my pores that I did not even know existed. After all the merriment the displaced sumo wrestler lathered me up, rinsed me off, and shampooed my hair. As I lay dazed on the marble slab, a few well placed few karate chops up and down the spine served as the *coup de grace*.

Turkey is the land of the carpet salesman and we encountered rug merchants of every persuasion. From upscale shops to tumble downed stalls, the rug merchants are an integral fabric of Turkish life. Carpets are priced according to the quality of the weave and age of the piece, the older the better. On a hot afternoon in Istanbul we visited a beautiful tea garden agreeably situated in a shady courtyard. The idea was to rest our tired feet. PL sipped apple tea and I fired up a Turkish water pipe. As I lounged on the huge cushions puffing the sweet fragrant tobacco, Furuk happened by. PL and I followed the personable university student to his uncle's adjacent carpet store, and after two hours of chatting and haggling, we bought a "treasure of a carpet." Furuk claimed the carpet is over a hundred years old and will just continue to become more valuable. Every year a Christmas email greeting arrives from Furuk, so he remains our resident carpet guy and who knows, maybe we even got a good deal.

Just a stroll away the Grand Bazaar, or *Kapali Carsi*, boasts an intricate maze of arched passages and tiny alleys leading to some 4000 shops spread out over fifty acres. Eager vendors entice unwary tourists into their shops with an offer of tea and conversation. The merchants insist that today is the doe eyed visitor's lucky day—the shop just happens to have a special treasure perfectly suited to the hapless shopper.

The Topaki Palace was the home to 25 sultans over the course of four centuries. Prior to the nineteenth century, 40,000 people lived on the palace grounds at any one time. Incredible wealth poured into the sultan's coffers. Sheiks and emirs bestowed incredibly lavish gifts on the sultan in exchange for his favor—a shrewd political move at a time when the fierce Janissary warriors of the Ottoman Empire ruled the region. Just a peak at the Treasury gives you an idea of how a sultan scored. Although much of the collection has been ripped off through the ages, there are a few choice baubles left, such as the Topaki dagger with its massive emeralds and the Spoonmaker's Diamond that happens to be the fifth largest diamond in the world.

Harem is Arabic for forbidden. According to our guide, the sultan would stroll down the hall of the Harem where 1000 of his special women lived and then toss a gold coin to the lady chosen to join him for the evening. Ruling the Harem was the valide sultan, the mother of the reigning sultan. Black eunuch servants did her bidding. The valide sultan wielded incredible influence with the sultan and she was personally involved in his selection of wives and concubines. Mom had a vested interest in producing little sultans and future heirs. A silk bowstring wielded by the sultan's henchman was used to kill young sultans who were not ordained to rein.

The chance to be a sultan sustains a fascinating Turkish ritual. We jumped back as a horn blaring procession of cars paraded through the crowded streets. A gaily-decorated pickup truck led the pack. A smiling seven-year old boy waved to the appreciative crowd from the back of the truck. Obviously the star of the day, the young "sultan" was dressed in a gold and white satin robe trimmed with fur. A huge golden crown was perched on his rather small head. The young star was actually the main player in a circumcision party. The circumcision ceremony is a major family event that can be more costly than a wedding. Perhaps all the hype was meant to carry him through the ordeal. We wondered if the star of the show would give his younger brothers any hints when their time came.

Andrea's vacation was over so he flew back to Chicago. Kate was still on her work break so she decided to join PL and I for an extended bus trip to Cappadocia, the ancient heart of the Hittite Empire. As our little trio boarded the long haul Turkish bus, PL caught a whiff of "Jean Nate," a fragrance she did not associate with the Muslim clientele aboard our coach. It turns out that the cross-country busses employ an extra hand who collects fares and periodically sprays the sweaty seats with deodorizer. At least everyone aboard ends up smelling the same.

Our fragrant bus lurched into a rest stop every few hours and we braced ourselves for the hideous public bathrooms. The consolation was a chance to stretch our cramped legs and indulge ourselves in a cup of the delicious local yogurt. Although Turkey has a ways to go in the public bathroom department, their fruits and vegetables and dairy products are world-class stuff.

After a long day, and an even longer night, our driver deposited us at a ramshackle bus station outside of Goreme. We staggered off the bus into the chilly predawn of Central Anatolia, still wiping the sleep from our eyes. A *dolmus,* the ubiquitous Turkish minibus, delivered us to a charming pension that mercifully boasted great showers and a good breakfast. Now that we were fed and watered, it was time to check out the rock-hewn churches, lunar landscape, and underground cities unique to Cappadocia.

In primal times the locals hollowed out soft volcanic tufa cones to create their original version of a multistory condo. The phallic shaped fairy chimneys of Cappadocia project an eerie moonscape impression—a unique look that was featured on the *Star Wars* movie set. The distinctive volcanic rock can be whittled like a cake of soap, then the tufa hardens when it exposed to the air. Apparently living in a stone chimney cone has appealed to Cappadocians for almost 4000 years. Even today many of the fairy chimneys are occupied by troglodyte-types who probably consider their digs the ultimate in affordable housing. It is just a matter of whittling out another room or two as the family grows.

None of us bumped into *R2D2* when we explored the steep, narrow passages of the ancient underground city of Kaymakli. Maybe it was because we were not ready to wander off through a claustrophobic maze of tunnels carved four stories under the earth. As early as seventh century BC, inhabitants of the region have taken to the subterranean city whenever invaders sweep through their land. As our guide explained, the ancients realistically preferred to live in peace above the ground as opposed to hiding out underground for months at a time—I could see their point.

Joan and Nick rejoined us in early October for a road trip into the Turkish hinterlands. We rented a car and toured the spectacular Turkish coast from the Aegean port of Kusadasi in the northwest to the Mediterranean port of Antalya in the southeast. The once pristine Turkish coastline has suffered at the hands of developers, but the ancient ruins, fishing villages, and orchards of figs and olives survive in spite of the influx of speculators.

Perhaps the most innovative salesman was the forest ranger who perched atop a forest fire lookout tower on the mountainside above Antalya. After our foursome plodded up the mountainside, we trudged up a steep flight of stairs to the lookout tower. The wizened ranger graciously pointed out the expansive view of the ancient fortification of Termessos on the hillside below us. After we checked out the centuries old stone sarcophagi scattered across the steep meadow, our host demonstrated his entrepreneurial skills by selling us bottled water...and a rug. The ranger assured PL that the carpet was weaved by local artisans. The rug did have a good look, so I found myself hiking back down the hillside with PL's new purchase rolled into my backpack.

Ephesus is the most well preserved classical city in the Mediterranean and home to the temple of Artemis, one of the Seven Wonders of the World. The extensive archeological digs recapture the essence of the once mighty city, considered by the Romans to be the first and greatest metropolis of Asia. Marbled streets rutted from ancient chariot wheels lead to the remnants of magnificent temples and fountains and villas. Unlike the Turkish counterparts of today, the ancient toilets would make any resident happy. The thrones are way ahead of their time with comfortable marble seats, a commanding view of the town, and innovative sewer pipes plumbed with running water from the city's aqueduct system. Armed with a trusty *Lonely Planet*, our quartet wandered through the ruins as each of us tried to envision the city in the glory days of the third century BC. The Great Theatre was built almost 2000 years ago to accommodate up to 25,000 patrons and it is still in use. St. Paul preached at Ephesus and St. John wrote some of his gospels on the grounds. Legend has it that the Virgin Mary lived out her days in a hilltop cottage above the city. At the time the marble paved Arcadian Way stretched from the Great Theater to the harbor. By the sixth century AD the "first and greatest metropolis of Asia" had lost its wealth as its harbor silted up. Today the ruins of Ephesus are stranded three miles inland. Ephesus is an easy bus trip from our home base in Marmaris. Since our visitors always have Ephesus on their agenda, PL and I became rather adept at giving guided tours. We figure if times get tough there is always a niche for us in the tour business.

By early December the Eastern Mediterranean weather turns chilly and damp. I dusted off our long neglected diesel furnace and we nestled in for the winter months aboard. Christmas is a grand event at Netsel Marina. PL and I celebrated the holiday with scores of other cruisers. Good will and cheer is the dominant theme regardless of the passport color, religious belief, or political persuasion. One of our frequent guests aboard was Peter, a freckle faced five-year-old Kiwi lad, who loved being my helper on boat projects. Santa brought Peter a new bike for Christmas, so naturally the little guy took his new wheels for a spin. As he was pedaling down our dock, Peter inadvertently drove off the pier. Peter could swim, but his new Christmas present was not amphibious—it plummeted to the bottom of the bay. Rob, Peter's exasperated dad, spent Christmas day grappling for the submerged bike, and then dismantling it for a rebuild after its salt-water baptism. Such is life in the cruising community.

Jerry and Gayle joined us in Istanbul for our farewell spring tour of Turkey, a road trip...but with a few complications. Initially I could not believe the good deal Jerry got on our rental car. About then the car guy blathered some unintelligible excuse about his "problem" with finding a proper vehicle for us. He insisted that Jerry take his personal car, a fifteen-year old Fiat with bald tires, feeble engine, and that special essence of stale cigarettes. Since the owner never bothered with seatbelts, he was mystified when PL and Gayle dismantled the back seat to retrieve them. Considering our questionable transportation and the deranged driving habits of the locals, strapping into a seat belt had a lot of appeal.

Assuring us that our car was first class, the rental guy counseled us to stay happy, *"Hosca kalin."* His whispered admonition of *"Caninizz sag olsun,"* or loosely translated, may your soul be safe from harm, fairly well summed our thoughts.

We fired up the beast, weaved through the exotic environs of Istanbul, and then boarded a ferry across the Dardanelles. Our road trip took us through the heartland past huge sections of farmland and miles of rolling wheat fields. As we roamed through western Turkey, Kurban Bayrami was in full swing. This important four-day Muslim holiday features ritual slaughtering of sheep so the haves can share with the have-nots. "Kodak moments" are easy come by. One unlucky sheep was trussed up and tossed into the trunk of a taxi. Another unfortunate animal was lifted up by its hind legs, and then wheel barrowed down the street with its front legs providing the pitter/patter locomotion. Dulled our taste buds for lamb.

A burly village cop rapped on our car window and in very broken English asked suspiciously, "Why are you here?" No good answer came to mind so I confessed that we were a bit lost. It could have turned ugly, but the senior guy at the helm of the weathered patrol car decided that we were to be escorted rather than ticketed. After a barrage of incomprehensible rapid-fire Turkish instructions, the boys in the police car motioned for us to follow them. Our official escort fired up their siren and flashing lights as they blithely roared the wrong way down one-way streets, scattering unsuspecting pedestrians. After we were suitably herded out of town, the cops slowed down and pointed to a road heading into the mountains—we were on our own.

A sudden snowstorm ambushed us as we motored along a twisting narrow road through the Beydaglari mountain range. Apparently hardy skiers frequented the place during the season, but this was not the season and the failing Fiat with bald tires was definitely not the car. Between the driving snow and the question-able Turkish roadmaps, my never fail internal compass was out of kilter. Jerry, being a mountain man at heart, eventually drove us out of the unexpected blizzard and down the icy ridge to the sun kissed Mediterranean coast. That evening we sat on the balcony of a funky seaside pension in Kas, toasted our reprieve over a few glasses of *raki,* and philosophized about our place in the universe—a much better alternative than dodging snowdrifts.

Our Turkish friends Christine and Beytullah lamented that Turkey suffers from growing pains—its citizens are torn between the rival cultures of the East and West. The conversation in their Royal Bistro & Café was usually lively, and at times controversial, but it was always an education. PL and I became regulars at their café, not only because we liked the owners, but also because the grilled entrees were superb. Christine and Beytullah catered a farewell dinner in our honor. Beytullah recharged our glasses with excellent French white burgundy as Christine served a sumptuous, multiple course seafood feast. Haunting strains of Middle Eastern music enveloped the room and the lights of Marmaris danced in the background. Later that evening it was time to say goodbye. After the kisses and hugs, our hosts insisted that the lavish meal was merely a token of their friendship. No payment was expected.

Turkey seemed to ground me. After years of globe hopping, the stability of the culture and the goodness of the people soothed my restless spirit. As the months rolled by, I recharged my wanderlust. But this time the path seemed less erratic as I learned a bit more patience and tolerance.

22

Come Fly with Me

Live as though you'll live forever.
And be prepared to die tomorrow.

—The Talmud

Coping with the regional quirks of the Turkish airports is a cold dose of reality therapy. Stray cats live in the baggage claim area of the local airport and happily ride the luggage conveyer belts. At such regional airports it is imperative to identify your luggage when the baggage is laid out in front of the plane prior to take-off. PL and I learned the Turkish system the hard way when we meekly deplaned, apologized to the perturbed officials, and positively identified the two remaining bags on the tarmac as ours.

Since our flight to Britain departed almost on time, we were not feeling too guilty about the luggage incident. Besides we were anxious to reacquaint ourselves with the civilized offerings of Western Europe. London's November weather was rainy and chilly, but our visit was warmed by the hospitality of a number of cruiser friends and their extended families. David and Kathryn spoiled us and soon we became rather attached to their cozy London flat. As PL and I strolled through the maze of dazzling Christmas lights and beautifully decorated stores, we caught a good dose of the Christmas spirit

London's venerable underground railway, better known as the Tube, was our link to the West Side theatres, Knightsbridge shops, and Westminster parliamentary sessions. As we wandered past Big Ben on the opening day of Parliament, the Queen's dashing cavalry escort passed in review. We stood in the drizzle gaping through a forest of umbrellas when the Queen's golden coach made its grand entrance. We were hooked as the regal surroundings of Europe's largest city reeled us into the cosmopolitan atmosphere.

At a homey pub on the Devon coastline, PL and I joined Jeremy and Bridget for a Plowman's lunch and a pint before trekking to their waterfront cottage. Our tramp took us past picturesque hedgerows bursting with foxgloves and wild roses. Since we were kitted out in sturdy English gum boots, cutting cross-country through the rough gorse and prickly brush was no problem. As we rounded the muddy, deep rutted country lane into the seaside village of Salcombe, we were flattered to see an American flag snapping in the breeze above our hosts' vacation home. Although Thanksgiving is a unique American tradition, our gracious British friends honored us by flying our colors. They genially invited a number of fascinating guests to share their table and celebrate our heritage. Rather than a turkey, we enjoyed a brace of fresh English quail.

Andrew and Sheila welcomed us for a weekend retreat at their country manor in Kent, the 'Garden of England'. Andrew, a veteran member of the British Parliament (MP), explained that a British politician is judged on the ability to speak with wit and vigor. The verbal jousting, so much apart of parliamentary debate, can either establish or destroy a politician's reputation. Andrew provided us with passes to the House of Commons so we could watch the action. The clever verbal cuts, brutal character assassinations, and inane banter from the floor of the convened House is definitely one of the best shows in town and, unlike the West Side theatres, the entertainment is free.

As our train chugged into Bath, we spotted our cruising sidekicks from Thailand, Jeremy and Sandrene. After checking out the medieval charms of Bath, Jeremy piled all of us into his tiny sedan and then we headed off for a weekend in the Berkshire horse country. Jeremy's sister and her husband hosted us in their huge nineteenth century country manor. The décor is original and the antique furniture authentically scruffy. The next morning was on the nippy side. When I rolled out from under the huge down comforter, I could see my breath. Downstairs in the enormous disheveled kitchen the kettle was on, but the morning uniform was definitely sweaters. The English penchant for frumpy furnishings and minimalist creature comforts is charming, but a set of long underwear would not be remiss.

A few days after Thanksgiving, PL and I hopped the overnight train to Edinburgh, Scotland. Spending a bit of time in the ancestral country of bagpipes, kilts, and clans appealed to us. Even though golfing is not my karma, I know that the Old Course at St. Andrews is a mecca for hard-core golfers. That was about it for my bit of Scottish local knowledge. I was focused on the Loch Ness Monster and Scotch whisky, not necessarily in that order.

Edinburgh Castle, the focal point of the city, is perched on the crater of an extinct volcano. As we hiked along Edinburgh Castle's Royal Mile and gawked at the old fortress, we rounded a corner and stumbled across a British Army awards ceremony. Prince Charles was doing the honors, but the guy looked a bit preoccupied. Since we had already seen his 'mum' with her entourage in London, we felt free to pursue other matters. We were off to the Scotch whisky show.

In the shadow of Edinburgh Castle the thoughtful Scottish distilleries have constructed a Disneyland sort of ride for Scotch aficionados. A miniature train loops around colorful displays depicting the major Scotch whisky players in the country. I am a single malt sort of guy, so I zeroed in on the Grampian Highlands and the fine offerings of the Spey Valley. After the train ride samples of Scotch, the "water of life," are the order of the day. Each distillery clings to its own unique combination of water and barley for the brew and then customizes the amount of peat in their fires. With over six-dozen single malt distilleries in the country, variety is not a problem.

Scottish food is an acquired taste and the innkeepers are sometimes a bit surly, but Loch Ness is worth the hassle. The fabled loch, tucked into the heather cloaked Highlands of Scotland, is deeper than two football fields stacked end to end. Nessie, the resident monster, has a lot of room to roam since her territory is about 26 miles long—the same distance as the passage between Catalina Island and Los Angeles. Although Nessie and her ancestors have supposedly been paddling around Lock Ness for the past fourteen centuries, we could not claim a sighting. However we did manage to soak up a wee bit of the mystic spirit coursing through the glens and lochs of the Scottish Highlands.

A January visit to Chamonix was our first chance to ski since *Osprey* sailed from Seattle four years prior. On a spectacularly clear day, PL and I boarded the highest cable car run in the world for an awesome ascent to the 12,600-foot peak of Aiguille du Midi. Massive glaciers, glistening snowfields, and icy spires dominated the view. The cold thin air of the French Alps etched a razor sharp panorama of the Matterhorn and Mt. Blanc, Europe's loftiest peak.

Our temporary home was a charming riverside inn in downtown Chamonix. Our bedroom was cozy and the food was memorable. The pub in our hotel served as the watering hole for the film crew of the latest James Bond movie. At sunrise prisms of sunlight shot through the high cloud layers and scattered across the icy peaks towering over the valley, an impressionist portrait of fire and ice—the perfect gig for 007.

For the first few days PL and I enjoyed the luxury of relaxed spring skiing under warm, crystalline blue skies. The new generation of shaped skis made our transition from sailing to skiing much easier. Lunch was a rather relaxed outdoor affair as we soaked up French sun, sipped Danish beer and, depending on the direction we looked, enjoyed the spectacular scenery of the Swiss, Italian, or French Alps. Admittedly we tortured the French language, but the locals still treated us very well. The European skiers were courteous, the skiing terrain was awesome, and the scenery defied description.

Towards the end of the week a large storm enveloped the French Alps. Thigh deep powder snow and phenomenal off-piste skiing awaited us. Although I am into powder snow, PL favors the packed stuff. About midday I found a ridge full of untracked powder so I went for it. PL agreed to ski down a well marked groomed run and meet me at the base of the chair lift. Just after PL had gone on her way, a blizzard swept through the area and the mountain was engulfed in a white out. I followed the vague outline of the ski chairs and eventually found our rendezvous…but no PL.

After a long while I began to worry. PL was lost somewhere, neither of us was familiar with the area, and there was not a ski patrolman in sight. I hopped the chair and skied down the run that PL had supposedly used, but no luck. For over an hour I crisscrossed the mountainside in a fruitless search. I was numb with fear and self-recrimination. My soul mate was lost and alone somewhere on the steep slopes. Suddenly I spotted a bedraggled skier tromping out of a snowdrift and waving at me—my desperate search was over. As we debriefed over warm cognac, PL's teeth still chattered as she relived her ordeal. The snowstorm had obliterated the trail markers, so she inadvertently skied over the edge of the narrow path and tumbled down the steep ridge into hip deep snow. The howling blizzard drowned out her cries for help and she could not hear my calls when I swept the trail looking for her. Although her lips were blue and she was physically exhausted, PL arduously slogged back up the snow swept hillside and eventually reached the ski trail.

PL's misadventure in the French Alps could easily have proved disastrous, but luck was on our side that day. Her brush with the malicious storm left both of us emotionally drained. Each of us murmured a prayer of thanks as we considered what could have gone down. Although no one would wish for such a moment, unforeseen and chaotic outcomes allow us to look deeply into life as it is, a razor sharp study of the here and now. She had been spared from a malevolent twist of fate—the virulent mix of random circumstances that overwhelmed Tyler and Ashley in the Indian Himalayas.

23

Greek Salad

Carpe Diem. Seize the Day, Boys! Make your lives extraordinary.

—*Tom Schulman,* **Dead Poets Society**

Osprey sailed for Rhodes in early April. At the heart of Rhodes city are the 12-meter thick walls of the old town. The medieval fortifications provided the Knights of Saint John with over two centuries of mastery over the ancient capital. The Christian era ended when a massive attack by the Ottoman Empire in 1522 brought the Muslims to power for the next four centuries. In the twentieth century, the Greek Orthodox Church emerged as a power to be reckoned with. Unfortunately the Greek bureaucrats who deal with visiting yachtsmen also consider themselves omnipotent.

The smartly dressed young people at the local Harley Davidson Café looked the part in their designer shades. The liberal Western European mindset of the dashing young Greeks is a stark contrast to the more conservative Eastern European philosophy of the less affluent young Turks, just over the horizon in Marmaris. Upscale Greek coffee houses serve espresso and lattes, quite a change from the ubiquitous apple tea synonymous with Turkey.

As we strolled along the waterfront, we bumped into the *Dolphin Spirit* crew. Our friends related their latest story—*Dolphin Spirit's* seaborne imitation of a ballistic missile. The saga unfolded in Mandraki Harbor, the busy commercial port just around the bend from our moorage. On one side of the main harbor, mammoth Greek ferries offload cars and trucks at the huge ferry terminal. The opposite side of the busy waterfront is supposedly reserved for visiting yachts. In the yacht anchorage a beautiful 100-foot British ketch was Med-moored adjacent to the 54-foot *Dolphin Spirit*. Typically a fast moving, incoming ferry drops its anchor to slow down inside the harbor. As the ferry slows, the anchor is used as a pivot to spin the big vessel 180 degrees so the skipper can back into the ferry dock. The ferry captains are clever and the technique is pretty slick. After the lumbering ferry is offloaded, the ferry captain slams the throttles to the stops and steams out of port at full tilt, cranking in the anchor on the fly. Unfortunately one of the ferries was hightailing it out of the anchorage when its huge anchor snagged the British yacht's anchor. The big ketch was unceremoniously yanked from the dock and dragged across the harbor. Snapped mooring lines, bent stanchions, and a crushed dinghy were just the beginning as *Dolphin Spirit* was also launched into the fray, still tied to the huge British yacht. Unfortunately the surprise rocket ride was on the Brits nickel—the ferry skipper denied that he could have done such a thing.

Terry and Lou came aboard just in time to witness the grand spectacle of Orthodox Easter, Greece's most important festival. In the Greek tradition emphasis is placed on the Resurrection more than the Crucifixion and families gather for the traditional feasting. Since *Osprey* was moored in front of the Greek Orthodox Cathedral, our crew had ringside seats for the massive candle-lit procession and the subsequent fireworks display.

Over the next few weeks our travels took us through the Dodecanese and Cyclades Island groups as we soaked up the beautiful spring weather, as well as our share of gyros and calamari.

Kos is the home of Hippocrates. It also seemed like a great place to celebrate my birthday. In the early '90's our foursome celebrated Terry's birthday at the Mount Kenya Safari Club, so the pressure was on. Under PL's watchful eye Pelagos Restaurant did it up right. Kate, our charming Greek hostess, greeted the *Osprey's* skipper with fresh roses. Then it was time for an awe-inspiring dinner of calamari, tzatziki, horiatiki salata, aubergine, and specially prepared wolf fish. The huge feast was presented in a grand unhurried manner with impeccable style and flair. I was at peace with the world as we toasted our good fortune and fine friends over a glass or two of *ouzo*.

My expansive mood evaporated the next morning as I searched for Nikki, the grizzled water warden. Nikki keeps the quay's single water spigot under lock and key and he was nowhere to be found. Eventually the water guy decided to shuffle our way and I was able to recharge our water tanks. Since most anchorages in the Med are polluted, using our onboard water maker in port was not in the cards.

Oleander, bougainvillea, and tamarisk draped from the balconies and walls in the small fishing village of Leros. Whiffs of hibiscus and jasmine perfumed the hillside as we hiked past sure-footed goats to a Venetian Castle perched high on a cliff. Along the way we met Gadi, a sparsely clothed expat who favors the moniker Oyster Catcher. The oyster guy's intriguing lifestyle involves naked walks along deserted hillsides while blessing the chosen island. Worked for him. As opposed to a naked stroll, our choice was a brace of fresh lobsters and a few Heinekens at the Psaropoyla taverna, a small seaside café overlooking *Osprey*'s moorage.

Our visit to the eleventh century Moni Hozoviotissas, a monastery literally plastered to the vertical cliffs of Amorgos, gave us a glimpse into the very private lives of its cloistered, silent monks. Although the monks require female visitors to wear the proffered long black robes, there are rumors about rogue monks who enjoy the charms of unescorted and uninhibited ladies. In any event we appreciated the local aperitif that the monks offered outsiders intrepid enough to make the long climb to visit their monastery and its beloved icons.

A little celebration was in order before Terry and Lou headed home. Consequently we hopped the *Jet Cat* in Naxos for a 40-knot ride to visit Santorini and soak in the majesty of her sheer cliffs. Santorini's imposing 83 square kilometer submerged caldera was violently created in 1678 BC by the largest volcanic explosion ever known to man. Nowadays the primitive upheavals are only a memory, but the burgeoning tourist industry has created it own landscape of upscale hotels and lively shops. We dined in style at the internationally renowned Selene restaurant, which was perched 900 feet above the deep indigo blue lagoon.

Our stay in Greece inadvertently coincided with the NATO bombing in Serbia. Since Greek sentiment overwhelmingly favored the Serbian cause, I temporarily struck *Osprey*'s colors after a very nationalistic Greek started screaming hysterically at us. We sailed from Naxos a few hours later. PL and I spent the next few weeks enjoying the laid back offerings of Paros as spring came to the islands. Since the Easter season is considered a time for rejuvenation, Greeks traditionally do their spring-cleaning. Gardens are lovingly tended and homes are given a fresh whitewash. Exploring the countryside aboard a motor scooter, we were captivated by the sparkling white houses and the brilliant wildflowers that spun a floral necklace over the arid islands.

One morning we decided to try something different. I drove our trusty scooter onto a small ferry and before long we were in Antiparos, economically a notch above its sister island. An aspirin white church with its bluebird colored dome lent its mystique to the place. Sugar cube shaped villas with classic windmills dot the coastline. The terraced hillsides of olive and fruit trees are sprinkled with cactus. PL really bonded with the place so she decided to start her own onboard cactus garden. I dug "Heckel," "Jeckel," "Archie," and "Barker" from a rocky hillside and popped the prickly newcomers into the storage bin of our scooter. The cactus quartet subsequently sailed with us until they were planted on Danzante Island in the Sea of Cortez a few years later.

Being footloose itinerant travelers pays unexpected dividends. A matronly storekeeper poured us shots of retsina, a gut wrenching concoction that tastes like pinecones. Now that we were acquainted, the proprietress informed my mate that Sifnos did indeed have the best olive oil in Greece. Alas, we had no bottle to hold this delicacy. As the accommodating woman washed down her retsina with a bottle of soda, she inquired if such a bottle was the right size? Yes, it was…so the obliging lady drained the soda, rinsed out the bottle, and proceeded to pour olive oil from her vat into the bottle that was now all ours. According to *Osprey's* very astute first mate, our skin would now be bathed in the warm caress of olive oil as the fragrant stuff seeped into every pore. An entrance sign at Moni Hrysopigis, a whitewashed church that straddles a rocky peninsula jutting into the Aegean, put such intricacies of life into perspective: *Respect the place—do not swim naked.*

Fog is unknown in the Aegean—or at least the British Admiralty publications advanced that theory. I reflected on this wisdom as I cautiously inched our way into a small inlet at Serifos. Naturally the relatively unprecedented fog coincided with our radar and anchor windless simultaneously packing it up. And, as luck would have it, I lacked a large-scale chart for our unanticipated visit to the island. It was back to the basics as PL listened for fog signals and I religiously stared at our depth sounder. Since sound travels a mile every 5 seconds, it is not much comfort to have the echo of our foghorn bounce back to us within a few seconds. Land was definitely close by, or so I thought. Dead ahead of us, a medley of bells and gongs echoed through the dense curtain of fog every few minutes. About midday the fog bank finally lifted and we motored to the source of the fog signals—a huge cruise ship anchored in the middle of the narrow entrance channel.

In mid-May Nick and Joan, together with a group of their friends from Port Orchard, sailed into our anchorage in Kithnos. The new arrivals chartered a couple of Athens based, fifty-foot sailboats to do their own exploration of the Greek Cyclades Islands. We were excited to see our good friends, but the Aegean Sea had its own welcome in store as gale force *meltemi* winds screamed down from the north into the Saronic Gulf. The newcomers were quickly initiated into the challenging business of anchoring in the weed-infested Aegean as their anchors dragged across the bottom and their sailboats slewed back and forth across the inlet. Our reunion was cut short until the howling winds moderated and the charter boats securely anchored. Since our radar and anchor windless were sick, PL and I sailed for Athens a few days later so I could sort out our boat's electrical woes. The charter boat flotilla resumed their cruise through the Aegean. We planned to meet them at the quay in Hydra a week or so later.

Athens is situated near the tip of the Greek mainland, a jutting peninsula about midway between Turkey and Italy. 40% of the country's population crowds into a congested and polluted metropolis about a third the size of Los Angeles. PL and I had already seen the historic sights and scoped out the Acropolis during a bare boat charter trip years before. We did not consider the city particularly appealing the first time around and not much had changed in the interim. Sea Trade Marine Ltd. is located in the seaport of Piraeus, about six miles from the teeming hordes in downtown Athens. Sea Trade's technicians are seasoned pros at marine repair, but radar parts are hard to come by. After a harried series of phone calls to Seattle, I located the necessary parts. Within a few days DHL, our favorite international delivery service, delivered new circuit boards for my ailing radar scanner. Since the Sea Trade technicians had the situation well in hand, PL and I poked around Piraeus's lively waterfront quarter while *Osprey*'s radar and anchor windless were resurrected.

One week and many drachmas later we rejoined the Port Orchard contingent in Hydra, a picturesque island renowned for its ban on motor vehicles—only donkeys allowed. Unfortunately this quaint ambiance spawns popularity and subsequent chaos in the yacht harbor. Hydra exudes the most panache of any of the Saronic Gulf Islands, but yachts are wedged into the tiny harbor like sardines jammed into a tin. My *Finger of the gods* not only proved itself, but was also was a real crowd pleaser as I unraveled assorted anchors, ropes, and chains from our anchor. Tangled anchors, scraped hulls, and frayed nerves are standard Mediterranean fare during the summer.

As the scruffy harbor attendant sagely observed, "Most of these people don't know a damn thing about boats, but I admire their enthusiasm."

In June we sailed from the gusty winds and shaky anchorages of the Cyclades into the calm, lake-like Ionian Sea. The Corinth Canal separates mainland Greece from the Peloponnesus and links the Aegean to the Ionian. Not only is the Corinth a gateway to the Ionian, the shortcut also saves a 300-mile detour around the tip of the Peloponnesus. Excavation of the steep sided narrow Corinth Canal was begun by Caesar in 67 AD and was continued by Nero. The waterway was not completed until 1893. Based on its length, the four-mile long canal transit is the most expensive canal passage in the world. We coughed up $120 for our 45-minute waterway excursion.

At Galaxidhi PL and I hopped a local bus bound for ancient Delphi, the "Navel of the Earth." The Sanctuary of Apollo, a mountaintop aerie overlooking vast olive orchards, was the home of the Delphic oracle—a legendary peasant woman. In the sixth century BC, priests translated the oracle's murmurings and ancients came to depend on the whispered prophecies. Whether the issue was an upcoming war or a proposed peace treaty, the oracle was the lady to see. Business types sought her advice and betrothed couples considered her predictions gospel. It was gypsy fortune telling and the Oprah show all rolled into one. Ignoring the tourist entrance, we decided to stretch our legs and stroll through the olive orchards to ferret out a possible back entrance to Delphi. If we had been able to read the Greek signage, PL assured me that our climb up and over a chain link fence could have been avoided since a perfectly serviceable gate was just over the hill. It was Greek to me.

One of our favorite cruising areas is the northern half of the Ionian, a placid inland sea perhaps fifteen miles wide and twice as long. Canny cruising folks tend to hang out on the lee side of Levkas because the mountainous island sentinel blocks the island-studded Ionian from the onslaughts of the Adriatic weather systems.

The pine forested, scythe shaped island of Meganisi offers sheltered anchorages, phenomenal views, and great swimming. Visiting yachtsmen actually care for the island much better than the locals. Cruisers habitually stroll the beaches picking up junk carelessly tossed away by the European Union crowd. A score of long-range cruising boats descended on our secluded cove as the time drifted by. During the day swimming and hiking occupied our time. The evenings revolved around socializing over beach barbeques. Magnificent sunsets melted into the western sky as chirping crickets and warm nights lulled us asleep. Our anchorage was only two miles from the Onassis island of Skorpios, a breathtaking study in landscape architecture.

As we shared stories with new friends in the cruising community, I was reminded that everyone has a story. Rather than dwell on our deceased son, I came to see our loss as a great equalizer. The revelation helped me to appreciate my humanity. I was coming to understand that I relied far too heavily on a false sense of control.

24

Italia

Love and desire are the spirit's wings.

—*Goethe*

We initially planned to sail north into the Adriatic, but war intervened. The Kosovo conflict effectively choked off tourism in Croatia, so we put the Adriatic on hold—a case study in going with the flow. As I explored my evolving persona, we sailed for the toe of Italy. A weather system pouring out of the Adriatic churned things up for us. PL and I just hunkered down as *Osprey* tore through the sloppy seas. As we dried ourselves out, a rising banshee scream bellowed from the bruised evening sky. A gray twin-engine jet shredded the low hanging scud and tore by us at masthead height. Although we were minding our own business, the US Navy "Prowler" was apparently checking us out to see if we posed any threat to the NATO taskforce operating in the Adriatic to the north of us.

The southern Italian port of Rocella Ionica introduced us to the Italian art of *fave una bella figura,* or "to put on a good show." The local officials had no idea of how to endorse our passports, but they did know how to praise my wife's charm and beauty. After the Italian studs had pledged their eternal devotion to the lovely PL, they saluted me. PL and I were in Italy—we assumed officially.

Though the violent whirlpools lurking in the Stretto di Messina horrified Odysseus of *Odyssey* fame, our team scored much better than his terrified crew. Of course we did have the benefit of computerized tide tables and a reliable engine. Much of the Mediterranean is fished out, but we encountered whales, porpoise, and flying fish off the coast of Sicily. Ungainly swordfish boats, sporting 16-meter bowsprits and 20-meter high control towers, harpoon swordfish sleeping on the surface. Small, brightly colored fishing boats depend on the Eye of Osiris, a huge eye painted on each side of the bow, to guide them and avoid the dangers of the sea. The Tyrrhenian Sea still summons images of tough warriors in copper helmets navigating the Italian coastline in sturdy galleys. The Tyrrhenian perpetuates the myths of Roman times—a place of omnipotent gods and exquisite scenery.

The picturesque fishing village of Acciaroli, reputed to be one of Hemingway's favorite towns in Italy, is just our kind of place. A monument sized bronze Madonna greeted us as we ducked into the breakwater. The Madonna must have been looking after us as I gingerly tried to wedge our 13-foot wide sailboat into a nonexistent space between two scarred fishing boats. Unannounced, Roberto deftly hopped aboard and expertly guided us in—*sprezzatura,* Italian for making it look easy. The village good will ambassador assured us the entire town was pleased to have us. Since our new Italian friend schmoozed us in his native tongue, I missed a few subtleties. But I did note that PL enchanted him. When Roberto theatrically gestured at the pots of red geraniums spilling from cozy balconies, PL demurely acknowledged *"magnifico."* Although the young Italian stallion was infatuated, I was getting hungry. In the nick of time, whiffs of garlic and olive oil and tomatoes from a local trattoria came my way. With a *"ciao"* to our benefactor, we bee lined for the great smells. On a bluff overlooking the Tyrrhenian Sea, we savored the good life over a bottle of Chianti and a plate of thin crust pizza, the southern Italian specialty.

The Isle of Capri is renowned for its sheer limestone cliffs. Exquisite villas hug the steep hillsides and precipitous roads wind through the pine forests. To the east, in the shadow of Mt. Vesuvius, the chaotic charm of Naples beckons. Mark and Redy, expat sailors from the East Coast of the US, suggested dining at Da Paolino. PL applauded the lemon motif, which is the cornerstone of the place. Dishes are emblazoned with the trademark lemon emblem, tables are strategically placed under a canopy of lemon trees, and mandolin music fills the air. The delicious Italian fare is as good as advertised.

No bargains to be had on Capri. Our obligatory visit to the *Grotto Azzura,* better known as the Blue Grotto, was a study in mass marketing. PL and I hopped into an overpriced wooden dory, and then the blasé Italian skiff driver jockeyed for position with a dozen other circling boats. Suddenly an outracing surge of water exposed a jagged four-foot square in the cliff side. Our dory shot through the hole and into a warehouse size underground grotto—our payoff was a glimpse of iridescent aquamarine water. Not bad, but the South Pacific spoiled us.

At an intimate sidewalk café in the port city of Gaeta, I had my first run in with a temperamental Italian chef. PL and I were enjoying superb seafood pasta when I requested a bit of Parmesan cheese—a big mistake. In broken English and uninhibited pantomimes, the chef went ballistic as he theatrically assailed my unthinking assault on his prize entrée.

Unlike the mafia thugs who insisted on "guarding" *Osprey* during our stay in southern Italy's Aeolian Islands, the professional armed guards at Base Nautico Flavio Gioia were actually on our side. In the Aeolian Islands, I quickly learned that a payoff to the scruffy looking guys on the dock basically insured that our sailboat would be there when we returned from lunch. In Gaeta, PL merely smiled at the well dressed, shotgun packing security guys as they pledged to look after *Osprey*. Since security was no longer an issue, we hopped a train to Florence.

Florence is the cradle of the Renaissance and home to Michelangelo, Dante, and Ghiberti. Renowned for its wealth of art, culture, and history, Florence is arguably one of the most fascinating cities in Italy. A few years prior to our sailing adventure, PL and I spent ten glorious days bicycling through the picturesque hills towns of Tuscany. During our bike trip we had a chance to check out Fiesole, the village perched above Florence. As it turned out Kate scored on a job in Fiesole the same year. Kate was hired as the resident advisor at the Georgetown University villa, which hosts a student abroad program. Not only did our clever daughter have an incredible opportunity to live in Florence for two years, she also met Andrea on a blind date at the local gym.

At Florence's crowded train station I spotted a very familiar young woman running towards us. As Kate got closer we noticed that she was flashing a rather stunning engagement ring. After a round or two of hugs and tears the story started to unfold. Andrea proposed the night before we arrived. Our short stopover in Florence morphed into a grand event as PL and I were caught up in a whirlwind of dining and socializing. Andrea's huge Italian family overwhelmed us with kindness as they welcomed us into their hearts.

Patriarch Roberto and his lady Anna, matriarch Theresa, brother Mario and his wife Ariana, Uncle Marciello and Aunt Lala, as well as Andre's good friend Letizia, wove us into the social fabric of Tuscany. Florence wins—I have never been kissed so much by so many. No matter how many times a day we encountered one of our new Italian family, they would shower us with kisses and then with an animated "*ciao*," they would continue about their business. Although we put our train passes to good use with side trips to Venice and Naples, Florence tugged us back time and again. Andrea, born and raised in Florence, assured PL and I that Florentines consider any area to the south, with the possible exception of Rome, to be on the primal side. The northern philosophy seems to be that perhaps the southern part of Italy should secede and go its own way.

Andrea flew back to Los Angeles and Kate sailed with us to Barcelona via Porto Cervo in Sardinia. Porto Cervo is an upscale marina community catering to the needs of yachtsman on the top end of the food chain. Our humble sailboat was anchored next to the Sultan of Brunei's mega yacht—a hundred million dollar showcase of floating conspicuous consumption. In lieu of a very hefty $150 per night marina fee, I opted for a small anchorage adjacent to the marina.

Our good fortune did not last for long. A French sloop motored into our anchorage to escape the howling *mistral* winds outside the marina. During an amateurish anchoring attempt, the sailboat's engine died. Things started to deteriorate as the 40-foot sailboat drifted helplessly downwind and pinned itself dead center on and perpendicular to our bow. *Osprey* now boasted an unsolicited Gallic hood ornament. Kate was the only one aboard *Osprey*, but she did a credible job of cursing the inept skipper even though the problem did not go away. Seeing the commotion from across the bay, I jumped in our dinghy and roared across the anchorage. In lieu of a better plan, I jammed our rubber inflatable between the errant sailboat and *Osprey* to hopefully separate the two grinding hulls. Our burley outboard screamed at full throttle. The tactic successfully pried the offending sailboat off our anchor chain, but our suddenly unencumbered dinghy popped out of the water like a champagne cork exploding off a bottle of bubbly. The dinghy shot to the sky and I was catapulted into the churning water.

Kate, trained since childhood to deal with overboard emergencies, threw me every piece of safety gear in *Osprey's* emergency arsenal. As I paddled around, I was joined by a flotation device, life ring, strobe light, man overboard pole, dye marker, and flares. Our unmanned dinghy rocketed through the breakwater and out to sea. Fortunately, a fellow yachtie took time to wipe the grin off his face and tear after our runaway inflatable. After the adrenalin rush, the contrite Frenchman made a soulful apology and even invited us aboard for a glass of wine. International repercussions averted once more.

There is nothing like being the reincarnation of a ground launched cruise missile. Although my fun quotient was on low ebb at the time, the tide turned with a couple of glasses of vino under my belt. The whole episode turned out to be quite a snorter. Going astray from a bit of respectability is not all that bad and it does set you free. PL was just concerned about my encore.

25

Spanish Eyes

We do not receive wisdom, we must discover it for ourselves, after a journey through the wilderness which no one else can make for us, which no can spare us, for our wisdom is the point of view from which we come at last to regard the world.

—Marcel Proust

In late July *Osprey* pulled into Marina Port Vell in Barcelona. Kate flew back to the States while PL and I started our exploration of the place. Barcelona is the crown jewel of Spain's fiercely independent and wealthy Catalonia region and a world-class city. Modernistic architecture of the late nineteenth and early twentieth centuries is a refreshing mix of Art Nouveau, Gothic, Moorish, and other innovative styles dominated by the brilliant creations of Antoni Gaudi. Gaudi's Sagrada Famili, his stunning modernistic cathedral masterpiece, is synonymous with Barcelona. Unfortunately for both Gaudi and Barcelona, the Art Nouveau cathedral is still unfinished. The eccentric architect was run over by a tram in the mid 1920's.

Although the city is bold, alive, and colorful, the people of Barcelona seem aloof and indifferent. Catalan and Spanish are the two official languages. English is rarely spoken. The inhabitants seem determined to maintain their own identity despite the huge influx of foreign tourists. Dinner in Spain is typically served just an hour or two before midnight, but if *paella* is on the menu, I will patiently wait for the bewitching hour. If my patience is in short supply that day, a *tapa* bar solves the early evening hunger pangs. Although PL is a little ambivalent about my discovery, I found that Barcelona offers Cuban cigars at civilized prices far below the typical Euro extortion rate—turns out to be the best price this side of Cuba.

A few days after our arrival we received devastating news from my brother Mark. His beautiful wife had just been diagnosed with a malignant brain tumor. Even after a prolonged neurosurgery procedure, Shannon's prognosis was very guarded. I immediately booked a flight out of Barcelona so I could return home to help Mark and Shannon through the coming ordeal. PL invited her sister Susie aboard *Osprey* until I returned to Spain.

My recollection of the flight back to Seattle is a blur, but the long sessions with Mark and Shannon at the University of Washington Hospital are crystal clear. Faced with a number of hard decisions regarding post surgical treatment of Shannon's tumor, there were not many options. I moved in with Mark and Shannon. We took thoughtful walks, investigated treatment options, and explored our most intimate feelings about life and death. Tyler confronted his mortality with bravery and determination—I considered Shannon in the same league. After Shannon had undergone several intense weeks of experimental radiation therapy, there was nothing more for me to do. Fate and time would determine the outcome. There were hugs and tears and fervent prayers. In the end I flew back to Barcelona, Shannon continued with her treatment, and all of us tried to move on.

As PL and I recapped our weeks apart, the importance of friends and family continued to be etched even deeper into our beings. We reaffirmed that our lives were precious and our days on earth numbered. Although eternity is a timeless place, the clock is always running on our day-to-day lives. After all we had been through in the past few years, neither of us would disparage a bit of supernatural intervention from time to time.

Just after I returned Salah and Liljana showed up for another visit. In late August the four of us sailed for the Balearic Islands off the east coast of Spain—it was a slow start out of the blocks. At full throttle *Osprey* just inched out of her slip at Port Vell. Very reluctantly I squeezed into my wet suit and scuba gear, then dove into the filthy harbor. A four-week growth of barnacles encrusted our variable pitch propeller in a hard embrace. In a swirl of brackish bubbles and unintelligible expletives, I managed to resurrect the propeller with a stiff brass barbeque brush. It was a rather inauspicious start for our overnighter to the Balearics. Lucky I had my shots.

The four main Balearic Islands, coupled with a number of small outlying islets, jut from the sea not a hundred miles from mainland Spain's Mediterranean coastline. Menorca and Formentera are the least developed of the lot, but the throngs of multinational tourists do not see the attendant simplicity and tranquility as vacation plusses. Mallorca and Ibiza are where it is at for the holiday hordes—the concoction of sun, sand, and sea, blended with innovative restaurants and wild nightlife chums in millions of annual visitors.

We made landfall at Puerto de Mahon, a long deep *cala,* or bight, on the southeastern coast of Menorca. The port is renowned as an ultimate hurricane hole and caters to commercial, naval, fishing, and pleasure vessels. We were searching for a little more peace and quiet. Over the next few days we anchored in a number of undeveloped, picturesque natural *calas* as we enjoyed the warm sun and the clear blue water along the leeward coasts of Menorca and Mallorca.

In a very compact rental car, our foursome zipped around the main island of Mallorca as we scoped out the subterranean caves of Porto Cristo. The northwest coast is a stunning mountainous region, where small villages and huge olive groves are the norm. It was a marked contract to the sophisticated environs of Palma, which is tucked into the southern side of the island. Although there are no bargains to be had in Palma, the restaurants are good and the people watching is first rate. The best deal in town is to sip *sangria* at a sidewalk café and admire the incredibly beautiful sunset over Bahia de Palma.

After Salah and Liljana ferried back to the mainland, PL and I sailed further west to Ibiza. Unhappily Shep, my faithful 3 hp Mercury outboard, finally expired at Cale Llonga in Ibiza. I tossed the unsalvageable motor in a dumpster and then rowed back to our anchorage. I was in mourning after dumping the overworked motor, so I was a bit inattentive as I snubbed our rubber dinghy to *Osprey's* transom. As the continuous surge burbled around the back of our boat, the very unforgiving sharp rudder of our wind vane steering gear punctured the very vulnerable inflatable tube on our dinghy. Although an extra outboard motor lived aboard, I only had one dinghy. Luckily I located my inflatable patch kit. While PL spent the next day enjoying our stunning anchorage at Isla Redonda, I entertained myself by resurrecting our wounded dinghy. Justice prevailed in the end. My inadvertent choice for our evening anchorage happened to be fronted by one of the Islas Baleares specialties, a nude beach.

September brought a big blast of fall weather to the western Mediterranean—a fickle season of contentious winds and spectacular lightning storms. We fled the balmy anchorages of the Balearics for the comfort and safety of the marinas that stretch south along the Costa Blanca and Costa del Sol of mainland Spain. Spanish marinas are well done and considerably less expensive than their counterparts in France and Italy. The new ultramodern marina at Alicante turned out to be one of our favorite stopovers on the Costa del Sol. We left

Osprey in the capable hands of the attentive marina staff and caught a flight to Lisbon.

Portugal seemed like a great place to celebrate PL's birthday. Our impromptu holiday not only provided a bit of diversion from full time cruising, but also gave us a chance to refocus on what was really important in our lives. Shannon's bout with cancer was just another reminder that life is a tenuous matter and each moment is a gift. We liked the feel of Lisbon so we checked into Residencia Lisbonense where our accommodating host lavishly welcomed us to his city. Although the ancient caged elevator that clattered to a stop next to our third floor room had seen better days, our room had all the amenities a cruiser could want—a genuine bathtub and air conditioning.

Even though Portugal is only about twice the size of Switzerland, it was a country of immense power and wealth in the fifteenth century, Europe's Age of Discovery. This was the era synonymous with lofty Moorish architecture—the time of discovery for such famous explorers as Columbus, de Gama, Magellan, and Diaz. Now it was time for the *Osprey* crew. Today the grandeur created by Prince Henry the Navigator has faded, but the locals are friendly and the prices are reasonable. Many Portuguese speak English, a welcome change from Spanish speaking Spain. Unlike the subtitled, foreign voice-over Hollywood movies endemic to much of Western Europe, cinemas in Lisbon feature first run, English-speaking movies. In recent years the European Union has infused Portugal with huge doses of capital—Lisbon resonates with the vitality of a healthy and successful city.

We explored the ancient alleys of the old Lisbon and strolled down checkerboard-tiled walkways on the tree-lined boulevards of Avenida de Liberdade. A clanking tram took us to Castel del Sao Jorge and its spectacular vista high above the city. With a manic day of sightseeing under our belts, we were tired and hungry. Our innkeeper insisted that Lisbon restaurants pride themselves on an unrushed atmosphere and excellent seafood. He directed us to the Bombia, a very fine eating establishment in the Baixa district. The birthday girl and myself dined late and ate well.

The city has a conscience. Huge black banners proclaimed "*Basta*" in blood red letters. The Portuguese demanded an end to the senseless killing in the former Portuguese enclave of Indonesia's East Timor. A few years prior we had cruised to East Timor, but we had been blissfully ignorant of the military's brutality. Our Indonesian army escorts had assured us that no problems existed.

Booming military cannons, blaring bugles, and a Spanish color guard introduced us to Cartagena, a strategic Spanish naval base dating back hundreds of years. *Osprey* was securely tied to a finger pier inside the very protected harbor while the violent winds from a Force 10 storm plowed through the area. From a vantage point high on the old castle, PL and I could see the awesome power of the storm as the onslaught of wild spindrift and savage seas hammered the coastline. The small yacht haven became a spider web of dock lines as yacht owners of every stripe banded together to lash all our boats securely together. Although we were stuck in the harbor until the storm passed, PL and I were more than happy to sit this one out.

As fate would have it, the annual *Carthaginesis y Romanos* extravaganza was underway. Locals dressed as Carthaginians advanced from the west while the appropriately attired Romans, their ancient nemesis, marched in from the east. The two make believe armies, decked out in their battle livery, fought staged battles and provided a great show for us stranded cruiser types.

When the next round of decent weather rolled in, we sailed for Estoponia. The marina is another first class operation. The staff presented us with a bottle of wine and assured us that they would look after *Osprey*. We decided that a fitting farewell to Spain would be a road trip to the interior. After our little rental car survived the motor mayhem of Costa del Sol, it was on to Fuengirola. Rattlesnake Annie, an eccentric expat rocker from Tennessee, put us on the inside track. Rattlesnake's advice was to head over the Sierra Nevada Mountains and explore southern Spain. Eventually our struggling Ford Fiesta wheezed over a summit and we were suddenly immersed in the exotic and colorful Andalucia region of Spain. It was as if a massive hand had splashed the rolling, arid plains in wide bands of gold and copper. We were bound for Grenada, so we just followed the groves of olive trees that stretched to the horizon.

Grenada's labyrinth of one-way serpentine streets is a driving nightmare, but visiting the Alhambra—one of the most spectacular buildings in Europe—was worth the aggravation. The Moorish rulers commissioned much of the spectacular Spanish Muslim architecture in the mid 1300's. The Christians finally overthrew the Moors in 1492, and then it was time for the Catholic monarchs to move in. Columbus was rumored to have taken his marching orders from Queen Isabella just after she took up residence. For more than two centuries, sultans wandered the fabulous gardens and sat beside the elaborate fountains. Today the Moorish art, manicured gardens, and intricate stonework are no longer the exclusive domain of sultans. PL let it be known that the sweet fragrances of jasmine, myrtle, and oleander permeating the still air made her feel like a princess.

> Washington Irving, a devotee of the Alhambra and a former ambassador to Spain, described the ambiance: *Simplicity matched only by its elegance.*

Located on the banks of the Rio Guadalquivir, Seville is reputed to be one of the most exciting cities in Spain. It is hard for us to get a read on that claim—our bedtime is well before the locals even eat dinner, let alone start partying. Since Seville is the home of flamenco dancing, we joined a gaggle of other tourists for an early evening show. Although the flamenco dancers strutted their stuff, the food was mediocre and the drinks were overpriced—a good reminder of why it is best to steer clear of tourist shows.

Seville boasts a magnificent bullring and the biggest Gothic cathedral in the world. I was more intrigued with the bullring since we had seen a fair number of cathedrals over the past few years. The matador hall of fame includes the sequined uniforms of matadors who had their careers abruptly ended by enraged bulls. A triumphant bull displaying such bravery and panache is allowed to live, but very few bulls escape the ignominy of having their ears or tail lopped off by a victorious matador.

One of our favorite Spanish communities is the mountain town of Ronda, the home of Spain's original bullring. Plaza de Toros was built in 1785 and attracted regulars such as Orson Wells and Ernest Hemingway. We put aside our westernized sensibilities and joined a crowd of Ronda citizens at the weekend bullfight, the *Gran Festival Taurino*. The apprentice bullfighters face a steep learning curve. The fickle crowd waves white hankies only if they are pleased with the skill of the matador. If a kill is sloppy, no ears are awarded to the matador. As a matador's skill, daring, and presentation improve, he can expect one ear or two ears for a job well done. The tail of the vanquished bull is the ultimate trophy for a matador. If eager young women throw flowers, so much the better.

A cocky young matador glanced towards a beautiful senorita in the viewing stands just about the time his bull decided to liven up the proceedings. The sly bull tossed the aspiring cape and sword guy across its shoulder, and then sauntered off. The gorgeous young woman coyly averted her eyes. Although the tattered young man limped out of the ring without the bull's ear or the lady's flowers, he had certainly acquired a more humble outlook.

I liken the inexperienced matador's troubles to an exaggerated sense of self-importance. Many of us cloak ourselves in arrogance: the arrogance of health, the arrogance of power, the arrogance of wealth—the list is endless but our lives are not.

26

The Pillars of Hercules

o o o o o o o o o o o o o o o o o o o o o o o o o o o o o o o o o

Knock on the sky and listen to the sound!

—*Zen saying*

The Rock of Gibraltar is a 2.5 square mile limestone monolith that happens to be the southernmost point of the Iberian Peninsula. The 1400-foot high Rock commands the western entrance to the Mediterranean, a fact that was not lost on assorted naval powers over the millenniums. In ancient times the stone mountains of Ceuta and Gibraltar were known as the Pillars of Hercules. The Pillars flank the ten-mile wide Strait of Gibraltar, the choke point between the North Africa's Morocco and Europe's Spain. The Spanish have unceasingly tried to reclaim Gibraltar since the British captured the strategic hunk of real estate in 1704. Today a British Royal Air Force runway is perched on the isthmus that separates Gibraltar from mainland Spain.

Gibraltar has an air of faded grandeur about it. Tourists suck up supposed bargains at the Gibraltar's duty free stores, but many of the buildings have seen better days. Just a tram's ride away the Barbary Macaques, the Rock's most famous inhabitants, scamper about the upper reaches of the huge headland. Actually the behavior of the less than savvy sightseers, naively hand feeding the unpredictably aggressive apes, is a fascinating study in itself.

There is always an easterly current of at least two knots coursing through the Strait of Gibraltar. It is much easier to sail easterly into the Mediterranean than westerly into the Atlantic. The incoming tidal flow sweeps around the Mediterranean counterclockwise in a rather predictable fashion. During our time in the Mediterranean, strong localized winds dictated our cruising schedule. Although conditions could be clear and dry, savage N-NW winds known as the Costa Brava's *tramontana,* the Aegean's *meltemi,* or the Golfe du Lion's *mistral* can ambush an unwary yacht without warning. *Siroccos*, hot humid winds blowing off the African coast, can obliterate the horizon with red rain that contains dust particles from the North African desert.

As we were getting adjusted to life on the Rock, a *levanter* arrived. An ominous dark cirrus cloud hanging over the Rock heralded the imminent ENE gale. A heavy swell moved into Marina Bay and the boats were shrouded in cold damp air. The gloomy weather was oppressive. An enraged British yachtsman threatened to toss an American yachtie's freaked out cat into the bay when the forlorn feline peed on the Brit's canvas awning. The Yank threatened to kill the Englishman if his cat disappeared.

Rather than be cooped up in Marina Bay waiting for the impending storm to blow through or for somebody to be killed, PL and I decided to visit Morocco. Since Spain is just a stroll away across the Rock's RAF runway, we walked across the border into the Spanish city of Algecirus, joined a Spanish bus tour, and hopped aboard a ferry bound for Morocco.

Morocco was home to the infamous Barbary pirates during the eighteenth and early nineteenth centuries. The ferociously independent Berber and Arab cutthroats haunted Morocco's Atlantic and Mediterranean coasts. The major European powers came to play in the mid 1800s, but the Euros proved to be just modern day pirates who carefully divided Morocco into various spheres of influence. About fifty years ago Morocco became an independent country, geographically a bit smaller than Spain. In 1975 Morocco decided to annex their southern neighbor, Western Sahara. Morocco ended up with about 30% more territory, but the land grab sparked a great deal of international controversy that is still unresolved three decades later.

Our Morocco adventure began as we hopped aboard a motor coach and rode a ferry across the Strait of Gibraltar to Tangiers. Although the trip was billed as a multilingual event, our tour was of the Spanish persuasion. Fortunately our guide was trilingual. Marc and Karen, as well as Iditha and Paul, hailed from Germany, but they were the only other English speakers aboard. The six of us bonded—we were excited to explore the exotic North African landscape and soak up the ancient offerings of Tangiers, Fes, Marrakech, Rabat, and Casablanca.

PL and I became relatively oblivious to the blaring Muslim call to prayer after eight months in the Middle East and ten months in Turkey. Now we were reintroduced to the five times a day ritual as we strolled through Tangiers. For us Tangiers conjured up images of secret agents and mysterious gambling dens. In fact Tangiers proved to be a world-weary port noted for drugs, prostitution, money laundering, and smuggling. On the plus side our group only spent the night. Morocco boasts some of the most beautiful countryside in North Africa—we were more than happy when our bus headed out into the hinterlands.

Each of us had heard stories about disillusioned Moroccans who sneaked across the Strait of Gibraltar any way they could. When the police forcibly removed a stowaway hidden in the engine compartment of our bus, the whispered stories suddenly became harsh reality. The pitiful local was so intent on fleeing to Spain that he failed to realize our bus was actually heading in country, away from his vague concept of deliverance. After our bus was thoroughly searched for any more hidden passengers, our party was good to go. In fact we were headed for the hometown of the recently arrested stowaway, the ancient Arab city of Fes.

Strolling through the medieval medina of Fes el Bali is a journey back in time. The old town is a warren of narrow alleys dishing up a mind-boggling assault on the senses. It would be dead easy to get lost in the winding alleyways and chaotic bazaars. Mohammad, our Fassi guide, kept us pointed in the right direction. Stretched out before us was Kaivaouine University and Mosque, one of the oldest universities in the world. In 859 AD the concept of a facility for higher education was ahead of its time, but then again so was the builder—Fatma bint Mohammed ben Feheri just happened to be a woman. Although the buildings are said to contain one of the finest Muslim libraries in the world, non-believers are not welcome.

Later PL traced a disgusting smell to the centuries old tanneries and dye pits which use a caustic brew of pigeon poo, cow urine, fish oil, animal fats, brains, chrome salts, and sulphuric acid to give their leather products that unique look. The telling whiff of the dye pits is long gone, but the handsome leather hassocks PL bought that day are still with us.

Our bus wound down the rugged Atlas Mountains and descended into the high desert country of North Africa. Towards dusk the red hued city walls of Marrakech glowed crimson as we rolled into town. The Beetles immortalized the place in a song and a generation of hippies considered the city nirvana. As we strolled past walls brimming with bougainvillea and hibiscus, hints of jasmine and rose filled the air.

PL and I splurged on an evening at *Fantasia,* an exotic extravaganza featuring Berber horsemen, lumbering elephants, and lavish Moroccan dishes. Under huge sprawling tents we dined on all manner of North African fare, but the kebabs and couscous won. We passed on sheep brains cooked in their own skulls. As luck would have it, the only rainstorm to hit Marrakech in months drenched our desert oasis that night—the downpour did not faze the proud Berbers. The cavalry tore around the flooded arena with mud on their faces, blood in their eyes, and wicked looking scimitars swirling above their heads.

A horse and carriage was our magic carpet ride into the Djemaa el Fna, the focal point of the city. The huge town square is action central where acrobats, jugglers, storytellers, fire-eaters, snake charmers, magicians, and assorted free spirits ply their trades. I was not happy when a snake charmer draped his personal snake around my neck, but PL figured my plight made a great photo op. Both of us enjoyed the storytellers at Djemaa el Fna. A huge crowd of locals gathered around a wizened raconteur who would animatedly spin his tale. As the fascinating saga stretched on and on, the milling crowd really got into it. At about that time the narrator would put his story on hold. If the crowd paid up, then the yarn would continue. If not, the throng was left hanging.

Casablanca is not what we expected. It turns out that the film *Casablanca* was shot on a Hollywood sound stage, so a drink at Rick's Bar was not in the cards. Instead of reliving the bygone days of the Bogey era, PL and I visited the biggest religious monument in the world outside of Mecca. The new and startlingly beautiful Hassan II Mosque is situated on a bluff high above the Atlantic Ocean. The ultramodern mosque accommodates 25,000 worshippers. Infidels such as us can only sneak a quick look inside the mammoth doorways, but the opulence of the mosque carries outside to spectacular cascading fountains and massive courtyards. Atop the 210-meter minaret a pulsing laser fires bursts of light toward Mecca.

Following a beam of light must be a comfort if you are of that religious persuasion, but there are many religions from which to choose. Some organized religions are in the mainstream while others preach their gospels on the periphery. Certainly a thoughtful personal viewpoint can be a religion in itself. As I continued to explore my life, I considered *Osprey* my personal passport into worlds and philosophies I had never visited before.

27

Canary Island Jump-off

○ ○

All that is gold does not glitter, not all those who wander are lost.

—*JRR Tolkien*

While PL and I were on our Moroccan jaunt, the weather at Gibraltar had sorted itself out and Terro Hammond arrived on board. Terro, our good friend from Brisbane, is an accomplished sailor and a good man to have aboard for a long ocean passage. If nothing else Gibraltar proved a great place to repair gear, download weather charts, and provision for the upcoming offshore jaunt. In mid-October the three of us sailed for the Canary Islands, a 700-mile passage.

Although the navigation books warned of treacherous tides and wild seas, our transit through the notorious Strait of Gibraltar was relatively hassle free...until I considered the implications of being hit by an errant artillery round. As *Osprey* hugged the Spanish coastline in the predawn hours, our radar suddenly painted a tug towing a massive barge just a few miles ahead of us. With no warning, a battery of Spanish artillery battery engaged the barge. Luckily the towed target barge got shelled instead of us.

Dolphins surfed down the face of the green Atlantic rollers as *Osprey* caught a fine ten-knot northwesterly on her outbound track. A great start but the breeze only lasted a day. Our choice was to gaze at the limp sails or fire up the diesel. When we finally putted into our landfall five days later, I was tempted to change the designation on our sloop from S/V (sailing vessel) *Osprey* to M/V (motor vessel) *Osprey*. Although I did not appreciate the implications at the time, the very unusual light air pattern would plague us all the way across the Atlantic.

The Canary Islands are 700 miles southwest of Gibraltar, but only 150 miles west of the North African mainland. The seven main islands constitute an autonomous region of Spain. Historically the strategic location of the islands made them ideal as repair and provisioning stops for westbound vessels crossing the Atlantic. Today tourism is the guiding economic force.

Terro reunited with one of his Aussie mates at Puerto Calero, our first port of call on Lanzarote. Terro's mate was on his third voyage around the world and not in any hurry. A mega yacht skippered by our friend Paul and crewed by four woman showed up the next day. It was party time.

Cesar Manrique is the man in Lanzarote. A modern art stylist of the Picasso and Matisse schools, Manrique devoted himself to preserving the surreal volcanic moonscape of Lanzarote and infusing the locals with a zest for his art. Taro de Tahiche, Manrique's former home, is a series of sublime subterranean vaults under a massive lava field. Even the underground swimming pool is carved out of a lava tube.

The Parque Nacional de Timanfaya is the eerie site of a still simmering volcano which exploded cataclysmically in 1730—one of the greatest volcanic eruptions in history. Our lunch at the Manrique designed Restaurante del Diablo featured main entrees grilled over an active volcanic steam vent. That was a new one on us. The grapes for the tasty local wine seem to flourish in the rich volcanic soil.

With over a thousand varieties of cactus, the magnificent Jardin de los Cactus is a place where PL, our shipboard cactus aficionado, could roam to her heart's content. Our miniscule seagoing cactus collection aboard *Osprey* paled in comparison to the estate's incredible gardens, but the prickly hitchhikers still thrived in PL's onboard cactus plot.

Las Palmas, on the north edge of the mountainous island of Gran Canaria, was our next stop. In November the cosmopolitan city hosts the annual Atlantic Rally for Cruisers (ARC) as hundreds of sailing yachts prepare for their Atlantic crossings. PL strolled the city's boulevards while Terro and I checked out the seminars presented by the Sir Chay Blyth's ARC staff. Although PL and I had sailed thousands of miles and Terro already had a circumnavigation to his credit, most of the rally participants had never crossed an ocean even though their yachts dwarfed *Osprey*.

Grocers, fruit vendors, and beer salesmen brought truckloads of supplies to the scores of sailing vessels jammed into the marina. The local merchants definitely had the logistical challenge handled. Rookie sailors lovingly washed each piece of fruit, and then consulted their lists as each item was stowed just so. Unlike the neophytes, PL is an expert at stocking for an ocean passage. She casually tucked our transatlantic supplies away with no muss or fuss. After our home-town friend Terry flew in to join us for the upcoming transatlantic crossing, our foursome launched into a never-ending cycle of boat chores.

After a few days the boat was in good order and we needed a diversion. I rented a car and our gang took off for a Saturday cross-island drive. Little did I know that the Gran Canaria rabbit hunters do their thing on Thursdays and Saturdays. On the designated days hordes of local rabbit hunters motor around the countryside dragging trailers packed with skinny hounds. The hound's sole purpose in life is to wiggle down narrow rabbit holes and snag rabbits. The baying hounds and their hyperventilating masters definitely get into it, but the challenge of the sport eluded us—perhaps the fuzzy bunnies are displaced attack rabbits.

Gran Canaria enjoys a unique series of microclimates. Arid heat in the south coast resort region is swept away at the chilly and sometimes snowy summit of Roque Nablo. To the west, windswept cliffs and jagged coastline dominate the panorama. We drove down the southern flank of the island and on to the charming seaside town of Puerto de Mogan. The place has the good honest feel of a genuine fishing port and yacht harbor, unlike many of the glitzy tourist villages hacked out of the barren coastline. An excellent seafood lunch came our way from Restaurante Cofradia, the fishing cooperative restaurant on the quay—nobody ordered rabbit.

A few days later the *Osprey* crew, along with our cruising mates from *Madjk*, celebrated Terro's birthday. Even though our navigator is a digit or two past his seventh decade, Terro is renowned for having the spunk and enthusiasm of pups half his age. After Terro was duly nominated an ultimate role model, we strolled back to our moorage at Muelle Deportivo.

Many of the folks in the ARC rally paint their ship's logo or a favorite quote on the marina's seawall prior to the start of the Atlantic crossing. On this occasion I thought long and hard about how I had come to this point in time. Many of the messages revolved around subtle themes of letting go. There was nothing subtle about my epiphany years before—I was blindsided when Tyler's shooting star logo seemed to leap off the hotel register in Manali. Ever since that time I found myself more willing to shed many of my precious attachments, but so far the process had been erratic and untidy.

28

Atlantic Crossing

In late November we sailed from Las Palmas de Gran Canaria bound for the St. Lucia in the Caribbean, 2700 miles away. There were 250 yachts in the 1999 Atlantic rally for Cruisers (ARC 99), not to mention scores of NARC (non-ARC) yachts crossing "The Pond." A 20-knot northeasterly greeted us as *Osprey* blasted through the four-foot seas. Billowing cumulus clouds scudded across the horizon. With sea and air temperatures in the 70's, the spray bursting across our windward rail seemed a fitting baptism as we broad reached into the Atlantic. It looked like a great start to the fabled trade wind passage. A number of the ARC entries were a bit on the over anxious side as they sailed up to the starting buoys. The resultant collisions, torn sails, jangled nerves, and even an inadvertently inflated life raft are not in keeping with the laid-back cruiser persona that the aspiring sailors shoot for.

Our fourth day offshore dawned with a fitful breeze, clear sky, and long ocean swells. It was also Thanksgiving. Although we were 500 miles downwind from Gran Canaria, the trade winds had failed to materialize. With little prospect for a legendary Atlantic downwind sleigh ride, we began to reconsider our limited options.

Suddenly the steering wheel spun wildly and our sloop slewed sideways down the face of a steep swell. *Osprey* yawed sickeningly as the sails slatted and banged against the rigging. After I disconnected our wind vane steering system and engaged the heavy-duty hydraulic backup system, I ripped open the access hatch to the steering system. After all sorts of spares and stores were tossed aside, I dove into the small locker headfirst. There was no song in my heart and island time eluded me as I roundly cursed the fates. Bathed in sweat, sickened by the lurching motion, and hanging upside down with a flashlight in my teeth, I found the problem—the stainless steel steering cable had parted. Over the next few hours I renovated the steering system as the boat wallowed in the swells. When steerage is lost in the middle of the ocean, bad things can happen. Fortunately for us the weather was benign and a repair was possible. Extra cable, clamps, and swages lurked in the bowels of the boat so by and by we sorted things out. Rather than a knock out punch, we had just been gently tagged by the fates.

As the days dragged by, the trade winds continued to elude us. Our diesel chugged along burning less than a gallon per hour at five knots. But with only 120 gallons of fuel aboard, motoring across the Atlantic was not an alternative. I only fired up the iron spinnaker when Osprey's speed fell below three knots.

Because the still mid-Atlantic resembled a vast cobalt blue landing strip, an ocean swim had lots of appeal. Powder puffs clouds skirted the horizon as the scorching sun baked the crew. But when the skipper announced swim call, there were no takers. Rather than consider what sort of malicious marine life might be lurking under the placid surface, I dove off the bow into my personal 13,000-foot deep pond—a letting go, leap of faith moment. The crew peered down at me from the security of the deck and assured me they were just keeping their swimming options open. They confidently offered to back my play in the event a marauding tiger shark jumped me. Just so I would not be mistaken for a struggling Happy Meal, I figured it was prudent to minimize any splashing. I judiciously paddled around the boat and then scrambled back aboard with my limbs intact—there were still no other takers.

With a crew of four aboard, as opposed to just PL and I, passage making is a much more civilized affair. Long ocean passages tend to wear down cruising couples since someone is always on watch. Eventually the constant watch routine of 4 hours on…4 hours off…4 hours on…4 hours off…gets old. Extra hands aboard translate into shorter watches for the person on duty, as well as longer periods of uninterrupted sleep for everyone off watch.

PL and Terry, our resident chefs, whipped up all sorts of tasty meals and presented their creations with flair and panache. Brilliantly colored dorado favored our trailing fishing lures—a steady source of fresh seafood. After we dispatched the struggling dolphin fish with a dose of tequila poured into its gills, the chefs magically transformed the flopping fish into a superb dining entree in very short order. Our freezer was stuffed with fish by the time we sailed into St. Lucia.

Terro, the consummate ocean navigator, figured the navigation competition between the boats in ARC 99 was made to order for him. Armed with a sextant, Terro ignored our bank of shipboard electronics as he worked out our daily position plots. Twinkling navigation stars and glimmering constellations seemed to come alive against the black chamber of the immense Atlantic sky as each of us took sextant sights under the tutelage of our master navigator.

"Mayday—Mayday—Mayday, man overboard." The desperate distress call was broadcast over the ARC fleet's radio net when the young skipper of the Norwegian thirty-two foot ultra light sailboat *Jagermeifter* fell overboard early in the morning. Petter had just come on watch when his boat accidentally jibed. Since Petter had yet to secure his safety harness when the low hanging boom violently slashed across the cockpit, he was catapulted across the deck and into the churning Atlantic. The small sloop had been sailing fast on a downwind spinnaker run, so the frenzied crewmembers lost precious minutes as they struggled to douse the billowing sail. Although the crew bashed back upwind to the coordinates punched into the GPS when the skipper went over the side, the sea was empty.

The frantic crew triggered their 406 EPIRB (Emergency Position Indicating Radio Beacon). The beacon uplinked an emergency message to orbiting satellites, which then downlinked the position of the beacon to the Rescue Control Center. The RCC then launched a search and rescue effort. Within hours a multinational collection of aircraft and ships were diverted to hunt for the missing man, but Petter seemed to have vanished from the face of the ocean. Petter's odds of survival were not good, but the massive search continued throughout the day. Every sailor in the ARC Rally was very aware that the inexplicable horror of falling overboard at night could happen to any of us.

In the late afternoon a Norwegian yacht changed course to skirt a squall line and miraculously spotted Petter. The indomitable skipper had been in the water for 12 hours. Apparently Petter had been knocked unconscious when he fell overboard, but his life vest inflated automatically, the water was 80 degrees, and he was extremely lucky. Apparently Petter saw his boat sail quite close to him as his crew searched for him in the dark, but they did not hear him or see him. If he had been equipped with a strobe light, he probably would have been back on board within an hour.

After his rescue Petter tanked up on water, enjoyed a hearty meal, indulged in a hot shower, and then asked to be reunited with *Jagermeifter*. Petter not only survived the experience, but also continued the passage to San Lucia aboard his own vessel. There are not many old salts around who can compete with Petter's sea story.

Christopher Columbus spent 22 days at sea during his fastest transatlantic crossing—we followed his lead. Unlike Columbus, we motored ten percent of the distance because the NE trade winds never materialized. Most of our weather consisted of southerly winds and unexpected calms. Typically November signals the end of the Atlantic hurricane season and is renowned for consistent trade winds. Hurricane Lenny, a category 4 storm, changed the rules for Atlantic hurricanes without telling anybody. Lenny, only the fifth major November hurricane on record, was the only late season hurricane to track from west to east in the last century. I breathed a lot easier when Lenny passed well north of our course. The mega force storm carved a brutal swath through the Atlantic after destroying hundreds of boats in the Caribbean.

As *Osprey* neared St. Lucia the winds finally piped up. Fifty miles to the west of us a sailboat surfed down the face of a large swell and inadvertently hit a sleeping whale. Luckily for the sailboat's crew the whale did not take offense to the ill-timed wake up call. Yachts straggled into Rodney Bay for a month. A few vessels suffered rigging failures and were fortunate not to be dismasted. Several others ran out of diesel fuel.

The whale incident did grab the attention of the ARC radio net—collisions with whales are notorious for sinking unlucky yachts. We have since learned that baleen whales, such as the humpback and the gray, only have passive sonar so they cannot hear a yacht that is relatively silent under sail. Tooth whales, such as the sperm and the killer, have active sonar so not only can they seek out prey, but they can also avoid non-menu items such as sailboats.

Just a few months after our Atlantic crossing, a humpback was credited with sinking a 75-foot wooden schooner. The century old vessel was anchored in Still Harbor off the wild western coast of SE Alaska's Baranof Island. Ward, the skipper of ill-fated *Merlin,* was by himself at the time. He decided to hop in his friend's borrowed kayak and paddle out to watch the humpbacks breaching in nearby Whale Bay. One of the huge leviathans did indeed breach, but it was right under Ward's classic sailboat. *Merlin* quickly sank after being torpedoed by the frolicking whale. With just a backpack and his .44 magnum bear gun, Ward eventually made his way back to Sitka. When *Merlin* was finally salvaged, the state biologist found baleen plates stuck inside a five-foot diameter hole punched through the splintered hull. A humpback had left its calling card.

For those not willing to sail across oceans, but definitely inclined to enjoy their yachts in a variety of foreign ports, there is the modern alternative of a motorized floating dry dock. The cleverly designed ship stores yachts in its hold, and then crosses the ocean on their behalf. If speed is a concern, nothing sails to windward faster than a jet.

Blue water sailing is an acquired taste—it is a wet, slow, uncomfortable, and challenging alternative for crossing an ocean. Of course there is the mystique. The romantic illusion inspires otherwise sane individuals to invest in a sailboat, put their careers on the backburner, and follow their hearts. Although the recipe calls for a dash of loose pocket change here and a pinch of courage there, the final product is an incomparable life style change. *Osprey* allowed PL and I to constantly reinvent ourselves—each time *Osprey* sailed across the horizon it was a new beginning.

29

The Windward Islands

○ ○

An adventure is an inconvenience rightly considered.

—*Stokey Woodall, ARC official*

A thin strand of gold caressed the pale Atlantic rollers as the star spangled ebony sky faded into a salmon pink dawn. Suddenly the molten rim of the sun catapulted into the powder blue heavens and puffy white cumulus clouds marched across the far horizon. Although the description sounds incredible, in actuality it was a rather ordinary morning in the Caribbean. But it just so happened that a welcome phone call from my brother Mark coincided with the sunrise. Since his news was so positive, my take on the tropical dawn was just as upbeat.

Mark recapped Shannon's progress since my visit a few months prior. He explained that after Shannon's regimen of intense radiation therapy, a follow up PET Scan and MRI showed no brain tumor activity. Shannon's oncologist was astounded by her almost unprecedented healing response. PL and I felt that just maybe the black cloud hanging over our family was starting to clear. The day was definitely getting brighter.

Years before our return to San Lucia, PL and I had charted sailboats in the British Virgin Islands and the Windward Islands of the Grenadines. Although the cruising grounds in the BVI are idyllic, the islands have been discovered by cruise ships and yacht flotillas. Our latest visit to the Caribbean was a homecoming—a chance to revisit some of our favorite haunts in the Windward Islands almost two decades later.

The Windward Islands, extending from Martinique in the north to Grenada in the south, are exposed to the full onslaught of Atlantic trade winds—protected anchorages only exist on their leeward sides. Sailing between the islands is habitually a lively affair in boisterous conditions. The native population tends to be a surly lot. After being exploited by assorted seafaring nations throughout their history, the latent animosity of the locals is understandable, but it is still not to our liking. For the most part food is mediocre and expensive.

The Caribbean Safety and Security Net, daily radio bulletins broadcast to the cruising crowd, periodically throws a cold dose of reality therapy on Margaritaville. Lots of places in the storied islands are rumored to be not all that safe or secure anymore. Many cruisers favor state of the art inflatable dinghies powered by muscular outboard motors. A motorized dinghy is to a cruiser what a car is to a suburban home dweller—a necessary mode of transportation. Enterprising thieves prowl the Caribbean anchorages always on the lookout for a likely hit—the fancier the ride, the more likely the rip off. The Safety and Security Net always signs off with the warning, "Lock it or lose it."

St. Lucia is one of the most eye-catching islands in the Caribbean. The lush countryside is alive with gorgeous orchids, bougainvillea, and frangipani. All manner of dazzling red, green, and yellow tropical birds flit about the verdant tropical rain forests that blanket the steep volcanic slopes. Along the coast islanders have hacked away at the jungle and cultivated bananas and coconuts, but tourism is now the main source of revenue. Even though St. Lucia gained independence in 1979 after 165 years of British colonial rule, the original French settlers still left their mark on the island's architecture. Francophiles can rejoice that French patois is spoken by many of the islanders.

Although the sandy beaches are pleasing to the eye, Hurricane Lenny effectively wiped out the undersea coral in the normally protected westerly coves. Because of the heavy silting from the unexpected storm, a full time dredge worked round the clock to reopen the entrance to Rodney Bay before the ARC 99 sailboats arrived.

During the Atlantic rally a becalmed sailor wrote "The Trade Wind Blues." The tune became a hit with the ARC sailors—the lyrics humorously revisited the unseasonable calms that plagued most of the sailboats crossing the Atlantic in November 1999. The ARC awards ceremony at Rodney Bay featured rum as the favored prize and our crew scored more than its fair share. *Osprey* and crew won the ETA award. Our arrival was only 41 minutes shy of our projected finish time that was radioed in a week prior to landfall in St. Lucia. Since Terro opted to use only a sextant for our Atlantic crossing, he walked off with the Five Star Navigation award for the most accurate sextant navigational plots of any vessel in the rally. Using a GPS is not much of a challenge for a guy who likes to write his own computerized navigation programs and relies solely on sextant sights.

Since *Osprey* sailed from Turkey eight months earlier, some 6000 miles had passed under our keel—a fair bit of voyaging by most standards. Now, for the first time in years, we were beginning to see a number of American boats. Many of our friends were sailing north to Florida. Thoughts of home started to tug at our well-worn cruiser persona.

With only intermittent doses of trade winds to cool the land, silhouettes of the anchored boats in Rodney Bay blurred in the heavy haze. Shorts and flip-flops became our standard tropical uniform, but the humidity and oppressive heat seemed to win in the end. For local color Caribbean style horseracing on a dusty oval was just down the way from Rodney Bay. Islanders sported cowboy hats that capped Rastafarian hairdos. A few of the guys had even traded in their sandals for cowboy boots. Although the locals love to wager on the races, the serious bettors strolled down a winding dirt road to the cockfights.

Christmas became extra special when PL's family, the Keithly clan, flew in for the holidays. Our last family holiday had been celebrated with Kate back in Thailand. We were nostalgic for a touch of home. Grandma ML, together with Pete and Phyllis and their offspring, made our celebration. *Madjk*'s Mike and Amy, along with their children, joined us for a bit of seasonal caroling from the back of a pickup truck. In northern climes hot chocolate would be the caroler's choice, but fresh coconut juice went down much better on that humid Caribbean evening. Instead of traveling over the meadow and through the woods to grandmother's house, the lumbering truck delivered us to Henry's Panache—a funky restaurant rendition of the Swiss Family Robinson tree house.

The kinfolk voted for a bit of sightseeing so PL and I piled everyone, sans ML, aboard *Osprey* and sailed north to the French island of Martinique. The reinforced trade winds that eluded us in the Atlantic materialized that day as Rodney Bay faded over the horizon. Some might say it was a spirited ride in a fresh breeze, whereas others might say it was rough as hell.

Fort de France has seen better days. The place was a little on the seedy side, but it did exude a decidedly French mystique. Although the Super H market displayed a few European delicacies, it is not on a par with the sumptuous supermarket offering of Spain's Corte Ingles and the Canary Island's Continente. Perhaps the fact that Napoleon's empress Josephine lived on Martinique as a young girl provides a bit of solace to the Gallic spirit. After scoping out the town, we sailed down the rain-forested western coastline to Grand Anse D'Arlet, a superb anchorage bordering a picturesque fishing village—more of what I had in mind. After an afternoon swim in the clear, warm lagoon, the crew dined on the spicy flambé offerings of the village's French Creole restaurant.

The 40-mile slog back to St. Lucia was a bit lumpy, even by PL and Kurt standards. Our novice crewmembers were rethinking their options, but basically they were stuck aboard a hard charging sloop bound for St. Lucia. I assured one and all that the boat would not turn turtle and to consider the flying spray a gentle tropical caress. Once everyone was harnessed safely in the cockpit, I fired up a few Caribbean tunes. I actually saw a smile light up a greenish face or two as my Jimmy Buffett CD extolled the virtues of a seafaring life.

Sailing between the islands is challenging, but apparently just negotiating the twisting island roads is too much for some local drivers. I was sitting in the cockpit minding my own business when a speeding Mini Moke, the classic island ride, launched off a tight curve on the Rodney Bay beach road and careened into the water not far from *Osprey's* stern. The driver nonchalantly crawled out of the window as the car sunk from sight. Since the locals are not blessed with a strong work ethic, the errant driver and a few friends took hours to mount their Mini Moke rescue campaign. Regrettably the grapples and cables, combined with the inept tow trick guys, reduced the previously unscathed car to a dripping pile of scrap. But then again, nobody got hurt and certainly nobody got excited.

In the wee morning hours I spotted vague shadows scurrying around inside our boat. In the feeble glow of a flashlight there was a quick flurry of retreating figures as the shadows ricocheted towards an exit. The curse of the tropics was back. Cockroaches, prime examples of nature's ultimate survivors, were living large again. After our hard learned lessons in Pest Control 101 in the South Pacific, PL whipped up a batch of cockroach cookies—the ultimate exterminators.

PL's award winning cockroach cookie recipe: *Liberally pour boric acid powder into a bowl of condensed milk; beat the mixture to the consistency of pudding; pour the concoction into a cupcake tin; bake until golden brown.* The ugly little critters loved it and before long, no more nocturnal visitors came to call.

Once the parties and socializing and millennium celebrations wound down, PL and I sailed south in hopes of rediscovering the tranquility that was so much a part of our cruising agenda. Although our shortwave radio brought BBC news to us every day, the harsh realities faced by much of the world saddened us so I turned it off. Our upcoming cruising schedule promised something different.

Soufriere Marine Park, tucked into the lush southwest section of St. Lucia, got us back in the mode. The spectacular twin volcanic domes of Gros Piton and Petit Piton towered above our anchorage in Hummingbird Cove. An afternoon shower sputtered across the 2600-foot peak of Gros Piton kindling a vivid rainbow from its misty slope. Our spirits soared as if we had found the fabled pot of gold. PL and I popped into the cove for a bit of snorkeling, but the water was a tad bit murky.

When I asked the local park ranger about the poor visibility in the supposedly pristine cove, the gangly local just shrugged his khaki clad shoulders and mumbled, *"De Hurricane Lenny, mon."*

In recent times St. Vincent has shed its colonial ties and become an independent nation. The main island of St. Vincent is an appealing tropical isle, but the local boat boys still give the place a bad name. The boat boys demand money in exchange for their questionable services such as "guarding" a dinghy. In the early '80's PL and I had sailed through the same area aboard a chartered sailboat and encountered the same problem. Apparently the authorities still do not get it—most visiting cruisers wisely avoid the main island and opt to sail south through the thirty other small islands in the Grenadine archipelago. Rightly so the Grenadines are billed as one of the great yachting destinations of the world. Boisterous NE trade winds provide challenging sailing between the scores of islands. The long strands of white sand beaches and vibrant coral reefs are the Caribbean's answer to the South Pacific.

Bequia is a former whaling town with a rich seafaring tradition, but nowadays Bequia's Admiralty Bay is a favorite hangout for charter boats. Over a hundred yachts were anchored in the harbor, so PL and I relied on stealth and cunning to tuck *Osprey* close to shore, away from the maddening crowd. The jammed anchorage is not much of a problem in settled weather, but towards the end of our stay a bout of nasty cold fronts decimated the transitory command at sea persona of many fledgling skippers. Dragging anchors transformed their rented beauties into bumper cars.

Although it had been awhile since our last visit, village carvers still produce excellent scrimshaw and the local boatyard still launches a wooden dory every now and then. Inviting shops and innovative restaurants add to the appeal. As PL and I waded in the brilliant sapphire blue water fronting the charming Frangipani Hotel, pink cedar blossoms bobbed around our legs and colorful reef fish darted about our toes. Mac's Pizza lived up to their reputation as the place for lobster pizza. After a day or two the *Osprey* crew became addicted to the lobster hit. PL suggested that a cross-island hike would ease our consciences and stretch our sea legs. At Friendship Bay, well-tended homes dot the countryside and the locals are friendly—a nice change of pace from our St. Lucia experience.

A few days after our cold turkey withdrawal from lobster pizza, we hopped aboard our dinghy for fish and chips at De Reef. What De Reef lacks in charm it makes up for in good food and local color. Yellow mooring lines are strung from the ramshackle bar to the bent coconut palms on the beach in the vain hope of resurrecting the leaning trees. Palm fronds interspersed with blue tarps barely keep out the afternoon showers. Islanders contentedly crunch on peanuts poured from Heineken beer bottles.

Tobago Cays is considered one of the premier anchorages in the Windward Islands. The low-lying islands demand a bit of careful navigation, but once *Osprey* was tucked inside the anchorage life was good. Horseshoe Reef provides protection from the pounding surf of the Atlantic and offers visiting yachts an ideal setting to savor the lazy Caribbean lifestyle. The dazzlingly clear turquoise lagoon is alive with all sorts of brilliantly colored tropical fish—humbugs, clownfish, triggerfish, angelfish, boxfish, trumpet fish, parrotfish, and many more wonderful creatures swim about in the sanctuary of the national marine park.

Carriacou is just a dot on the Caribbean map, a small blip in the long string of Windward Islands running from Martinique to Grenada. Although officially part of Grenada, diminutive Carriacou has a more insular feel. In the old days Carriacou was renowned for its fast handcrafted cedar hulled workboats. These days the boatyards are almost empty as the locals struggle to promote the island's tourist potential.

The folks at Carriacou Yacht Club in Tyrrel Bay treated us right. The mom and pop operation is tucked into a very protected cove so they escaped the wrath of Hurricane Lenny. After gorging ourselves on the CYC specialty of curry and lambi (conch), PL and I decided a hike would be therapeutic. Our little trek wound along a dusty island road and eventually led to a beach fronting Tyrrel Bay. The hurricane had smashed into the normally protected westward facing bay and trashed everything in sight. The washed out bulkheads, downed palm trees, improbable sand dunes, and wrecked waterfront businesses resembled a war zone.

Back at the CYC bar I met Chris Doyle, a Caribbean veteran and publisher of the Doyle Cruising Guides. Although Chris had seen hurricanes come and go over the years, he deemed the storm damage resulting from Lenny's aberrant eastward track to be unprecedented. He stared at my dog-eared collection of cruising

guides and suggested that perhaps the best way to stay current on cruising information in the Caribbean was to access his website. I was a holdout at the time,
but electronic charts and web based cruising updates have since become an integral part of a navigator's bag of tricks.

Grenada, a British Commonwealth dominion, is our favorite destination in
the Windward Islands. In October 1983 President Reagan authorized a military
invasion of Grenada to force out the Soviet and Cuban backed government that
had just staged a military coup. No contest. These days cruise ships have replaced
warships and the natives are not restless—the living is easy and the food is terrific.

Our anchorage at Prickly Bay fronted Grand Anse, a two-mile stretch of white
sand beach custom made for just hanging out. Since PL and I had no wheels,
Henry told us he was the man to see for our guided tour of the Spice Island.
Henry went on and on about the plantations. Besides the requisite bananas and
papayas and cocoa, Grenada's claim to fame is the abundance of cinnamon, bay
leaves, cloves, and nutmeg. It is no wonder that cruise ships stop at the colorful
West Indian port city of St. Georges. The open-air market is awash in island
spices and the turbaned ladies are not bashful about pushing their wares.

From what Henry told us, the USA invaded Grenada to protect the American
students at the St. Georges Medical School. Now a miniscule US Embassy, rendered in sparkling Caribbean pastels, resides just down the road from the marina.
Personally I favored the White Lightning Factory, a weathered wooden barn that
distills 150-proof white rum. On the far side of the island Henry pointed out a
deserted airstrip with its resident Cuban bomber. The obsolete prop job was in
sad shape, but the surrounding jungle was doing its part by swallowing it.

At the Venezuelan Embassy high on the hillside above the horseshoe-shaped
port of St. Georges, PL and I met Forrest and Elly. Forrest is the professional captain on the mega yacht *Valkyrie*. Besides giving us the lowdown on Venezuela,
the charming couple gave us a ride back to town. That evening we were invited
for cocktails aboard the phenomenal yacht. Forrest is not only a genial host; he is
also the man who taught me the rhyme for a proper rum punch.

> *One part sour (fresh squeezed lime), two parts sweet (sugar), three parts strong*
> *(Mount Gay Rum) and four parts weak (water).* Mix sweet and weak, pour in
> sour and strong, then top with grated nutmeg and a dash of bitters.

PL and I got another dose of home when Spice Island Marina fired up their
TV for the broadcast of Super Bowl XXXIV. Although a few of the bar's patrons
were concerned whether the Rams or the Titans won, we were scoping out the

clever commercials. As we sipped our Carib beers and gazed at the lavish advertisements, we got the feeling that perhaps Grenada was on another planet.

As I considered the mass marketing hype, I realized that beneath all the tinsel, there is very treacherous quicksand. Accumulating and holding is a passion typically reserved for the more affluent citizens of the world. Unwittingly many of us become stuck—the heavy burden of too much stuff eventually costs us our freedom.

30

Carnival in Trinidad

Man, if you gotta ask, you'll never know.

—*Louis Armstrong*

The Andrews Sisters of World War Two fame made this place famous with their smash hit "Rum and Coca Cola." Trinidad has changed over the intervening years. Sixty years ago the port town of Chaguaramus was a strategic military base where Navy flying boats conducted antisubmarine warfare in the Caribbean. Today Chaguaramus, safely south of the Caribbean hurricane zone, caters to visiting yachties. Trinidad is also blessed with 460 species of birds, 650 kinds of butterflies, and 200 types of orchids.

PL and I sailed into Chaguaramus just about the time Trinidad was gearing up for their world class Carnival, a flamboyant tribute to the Creole culture. Considered the biggest and most famous Caribbean Carnival, Trinidad produced calypso in the nineteenth century and the steel band in the twentieth century. Soca, the trademark of local vocalists, is a musical form unique to Trinidad. Slaves emancipation in 1830 transformed Carnival into an African street festival sated with singing, dancing, drumming, stick fighting, and uninhibited partying.

Bands and masqueraders prepare a year in advance for the festivities that explode in a sea of calypso music and extravagant costumes. Trinidad's six-week recipe features catchy calypso tunes with a backdrop of lavishly costumed masqueraders, nimble limbo dancers, vibrant pan bands, and clever extempore entertainers. Action central is in Port of Spain, the nearby capital. The weekly Taste of Carnival, beginning six weeks prior to the Opening Day or *Jour Ouvert*, introduces yachties to many faces of the huge Mardi Gras celebration. Mike and Yvonne, fellow Washingtonians aboard *Pacific Grace*, befriended us and showed us the ropes.

Trinidad offers professional refit and haul out services, comparable to yards in New Zealand or the USA. Hundreds of cruising sailboats descend on Trinidad every year. It is one of the few places in the world that you can have your boat painted one day and have your body painted the next. I treated *Osprey* to some pampering at Power Boats Marina—she deserved a few upgrades after all her faithful service. It is not often that I can indulge our talisman in such style.

Some of our cruising amigos got caught up in the festivities and went native. Between the local seafood specialty of Shark & Bake and the modestly priced Cuban cigars, I was feeling a bit native myself. PL and I got into the calypso music. Mighty Sparrow, the 70-year old lord of calypso music, is Trinidad's consummate showman. Although Sparrow is a dead ringer for a retired football linebacker, his two-hour nonstop show of dancing, singing, and impersonations would leave most NFL bone crushers dragging.

PL and I liked the Caroni Bird Sanctuary. The place resembled the Everglades but with a twist. At sunset returning flocks of brilliantly colored scarlet ibis and dazzlingly white egrets filled the clear blue skies of the forty square mile mangrove swamp. As if on cue the stark green mangroves were magically transformed into crimson poinsettias as scores of the birds roosted for the night. After the evening fly-in our guide pointed out a couple of mellow boa constrictors eyeing our passing skiff. Conservation in Trinidad is on the upswing, but as our boat guy observed, "Most animals that live in Trinidad fit into a stew pot and go well with curry."

As we got to know a few of the local folks, the undercurrent of racial and political tension became quite apparent. Jesse James, whose yellow maxi van caters to yachties, was a font of local knowledge. Jesse considered the thriving cruiser hangouts and tourist resorts relatively secure, but he warned us away from the back streets of Port of Spain.

Throughout our travels, the specter of grinding poverty and ethnic violence seems to be the driving theme behind desperate, impoverished people with no hope. During our circumnavigation my sense of entitlement and my unassailable opinions were being called into question as I witnessed the hapless lives of so many of the world's citizens. I was extremely fortunate to be born as a white, middle class citizen of the USA. My education, lifestyle, and economic status are a result of lucky happenstance. Billions of people are simply not blessed in the same way. Although I know that life is not fair, I received a much better shake than most. When I start to lose touch with such a basic fact, a good dose of introspection and empathy is good medicine. It jolts me back into the real world of ordinary people.

31

The Haves and the Have-Nots

∘ ∘

Despite the intricacies of Buddhist metaphysics, all of it can be distilled into two sentences: If you can, help others; if you cannot do that, at least do not harm them.

—*Dalai Lama*

The Paria Peninsula of Venezuela is only an afternoon sail from Trinidad, but the troubled Latin country is eons away culturally and politically. The transition from the user friendly, English-speaking ways of Trinidad to the divergent Spanish cultures of South America was about to begin. Our first introduction to Latin American bureaucracy was the *zarpe,* a sort of a multiple country visa. To check into a Central or South American country, we were required to present an international zarpe endorsed by the country we had just sailed from. A *y puntos intermedios* endorsement on a zarpe allows us to visit assorted intermediate ports en route with no hassle from officials—a very big deal. No previous endorsement, no entry. Every now and then we encountered a distraught yachtie who had vainly pleaded their case to an unrelenting bureaucrat. The unfortunate cruisers were obliged to sail back the way they came in search of their missing exit endorsement.

Reaching down the Venezuelan coastline, PL and I enjoyed the best trade wind sailing since our days in the Indian Ocean. We coast hopped our way through the stunning anchorages of Mochina National Park, then checked into the country at Puerta la Cruz. Turbulent political unrest and security concerns have severely dampened tourism in Venezuela—our thought was just to keep a low profile and not dawdle in isolated bays. The philosophy worked for us, but sporadic tales of blatant piracy and armed robbery were unnerving.

Leo, a fellow cruiser aboard the sailboat *Baltic Heritage*, flew back to Canada for a visit. When our friend returned there was no boat to be found and no forwarding address. Neighboring yachties saw the sailboat leave its berth, but they just figured Leo had hired a few locals to work on his boat. Since theft was always an underlying threat, we became a bit more wary. On the positive side diesel fuel was only 30 cents per gallon.

Four months prior to our visit, a torrential downpour flooded a ravine by the coastal town of Carmen de Uria. The government had diverted the ravine's river fifty years ago and poor coastal residents had subsequently moved into the area. The flood and mudslides killed thousands of people. President Hugo Chavez, a Castro sympathizer and vehement critic of the USA, refused our ambassador's offer of help. American medical teams were ordered to stand down, and then the populist president imported Cuban medics—too little and too late.

Alfonso guided us to the mountainous interior east of Cariaco. I had never heard of a guacharo, or oilbird, until we found ourselves tramping though a primal, mile long cavern in search of the radar-emitting nocturnal specimen. No luck. But Alfonso and driver Mario had something even better in mind, a tour of a mountain village. PL and her friend Yvonne zeroed in on the cute guinea pigs. Mario, using his only English words, christened two of the little creatures "Oh my" and "Oh my God." As our van headed off, the ladies wondered why the poor village held guinea pigs in such esteem. Alfonso shattered the illusion. "Oh my" and "Oh my God" were village dinner entrees, a taste shared by many South American cultures.

Maremares Marina and Hotel is about as upscale as it gets in Puerta La Cruz. Although a huge section of the city is a sad barrio of have-nots, the local high rollers have carved out their own niche. The haves favor waterfront mansions perched on the shores of winding man-made canals that front the Maremares complex. For the price of moorage, PL and I had access to the facilities at the marina's 5 star hotel. It was a nice lash up but the wave-making machine in the Olympic size pool was a little over the top. From the marina the luxurious Plaza Mayor shopping mall is only a dinghy ride away. Huge yachts moored in front of the grand waterfront estates brought to mind the whispers I had heard in Trinidad—the area was allegedly rife with drug lords and laundered money. Shotgun toting guards patrolled the marina complex and razor wire topped the perimeter fence. Have-nots were not welcome.

The languid pace and luxurious accommodations were addicting at first, but then PL and I met the Operation Rainbow team. The dedicated group of volunteer physicians and nurses happened to be headquartered at our hotel for the week. Rick, a plastic surgeon from Florida, invited us to join their team. I assisted Rick in the operating room and PL helped out in recovery.

Rassetti Hospital is a public hospital on the outskirts of Puerta la Cruz. Although the neighborhood was not the best, the locals were. When our Operation Rainbow crew hopped off the bus and entered the hospital, the place erupted with cheers and whistles. During the very intense and hectic week, needy children from throughout Venezuela were treated for disfiguring problems such as cleft palate, cleft lip, and clubfoot.

The patients and most of the staff were very appreciative of our efforts, but local politics occasionally got in the way. Some of the hospital's in-house docs were very protective of their turf and felt slighted that the American medical personnel were treated as white knights and conquering heroes. Since the hospital's stores were limited and some of the surgical equipment was not up to par, the Rainbow team brought their own. My personal introduction to Third World medicine had to do with supplies, or rather the lack there of. When I requested 3-0 silk sutures, the OR nurse sadly announced that there was not much suture left. Apparently someone had ripped off a fair amount of Operation Rainbow's imported surgical supplies.

After a long morning assisting in the operating room, I took a break. Rather than the hospital's cloying odor of antiseptic and alcohol, great smells percolated from the doctor's lounge. An ancient little woman tugged on my sleeve and pantomimed that she had brought me lunch. Once again people who had little made it their business to treat us with kindness. A disfigured child's new smile and a grateful parent's hug were payment in full.

Following our hospital commitment, PL and I needed an adventure fix. We joined the *Pacific Grace* crew aboard a WW II vintage DC-3 for a treetop flight across the sprawling Orinoco Delta and on to La Gran Sabana. We were winging over a huge river drainage second only in size to the Amazon. Ahead of us lay Venezuela's Canaima National Park and its crown jewel, Angel Falls. In 1935 Jimmy Angel, an American bush pilot, inadvertently discovered the highest waterfall in the world. The awesome falls tumble 3212 feet from the summit of a huge sandstone mesa, Auyan Tepuy.

Our pilot was as classic as his airplane—the kind of guy who stoked up his cigarette as the aircraft was being fueled and who considered his young copilot to be the autopilot device. As our slow flying plane lumbered through a squall line, the grizzled captain opened the side windscreen, wetted his hand, and with a satisfied grin sloshed his face with rainwater.

The DC-3 tail dragger taxied off the dirt landing strip and there we were at Parakaupa Camp in the jungle village of Canaima. Fernando, our faithful Indian guide, was actually quite a little stud muffin according to our ladies. When he was not eyeing the latest crop of women tourists, Fernando was an articulate spokesman for the displaced Indian cultures of the Orinoco. During our dugout canoe ride up river, our guide explained that the indigenous people living in the thick of the vast Orinoco system were among the world's most untouched civilizations. Interestingly enough Fernando's tribe has its own website.

The Internet has allowed the Fernandos of the world a glimpse into the global community. Our young guide was passionate about preserving the unique culture of his tribe, but he understood the reality of encroaching civilization. Hopefully he will find that civilization is everything it is cracked up to be—I still have my doubts.

32

Winging It over South America

Osprey was tucked away at Maremares and the local travel agent assured us that our upcoming trip to Peru would be problem free. I should have known. Our plane landed in Lima about midnight. We paced around the strange airport, backpacks in hand, but our promised guide never showed. The consensus of the itinerant tour guide night shift was that our guy was probably drunk.

As the chilly early morning unfolded, actually I guess you could say unraveled, PL and I chanced upon Aquiles, who was hustling tour business in the wee hours. Aquiles found a hotel for us, joined us for breakfast, and then set us up with a few connections to make our three-week odyssey a grand event instead of an ongoing nightmare.

When Spaniard Francisco Pizarro invaded Peru in 1531, the Inca Empire was in the twilight years of its relatively short 150-year run. Although modern Peru is infamous as the world's leading producer of coca, the Incas left a legacy that is the basis for Peru's more legitimate commodity—tourism.

Cuzco, perched at the rarified altitude of 3326 meters, is the archaeological capital of the Americas. The colonial city of 11,000 souls was considered by the Quechua natives to be "the earth's navel." Interesting concept since PL and I could have sworn that ancient Delphi in Greece shared the same anatomical position on mother earth.

Since most visitors fly into Cuzco's high altitude airport from a sea level environment, the city is infamous for being the ground zero of altitude sickness. Peru has embraced the coca plant for many generations—the local remedy to alleviate altitude malaise is coca tea. Hotels, coffee shops, and restaurants make it their business to brew liberal amounts of coca tea so the tourists stay happy, symptom free, and free spending. The mild coca leaf is a non-addictive antidepressant, unlike the highly addictive cocaine hydrochloride powder made from the humble leaf. Besides combating altitude sickness, coca is the favored Andean medication for treating ulcers and enhancing endurance.

Our arrival coincided with Holy Week. Huge throngs of Peruvians descended on Cuzco to watch the epic-sized procession honoring El Senor de Los Temblores, Lord of the Earthquakes. Once PL and I got over the shock of being compressed in the trash masher of ardent believers, we enjoyed the spectacle. The Andes Catholic Church puts a decidedly different spin on the Roman Catholic Church liturgy. The life-size, black crucified Christ figure was paraded past the adoring crowds and then returned to the cathedral. Inside the cathedral the Quechua Indian visage of Christ was housed next to a huge painting of "The Last Supper" featuring the Inca delicacy, guinea pig. Brought to mind PL's fuzzy little Venezuelan friends, "Oh my" and "Oh my God."

We decided to splurge on a few nights in Hotel Monasterio, formally the seventeenth century San Antonio de Abad seminary. Our former monk's cell featured a marbled bath and antique furniture. Rather than serving coca tea, the hotel pumped oxygen into the guest rooms to assuage the effects of altitude sickness—a first in the hotel industry. The beautifully landscaped central courtyard and Spanish style fountains looked even better after we were snapped back by a jolt of oxygen.

Our train chugged out of Cuzco and then lurched its way to Ollantaytambo, an ancient Incan town that has managed to retain its authenticity. Wendy, of the El Albergue Ollantaytambo guest lodge, noted that her adopted village is the end of the road. The only way to continue on to Machu Pichu is by rail or foot. PL and I chose rail. Our destination was Aquas Calientes, where we boarded a bus for the 90-minute switchback climb to the most spectacular archaeological site in South America. Hiram Bingham, an American historian, stumbled across the long forgotten ruins of Machu Pichu in 1911. Today the "Lost City of the Incas" is famous throughout the world. Although the altitude was tough on us, the local guides who delighted in foot racing the descending buses back downhill to Aquas Calientes thought nothing of it.

From the Inca Trail aerie at *Intipunku,* or Sun Gate, PL and I soaked up the panoramic view of Machu Pichu far below. We tramped down a primitive trail that courses through the cliff-hanging cloud forest and eventually emerged at the famed remains. When we were guests at the elegant Monesterio Hotel in Cuzco, the concierge kindly booked us into a sister hotel, the Machu Pichu Sanctuary

Lodge—an intimate small hotel that is the only accommodation at Machu Pichu. Long after other tourists had left the mountain, we were free to wander the deserted ruins of Machu Pichu in the pale cold moonlight.

Good thing we got acclimatized in Cuzco because our gaily-colored bus was bound for Lake Titicaca, the highest navigable lake in the world. The Uros Indians maintain tradition by interweaving totora reed to fashion their canoe-shaped boats, build huts, and create their own floating islands on the lake. PL noted that although the thatched islands felt stable enough, it would not do to light a match.

After a three-hour boat ride from the lakeside village of Puno, our decrepit water taxi dropped us off on Taquile Island, the Peruvian equivalent of a Greek island. The altitude of the lake was 12,500 feet. After staggering up an additional 500 steep stone steps, PL and I flopped down exhausted. Eventually coca tea and a lunch of fresh king fish brought us around. Then we started to consider exactly what we had gotten ourselves into. Ernasto, a very shy islander, was our host. In his Taquile dialect he mumbled something incomprehensible, pointed to a few shacks even further up the rocky hillside, resumed his knitting, and trotted off. The men on Taquile knit hats and gloves. It is their deal and they are constantly at it. As PL and I numbly trudged behind, sandal shod Ernasto nimbly scampered further up the hill that was getting steeper by the minute.

My birthday was celebrated in an unheated mud hut featuring a dirt floor, piles of rough woven llama blankets, and a one-inch candle stub for light. Providentially I had my picture dictionary along. Rather than deal with language barriers, I just point to an appropriate picture—my proven point and shoot technique. When PL pointed to the picture of a toilet, Ernasto threw his arms open wide and replied, "Es natural, senora!"

The night was freezing. PL and I snuggled together under the gamey blankets, pulled our recently acquired Taquile knit hats over our ears, and prayed for morning. About the time we fell asleep the flutes started. A couple hundred meters below our hut the islanders were dancing in the pale moonlight that bathed the dusty village square. All was right with the world.

At daybreak PL and I sipped coca tea in the deserted village square and talked it over with an international contingent of backpackers. A couple of young Europeans were kicking around a hackey sack, which absolutely fascinated the grubby bare footed village kids. Another backpacker was taking it all in as he nonchalantly ate breakfast using his Frisbee for a plate. After his meager breakfast, the insightful good will ambassador flipped the Frisbee to the village children. The little ragamuffins spent the morning in ecstasy as they flew the magic dish. The young man's spontaneous act of kindness and empathy is still etched in our memories—shades of Tyler and deserving of our Shooting Star tribute. A Frisbee is now one of the essential items in my backpack.

PL and I were a good two decades senior to the other backpackers aboard the "peoples' bus." The bus had seen better days, but it was time to leave Puno so our fate was sealed. Our plan was to cross the frontier between Peru and Bolivia, ride a barge across the Bolivian corner of Lake Titicaca, and then visit LaPaz for a few days. Butch Cassidy and the Sundance Kid, as well as Che Guevara, hung out in Bolivia. Inaccessible terrain and corrupt officials ensured a measure of protection and anonymity back then. Not much has changed. Our introduction to the State of Emergency in Bolivia was in the form of large boulders. The local coca producers were unhappy that the government was burning their huge cash crops of coca at the behest of America's DEA. To graphically illustrate their disillusionment, the drug boys simply dynamited the roads leading into the capital of LaPaz. As our aged bus corkscrewed through the rubble, it occurred to us that there was much more to Latin American politics than colorful Quechua Indian women with their bowler hats and voluminous skirts.

On the outskirts of LaPaz, the grim faces and stark poverty was a harsh reminder that Bolivia had a lot of ongoing social unrest. Our wheezing bus edged through a dubious neighborhood, finally got a second wind as it crested the lip of a huge crater, and then backfired its way down the canyon's bowl and into LaPaz, a quarter of a mile below. The spectacular triple peak of Illimani shimmered in the distance, a reminder that we were still at altitude. PL and I explored the central area of the city and soaked up the Latin American flavor of the place. The Witchcraft Market seemed to feature a remedy or charm to ward off most any malady. Since our only complaint was sore feet, the proud *chola* women who sold all the charms and amulets did not extract much money from us.

After a fashionably late dinner, we strolled back to the Sucre Palace Hotel and chatted with the manager. He was appalled that we had unknowingly taken such a dangerous chance when it could have gone either way for us. Apparently Jose subscribed to the local Aymara belief that the world is a collection of friendly and not so friendly spirits. An early flight out of LaPaz started to make a lot more sense as the manager moaned that the city was in a state of chaos.

After touching down in Lima, we decided to take a few days and visit Islas Ballestas, billed as Peru's miniature Galapagos. The luxurious Royal Class motor coach, complete with a stewardess, was quite an upgrade from the tooth rattling bus of Bolivian extraction. Instead of dodging those irksome boulders that were rolled across Bolivian mountain roads, our fancy wheels high tailed down a well-maintained highway as we swept past enormous stretches of uninhabited beaches and mile after mile of austere sand dunes. We were reintroduced to our old friend the Pacific Ocean at our seaside digs in the Paracus Hotel. PL and I boarded a small launch for our jaunt to Ballestas Island. The Humboldt Current and the El Nino weather pattern produced an upwelling of warm, nutrient rich water that suited the resident boobies, frigates, pelicans, vultures, sea lions, and penguins just fine.

To cap off our excursion, a Cessna 206 buzzed us low over the mysterious Nazca Lines that cover 190 miles of Peru's arid desert coastal region. The obscure sand drawings are said to date back to 900 AD and mirror the figures embossed on Nazca ceramics. Aficionados claim the primitive desert etchings communicated with other interplanetary life forms. My personal favorite was the condor with its huge 390-foot wingspan. PL was quick to point out that the massive stick figures were within the artistic range of a 5 year old.

33

Island Time

○ ○

The life which is unexamined is not worth living.

—Plato

After coughing up a rather hefty fee for our long-term stay at Maremares, we sailed northwest bound for Venezuela's Los Roques Parque. The forty mangrove-covered islets of Venezuela's Los Roques encompass a 15 by 25 mile chunk of the Caribbean in a spectacular setting of massive sun drenched shallows that bristle with boat busting coral heads. The Los Roques feature over 300 bird species for hard-core bird watchers and the islands are also famous for world-class bone fishing. Floatplanes and fast sport fishing boats busily ferry fishermen from Franciquis Island to the shallow reefs where they can try their luck.

Mooring buoys are thoughtfully installed in ecologically sensitive areas of the parque to prevent damage to the huge forests of soft coral and the miles of hard coral barrier reef. All manner of brilliantly colored tropical fish inhabit the clear warm water. It is like skin diving in a gigantic aquarium—our best underwater hit since the Red Sea. After we had snorkeled away the afternoon around Sarqui Island, it was time to swim back to *Osprey*. But something new had been added. Two official looking skiffs, with Los Roques Parque emblazoned on their hulls, were pulled alongside our sailboat. Rather than deal with the mainland bureaucrats, we had sailed into the Los Roques without a permit. I figured the unannounced visit was not a good development. Actually the parque rangers were very hospitable and invited us to moor overnight without filling out any paperwork. To extend our stay, we would have been required to backtrack through a maze of coral reefs, pay $100, and jump through a series of ritualistic hoops. Our goal was to keep a low profile and avoid the clutches of the Venezuelan government. We had heard wonderful things about the sparsely inhabited Aves, just a day sail to the west. When morning rolled around, *Osprey* followed the sun.

The breaking seas cut a swath across a substantial chunk of the western horizon as the ocean churned along a jagged stretch of windward reefs that protect Ave de Sotavento. It is nature's way of saying be very careful. Unexpectedly kissing the edge of a hidden barrier reef would be bad form. A French fleet of 18 warships learned the tragic lesson late one night in the spring of 1678—a navigational error condemned hundreds of sailors and 17 ships to a watery grave as the knife-edged coral of the barrier reef at Ave de Sotavento carved up the proud fleet. The rusty hulk of the freighter *Mui Bien*, splattered across the windward fringes of the unforgiving coral reef, is a more recent addition to the carnage and definitely got our attention.

Despite the nasty coral reefs and the intimidating access, PL and I view the isolated cays of Venezuela's Aves as our favorite Caribbean anchorages. Only a few local fishermen, a couple of young Venezuelan coast guard light keepers, and an occasional cruising boat frequent the beautiful, primal atolls. Although the approach to the remote cays of Ave de Barlovento (Windward) and Ave de Sotavento (Leeward) can be hazardous for the unwary or the unlucky, the payoff is well worth it.

It was easy to idle away a couple weeks anchored inside the pristine reefs. The spectacular coral forests, endless parade of iridescent tropical fish, and clear warm water are addictive. I almost developed a permanent crease on the edge of my mouth from clamping down on my snorkel mouthpiece for hours on end. The cure for snorkel crease is simply to grin a lot and sip a medicinal G & T at sundown—worked like a charm.

For madam's dining pleasure a fresh selection of conch and reef fish was available at the live fish market just under our keel. In keeping with the food chain concept, I swapped a bit of cash and a few packages of Marlboros with the locals in exchange for lobster and orange ruffey. With few pleasures in their relatively short lives, the trio of fishermen was ecstatic about their Marlboro haul. Usually the fishermen barely get by. They harvest green patches of saltwort, dry the green clumps of weed, and then smoke the stuff. Oblivious to the surgeon general's warning and our rather prissy views, they sucked each cigarette right down to the stub. Perhaps the tattered threesome were very philosophical souls—they had looked deeply at life, and then decided that it is very here and now.

Turtles and rays would occasionally swim by, but a six-foot barracuda we nicknamed Jaws became a fixture under our boat. Jaws liked to hang out in the shade under our hull. Besides his telltale shadow on the white sand bottom, Jaws was bulky enough to trigger our depth sounder's shallow water alarm. If Jaws showed up, the buzzer sounded off. Before our uninvited mascot developed a taste for hairy white limbs with squiggling digits, PL and I voted not to fin around in the immediate vicinity of *Osprey*.

Philosophically I knew that mangrove branches did not sprout puffy white snowballs. The fuzzy trimmings turned out to be scores of snowy white baby boobies perched in the mangroves, a regular treetop nursery. Adult blue-footed boobies struggled to bring fish to their babies, but the predatory frigate birds would steal fish right out of their beaks.

From the western fringes of the Aves, Bonaire is downwind and less than a day away. Bonaire is renowned as a charming and quiet island, supposedly long on excellent restaurants and spectacular diving. Bonaire is the B part of the autonomous Dutch ABC Islands. Sister islands Curacao and Aruba lay a bit to the west. Tourism and salt seem to be the mainstays of the place. Mediterranean style bungalows with ochre walls and red roofs dot the western waterfront and brilliantly clear turquoise water laps the shores. However the glossy brochures failed to mention Hurricane Lenny's westerly surge that had decimated Bonaire's celebrated coral reefs.

Immigration and police officials were on strike when we sailed into the small port of Kralendijk. Even the customs guy told us to come back another time. Although the officialdom on Bonaire proved to be pretty loose, Uncle Sam's drug interdiction patrol was anything but. There was usually a visiting US Coast Guard cutter or a US Navy frigate tied up at the town's main pier.

An obliging coast guard chief showed PL and I around the USCG Cutter *Valiant*. We heard a few troubling tales about the ongoing drug operations off the coasts of Venezuela, Columbia, Panama, and Mexico. Intimating that bad things could happen if a cruising boat stumbled across a smuggling operation, the veteran chief warned us to steer clear of Columbia. Other cruisers raved about the charms of Cartagena, but after getting the lowdown we scratched the popular Columbian port off our list.

Now that he had our undivided attention, the chief gave us a bit more counsel. Since *Osprey* would be cruising the coasts of South and Central America in the coming months, caution was the operative word. In the case of a grave or imminent threat, the chief advised us to trigger an emergency signal on our 406 EPIRB without hesitation. This was the same type of emergency beacon *Jagermeifter's* crew activated on our Atlantic crossing. The cavalry, in the form of a military ship or aircraft, would theoretically charge to our rescue. The concept took some getting used to after being on our own for so long in the far reaches of the world's oceans. Our visit had been enlightening, but also a bit sobering.

Bonaire is only twenty some miles long so a motor scooter puts everything within reach. Bonaire produces and exports massive quantities of salt from the huge salt bogs on the south end of the island. The pastel shaded salt pens are also home to thousands of pink flamingoes. Solar evaporation is a clever way to extract salt from seawater and entice flamingoes, but the by-product is aggressive hordes of voracious mosquitoes. Uncharitably one could consider the wind swept wetlands a huge salt lick.

The northern section of the arid island is desert terrain that is dotted with scrub and cactus and inhabited by feral donkeys and goats. Towards the interior the Devil's Mouth is noted for its interesting caves and cliffs. Parrots, doves, and flamingoes make the area a bird watching smorgasbord. The jagged leeward coastline is renowned for exceptional diving, but since it was post-Lenny time good snorkeling was hard to find. 1000 Steps, a series of coral encrusted underwater slopes, turned out to be an exception. PL and I got our skin diving fix as we snorkeled in the warm embrace of the clear water and swam with the resident green turtles.

In 1979 the Bonaire Marine Park was established. The innovative park encircles the island and about half of Bonaire's marked dive sites are accessible from shore. Dive shops claim the local waters support over 80 varieties of coral and at least 350 varieties of fish. Although Lenny obliterated much of the coral on the western edge of the island, I figured the local dive shop must have some good diving venues in their bag of tricks. I joined Great Adventures for a deep-water dive on the wreck of 230 foot *Hilda Hooker*. I was not prepared for the immense assault as sixty divers from three dive boats spiraled down 120 feet to the wreck. As I watched the bubbling trails of the wet suited masses descend through the surprisingly murky water, I decided to keep our unbelievably good diving exploits in the Aves a secret.

From Harbor Village Marina it was just a short stroll along the waterfront quay to downtown Kralendijk. A couple of good local restaurants boosted our morale after we had been chewed on by mosquitoes and skunked in the snorkeling department. The hot sticky weather was tough on us aboard our non-air conditioned boat, but it was even tougher on our refrigeration system. Our shore powered electrical refrigeration compressor decided it was through. Sorting out the problem, ordering parts from the US, and reinstalling the replacement compressor kept me out of mischief.

As mother of the bride, PL was in the throes of planning an Italian wedding even though Bonaire does not have quite the same feel as the rolling hills of Tuscany. PL set up a charge account at Bonaire Live, the local Internet hangout, so she could stay in constant touch with our betrothed daughter. The logistics of booking airline tickets, securing hotel reservations, and coordinating wedding activities was thankfully not in my job description.

In the late spring it was time to reenter the real world and concentrate on the upcoming wedding festivities. We left *Osprey* in the care of Harbor Village Marina, trusted our fate to Air Jamaica, and then flew off to Seattle.

Prior to our circumnavigation, I had become rather attached to stories I associated with myself. As my cruising persona began to assert itself, the stories started to change. Change is difficult, but I was about to learn a few object lessons that would hasten the transformation.

34

A Florentine Celebration

○ ○

For my part, I travel not to go anywhere, but to go: I travel not for travel's sake…but the great affair is to move.

—Robert Lewis Stevenson

Snow capped Mount Rainier glistened in the afternoon sun as our plane made its final approach into the Puget Sound basin. Reentry is mind-boggling. PL and I felt like aliens as America's high tech offerings and the ferocious pace of consumerism besieged us. After our rather simplistic cruising lifestyle, just having easy access to a bathtub or phone was a new adventure. Over the last few years I had become quite adept at hauling fuel around in 5-gallon jerry jugs. The concept of slipping an ATM card into a computerized pay slot and magically unleashing the gasoline genie was an unheard of luxury. Priming the pump took on a whole new meaning. Things had definitely changed while we were away.

Sometimes our reawakening was a slow, thoughtful process—as if we were reading a fascinating book on a lazy Sunday morning in front of the fire. At other times the transition was a shock, like being dragged out of snuggly warm bed and tossed into an ice cold shower. PL and I roared into town full of enthusiasm with a tale or two to tell. Our outlook had changed and our values were different…but not many people really cared. Our bohemian personalities did not seem to register favorably on many heretofore-friendly radar screens. People got on with their lives and since we had dropped out for a long while, our reemergence was a peripheral event—unique for a short while, but mostly just way outside the norm. Assimilation, or lack thereof, occupied us as we grappled on the edge of our former lives. We made it a point to contact a former cruiser or two, but everyone shared similar stories.

Road trips were in our blood, so PL and I fired up a rental car and headed for points south. We explored the rim of the Grand Canyon, hiked the mountains outside of Bend, and celebrated my godson Joe's wedding in Montana. Our road trip was rather aimless, but our agenda was to hopefully rekindle old friendships and rejuvenate our flagging spirits along the way. The revelation slowly dawned that perhaps PL and I needed to move on. After Tyler died, our lives spiraled down into a living hell and our souls were scarred beyond recognition. We had endured a nightmare, suffered the unimagined consequences, and emerged in a different place and time with our love for each other intact. Now it was time to celebrate and get on with our journey. With a core of tried and true friends and relatives, the adventure moved on to Tuscany.

Fifty friends and relatives from the States joined us for one of Florence's grand events of the new millennium, the marriage of Kate Mondloch and Andrea Loreto. Italians love weddings and the delicious thought of adding an American bride to the Loreto extended family was all the more reason for a huge celebration. The ongoing festivities started off with a rehearsal dinner poolside at Villa Fioratti in Fiesole. Andrea's brother Mario and his wife Ariana graciously hosted the event for the American contingent.

A medieval chapel, bathed in the golden pink afternoon hues of the Tuscan countryside, became the center of our universe on September 2, 2000. Monsignor Timothy Verdon, a renowned Renaissance art historian, adroitly presided over the wedding mass in both English and Italian. The ceremony was evocative and inspirational. For the record the bride wore a fitted raw silk gown as she and I walked down the aisle at Chiesa Di Sant. There was no question—PL looked radiant and it was said that even I cleaned up well.

The evening reception at Villa Montalto, a beautiful villa overlooking the twinkling lights of Florence, was an extravaganza in the finest tradition. Excellent wine, exquisite food, and whimsical music made the party special—our family and friends made it incomparable. To PL and I the continual champagne toasts were more than accolades to Kate and Andrea. The good wishes and heartfelt sentiments, whether spoken in English or Italian, signified a new direction and a brighter future for our entire family. It was a fairy tale wedding that left us feeling very happy and content.

When the action wound down and the honeymooners were on their way, PL and I hopped the train bound for France. Riding the Euro Star through the Italian, Swiss, and German countryside was a much more relaxed affair than flying from here to there. We stopped overnight in Baden Baden, and then we were off to Strasburg. After the hectic action in Florence, the slower pace was a welcome change. All of a sudden an unexpected French fuel strike really cooled our jets. A cabbie befriended us and pointed out an unscheduled train that just happened to be whistle-stopping its way to the charming art nouveau city of Nancy. Hours later the little engine that could chugged into Nancy and we bailed. PL and I grabbed our duffels and hoofed it down to the municipal marina. We found *Liljana,* Salah and Liljana's shiny forty-foot steel canal boat, bobbing peacefully at her moorage on the Moselle River.

When Salah and Lilijana joined us at Kate's wedding, they graciously invited us aboard *Liljana* for a trip from Nancy to Paris. The invitation was too tempting to resist. If the locals are to be believed, France is geographically, culturally, and philosophically the center of Europe. Although the Gallic disposition can be trying, France projects an almost sensual appeal that keeps us coming back for more. Meandering 400 kilometers through the French Lorraine and Champagne regions promised to be a magical experience for us.

Over the course of two weeks *Liljana* negotiated 140 locks as we cruised down the Moselle River, intersected the Marne River, and continued on to the River Seine. Along the way we moored next to rural French farming villages and even motored *Liljana* under a mountain via the three-mile long Tunnel Souterraine de Mauvages. The four of us traipsed through the bubbly laden cellars of the House of Castellane in the Champagne capital of Epernay.

Three centuries ago Dom Perignon, the inventor of champagne, sagely observed that he was "drinking stars"—we had to agree.

Our crew tucked *Liljana* into her winter moorage at Port de Plaisance de Paris Arsenal, and then soaked up the ambiance of Paris. Salah and Liljana, as fellow cruisers, offered a bit of perspective as we related the trauma of our Port Orchard homecoming. They reminded PL and I of what we were about. Many of our friends had moved on, and we needed to do the same.

Although building and commissioning a canal boat in the Netherlands had been a challenging exercise for Salah and Liljana, their stories about blazing fields of tulips and miles of flat bike paths intrigued us. We were off.

A very fast TGV train whisked us from Paris to Amsterdam in four hours. I was still in the canal mode and Amsterdam was there for me. Over 1200 arched bridges cross 160 canals within the city's 60 miles of waterways. Amsterdam is one of Western Europe's favorite back packer haunts with its liberal drug laws and unobtrusive ordinances.

The Amstel River, with its picturesque gabled canal houses and sturdy wood houseboats, is the main drag through town. We slowly deciphered the map and finally figured out that any strange word ending in *gracht* meant canal and the city was full of them. During our informational hike we crossed a bridge at Korengracht and stumbled across the Hotel Hoksbergen, our kind of place—small, funky, and cheap.

Amsterdam is best seen astride a bike. PL and I rented a pair of basic one speeds, then we joined the masses pedaling to and fro around the city. Our cultural immersion continued. Bulldog and Pie were not selling pets and dessert—the main ticket items at a *bruine kroegen* were joints sold in small glass vials. Our little country mouse persona tickled the youthful clientele. To paraphrase our esteemed former president: "I did not inhale" or was it "Don't ask, don't tell."

Down the pike in the red light district, or *De Walletjes,* sleazy establishments give flesh a new meaning as the ladies of the night strut their stuff in the live window displays. Amsterdam is a live and let live city—the ladies of the world's oldest profession are not only regulated, but also unionized. I must have been gaping too much because PL flatly refused to visit the Erotic Museum, or for that matter, the Tattoo Museum. Actually the Van Gogh Museum was a much better choice and it was sure to score points with my art historian daughter.

Easy Everything, the biggest Internet facility in the world at that time, gave us our email fix from one of their 650 computers. Since I was behind the keyboard anyway, I downloaded Caribbean weather information from the NOAA website. The overall weather picture back in Bonaire looked promising. Now it was just a small matter of jetting back to the island and sailing west.

35

The Spanish Main

o o o o o o o o o o o o o o o o o o o o o o o o o o o o o o o o o o

The years thunder by. The dreams of youth grown dim where they lie caked in dust on the shelves of Patience. Before we know it, the tomb is sealed

—Sterling Hayden

After months of extended European travel, PL and I were wistfully philosophizing about the cruising life when our 747 touched down at JFK in New York. The huge plane disgorged scores of tired travelers, and then our group staggered towards the immigration officials. We dutifully presented our bulging passports to the bored looking officer, but suddenly things changed big time. The official snapped awake and halted the huge milling line behind us. He scrutinized PL and I up and down and then motioned us aside. I figured the computers had fingered us for visiting terrorist states and I was working on a good talking argument when the officer's voice broke through my reverie.

"How was your sailing trip?" Our starry eyed interrogator was fascinated by our adventure and just kept asking questions. The pressure was off—no strip search was forthcoming.

"Could I do it?" I assured the inquisitive inspector that such a trip was very doable, but the learning curve was a bit steep. The immigration guy gratefully thanked us for our time, stamped our passports, and motioned us on through the turnstile with an enthusiastic, "Welcome back!"

Impatient passengers moved in to take our place, but the harried bureaucrat was now a changed man. His eyes actually sparkled as he animatedly resumed his monotonous job. Dreams of distant sunsets and far away places can do that to a person.

In late September we were reunited with *Osprey* and found her to be in fine shape. My friend and former colleague Bob flew into Bonaire to join us for the offshore sailing passage to the San Blas Islands of Panama. The boat was stocked and ready to roll, but then the weather turned sour. Nasty weather systems can put a major crimp in the most carefully laid cruising plans. Surprise hurricanes are the worst of the lot.

We had recently resumed our weekly anti-malarial medication and I was aware that an uncommon side effect of our prophylactic Larium regimen was hallucinogenic episodes. After spending many seasons in the tropics, PL and I had taken the medication for months on end and had so far dodged both the attack dog moods and hallucinogenic trips. When I heard a hurricane warning being broadcast to all shipping in our vicinity, I just chalked it up to a hallucination. Such was not the case.

According to the conventional wisdom Bonaire is out of the Caribbean hurricane zone, but then Hurricane Joyce came to call. Over the next few days Joyce relentlessly headed our way, but she lost her lethal intensity in the process. Joyce was redesignated a tropical storm. The detuned storm eventually passed 80 miles north of Bonaire packing relatively sedate 30-knot winds. Most of the yachts anchored around Bonaire had initially wedged into our small marina because they assumed a catastrophic windstorm and ocean surge was headed for the island. Fortunately Joyce spun away to the northwest, but the giant conglomeration of tangled anchors, chafed lines, dinged boats, and frayed tempers took awhile to sort out.

Thanks to *The Finger of the gods*, no Larium induced delusions, and a bit of good luck we sailed two days later. The reinforced trade winds had piped up and my crew was smiling. Mindful that two boats had recently sunk after they collided with unidentified objects off the coast of Aruba, we decided to forego a visit and sail directly for the San Blas Islands.

The southeast corner of the Caribbean, from the shores of the Mosquito Coast to the coastal shelf of Panama and Columbia, transforms into an awe-inspiring wave-making machine during the fall and winter. Reinforced NE trade winds, originating thousands of miles away in the North Atlantic, sweep huge waves into this blind alley. With nowhere to go the waves pile up and create thundering breakers. The end result is a mind-blowing downwind sleigh ride for the sailor en route to Panama. *Osprey* spread her wings as she surfed down the face of the huge following seas. Boiling foam cascaded over the bow and sheets of spray glistened against the sails. Our rugged sloop tore through the bubbling foam with sheer abandon leaving a trail of sparkling phosphorus in her wake. We roared through the 720-mile passage in four days, a record passage for us.

It was all good—almost too good. Just to spice things up the servo rudder, the critical underwater part of our wind vane steering system, broke off and sank. Our boat suddenly became an unguided missile as she veered across the face of a massive wave, took a broadside blast from the pounding surf, and then wallowed in the huge troughs. Our hype vanished just like our steering system. As *Osprey* gyrated back and forth I checked out the carnage, rallied the troops, paid homage to our backup hydraulic autopilot, and then we were on our way again. The San Blas Islands were just over the western horizon and the prospect of a landfall looked mighty tantalizing at that stage.

The San Blas Islands lay about a hundred miles east of the Caribbean side of the Panama Canal. At first blush the miniscule islands are not very apparent on a world globe, but they are very real. 55,000 Kunas living in 48 island communities maintain their unique culture with a well-ordered independent government that could be the poster child for other banana republics in Central America.

We made a night landfall at Banedup Island, one of the 360 odd islands dotting the San Blas Archipelago. Rather than lying offshore for the night, our tired crew opted to anchor in a protected lagoon in the lee of the eastern Holandes Cays. Normally a night approach into an unknown cove is chancy at best, but I figured the pale moonlight bathing the placid water made it doable. Our night vision scope, radar, depth sounder, and GPS allowed us to thread the needle. Next morning I was jolted back to the harsh reality of cruising where inattention or bad luck can spell disaster. The lazy haze lifted like drifting gun smoke and before me a beautiful 45-foot sloop lay holed and abandoned on the reef fronting our anchorage. Eight months prior her owners had been living their dream when the unthinkable happened.

About midday *Kuna Freighter*, a twenty-foot wood canoe, putted into our anchorage and rafted alongside. Obviously the word was out that there were new kids on the block. Besides filling us in on the demise of the nearby sailboat, the four local Kunas had a few scrawny chickens and Coca Cola for sale. PL declined the unappetizing chickens, but our gift of a Marlboro welcome pack was a hit. The young entrepreneurs mumbled, *"gratias"* and then they were off in search of other potential marks…or customers.

The San Blas Islands are like a rerun of the South Pacific but on a much smaller scale. The exquisitely beautiful white sandy cays are dotted with waving palm trees and quaint thatch roofed huts. In the outer anchorages the warm, clear water is alive with colorful fish. Eagle and bat rays swoop around the coral heads. Spear fishing is fairly productive—many of the itinerant cruisers subsist on their catch of the day. Columbian schooners exchange gritty diesel and watered gasoline for San Blas coconuts. Apparently the stuff works for the locals, but it would not be a pretty picture if I ran it through my tanks.

Daily thunder and lightning storms roll through the islands as the weather transitions from the wet season to the dry season, although in Panama it is a blurred distinction at best. Blustery afternoons whipped the transparent waters into a foaming milkshake. Tropical cruising wisdom asserts that the darker the blue, the deeper the water—not necessarily so in the San Blas. Cruising waters close to the Panamanian mainland are on the murky side because heavy silt deposited by the jungle rivers mucks up the surrounding bays. Hidden rocks and jagged reefs could ruin our day so if water clarity took on that mocha look, my navigational plots and crosschecks increased exponentially.

Petty theft is an endemic problem since the Kuna society is based on communal sharing—visiting cruisers can unwittingly become unsuspecting donors. As in many parts of the Caribbean, the mantra still applied, "lock it or lose it." A decade prior PL and I had met an expat diver in Costa Rica who philosophically shared his views about petty theft in the Third World. His ultimate solution was to leave his house unlocked. The thieves did their thing and soon the house was cleaned out. With no more possessions to lose, the Costa Rican beachcomber insisted that his new minimalist existence set him free. I was not there yet—I installed fresh batteries in our motion detector and oiled up our padlocks.

One afternoon a crudely hollowed out log canoe carrying a couple of Kuna women and their barefoot children appeared out of nowhere. The paddlers were gaudily dressed in bright primary colors. Their wrists and legs were adorned with tiny strands of colorful beads that resembled multicolored socks. Gold necklaces, nose rings, and a midline tattoo on the bridge of their noses completed the Kuna look. Not the least bit intimidated, the tiny Kuna women pulled alongside *Osprey* and began hanging molas all over the rigging until our boat looked like a circus tent. The intricate appliqué designs are hand sewn onto clothing or used for decorative pillows and wall hangings. "*Mola bakke suli*," or "We do not buy molas," was our safety valve to relieve the high pressure selling of the aggressive ladies.

Kuna women are not easily discouraged. They also call the shots in their homes. It is the Kuna woman who makes the decision about who she wants to marry—the man she chooses must live with her family. If the relationship does not work out, separation is acceptable. Once the woman makes the decision to dissolve the marriage, she simply piles all her former husband's belongings outside the door and he must leave. The men may eventually remarry but unless the wife remarries first, her ex must wait to get her approval before choosing another bride. Never cross the Kuna ladies.

The ramshackle buildings on the edge of Provenir's miniscule airstrip housed customs and immigration, but there was a game to be played. The Kuna authorities enjoyed stamping our passports and *zarpas* even though the mainland bureaucrats do not always recognize their endorsement. Without suitable stamps on a *zarpa,* immigration officers in Costa Rica had been known to send yachts back to Panama. Just to be on the safe side I let the local guys stamp away.

A commuter turboprop taxied to the edge of the potholed airstrip and out popped Nick and Joan. Our good friends were back again for another visit. The pilot also unloaded an ice chest with my name on it—Panama Yacht Services had come through. A couple days prior I had called Julie at PYS, explained that our thirtieth anniversary was coming up, and that I needed her help. Since the local Kuna stores were limited to Quaker oats and Spam, Julie's timely delivery of prime cut steaks and chops added a civilized touch to our special celebration.

Brolio Henry is a Kuna guide who had spent a few years living in Newport Beach. Henry distained the California lifestyle and insisted that Sugtupu Island was where he belonged. As our crew wandered through the dusty traditional village of Carti Tupile, we had to agree that it was very unlike Southern California. We did not spot any surfers, but the village did have a basketball hoop. The closest thing to a Newport Beach sports car was the occasional wooden canoe with a small outboard slung on the backside.

Bob and Brolio Henry bonded. Henry, the consummate PR guy, assured Bob that a canoe trip up Rio Carti was not only doable but also the right thing to do. About 3 am a dugout canoe bumped against our hull and Bob hopped aboard. Henry and his helper insisted that they had the situation well in hand as the trio rowed off into the night. Although we were out of communication with Bob for weeks, he eventually paddled upriver and then, after a few misadventures, trudged out to the Pan American Highway.

As a Western Washington native I know about rain, or at least I thought I did. Portobelo, renowned as the wettest town on the coast, gives new meaning to being waterlogged. We sailed into town bundled up in foul weather gear, but about 8000 drenched pilgrims shrugged off the pounding rain as their slow procession celebrated the annual Fiesta of the Black Christ.

Sir Francis Drake used the soggy port as a base to rob Spanish merchantmen. Apparently the notorious pirate is still lurking in an elusive lead coffin in nearby coastal waters. The ruins of Fort San Fernando hark back to the early 1600's when the fort guarded the Spanish treasure fleet, or *flota*. The massive treasure galleons were loaded with gold and silver stolen from the Americas and destined for the coffers of the Spanish dons. Buccaneer Henry Morgan made it his business to relieve the Spaniards of a gold ingot or two whenever a galleon crossed his path. In the early 1900's the Panama Canal engineers formed part of the Panama Canal's Cristobal breakwater with huge chunks of stone from the old fort.

The El Torre Café is situated unobtrusively alongside the road leading into Portobelo. Vine covered beams supported the sagging roof of the café and delicate white flowers wove around the weathered window frames. The subtle fragrances of the small flowers lent a fresh sweet smell to the moist tropic air. Inside rows of wooden tables were draped with bright oilcloth and banked by scarred benches. Brown wrinkled men in worn cotton pants were seated companionably around one of the tables contentedly puffing their cigarettes—the smoke, dampened by the heavy mist of the almost continuous downpour, clung to the scarred rafters. At another table an elderly couple sipped Nescafe out of stained white mugs and stared at a psychedelic colored bus delivering pilgrims to the pageant.

As we ate our breakfast of melons and eggs, an unending throng of pilgrims passed in review outside the flower-draped windowsill. In the wake of the exhaust fumes, a devout man and his son walked hand in hand, their countenances serene and at peace. Three young girls could be seen following the man and boy. One of the teens was dressed in a bright purple robe trimmed with gold braid that flashed in the morning sun. Her robe symbolized their sojourn—a journey of the faithful in honor of the Black Christ. Thousands of believers rode, walked, or crawled past the El Torre Café in a serpentine procession towards town. Our most poignant memory was of a ragged pilgrim laying prostrate in the muddy rode. After reciting a litany of praise to the Black Christ, the bedraggled man staggered to his feet, walked a few more paces, and then flopped himself back into the mud while intensely praying to his lord and master. This man and many others of similar persuasion spent days crawling mile after mile towards Portobelo's cathedral and its elusive promise of divine intercession.

As a good Catholic boy, I attended a parochial school, memorized my catechism lessons, and put in my altar boy time. Although I followed a typical pattern of throwing off the constraints of Catholicism during college, I sought the reassurance of being in a church congregation as PL and I raised our children.

Any remnant of blind faith completely unraveled after the loss of my son.

I still grieved, I was still angry, and I still could not make the leap that losing Tyler was part of a natural plan that I was just not privy to. Although I admired the unwavering determination of the Portobelo throngs, the underlying dogma left me wanting.

In the far reaches of the ocean and on the isolated peaks of the mountains, I have come to know peace and perhaps to know something of God. Organized religions, no matter of what persuasion or pedigree, are ultimately creations of man. From what I gather, God has not endorsed one over all the others. I now find great comfort in the mystical philosophies of the East. The ethereal magic of Tyler's trademark shooting star has launched me on a fascinating personal journey of self-exploration.

36

The Ultimate Ditch

o o o o o o o o o o o o o o o o o o o o o o o o o o o o o o o o o o o o
Everything is on a colossal scale.

—*Scientific American*, March 18, 1911

In 1524 King Charles V of Spain presented his concept of a canal linking the Pacific and Caribbean, but the idea languished for centuries. In the twilight of the nineteenth century, the French attempted to build their version of a canal bisecting the Americas. Lethal tropical diseases, political squabbles, and inept engineering condemned the project so the Americans tried their hand at the canal business. After Doctor William Gorgas and his crew eradicated the breeding grounds for the mosquito, malaria and yellow fever no longer killed off workers by the thousands—the dream of a canal connecting the Atlantic to the Pacific became a reality. Colonel George Washington Goethals was the driving force behind the construction effort. In the midst of the canal construction, massive steam shovels excavated the equivalent of a Suez Canal every three years. American engineers dammed the Chagres River to create an artificial lake that provided water for the lock system and also served as the main waterway for vessel traffic. The canal was inaugurated in 1914 after 75,000 workers labored ten years to blast through the mountains, dam the river, and construct the grandest locks in the world.

The country of Panama owned and operated the Panama Canal for about a year when *Osprey* sailed into the Caribbean port city of Cristobal. The Panamanians were making up for lost time since the USA relinquished control in 1999. We were nicked $500 for our one-day transit. An $800 refundable deposit was also extracted on the off chance that our relatively miniscule 42 footer might damage one of the canal's gigantic 1000-foot long by 110-foot wide locks. A typical commercial ship pays around $30,000. If a skipper balks at the fees, or if your ship happens to be longer than 950 feet, wider than 106 feet, or draw more than 40 feet, then a trip around Cape Horn is the only alternative to the canal—I coughed up the money and moved on with my life.

The aging Panama Canal Yacht Club offered us a vacant berth on one of their rickety floats. Our crew was spared the poor alternative of anchoring in the Flats—a bay that funnels shipping in and out of the canal. Periodically large ships mangle small sailboats when mechanical problems or human error unexpectedly sends a wayward ship drifting through the Flats, a supposedly safe anchorage.

Beyond the concertina wire and cyclone fencing surrounding PCYC was the downtrodden town of Colon. Actually the place gave us bad vibes even in the daylight. Garbage was piled next to urine stained walls and graffiti, splashed in bold angry strokes, branded the buildings with despair. Tourist brochures extol the virtues of the Canal Zone but instead of tempting shops and intriguing markets, Colon's contribution is grungy buildings, barred windows, and well-armed security guards. Carlos, the resident taxi guy and gofer, sagely suggested that we were relatively safe from muggings if we confined our walks to daylight hours on Bolivar Street between 8th and 13th Avenue. Carlos wistfully assured us that Panama City, nestled on the Pacific side of the canal, was a radical departure from the likes of Colon.

The Panama Canal operates 24 hours a day, 365 days a year so the canal employees get lots of practice. Actually the entire process was relatively efficient, especially by Central American standards. Carlos was a master at ferreting out the local bureaucrats and expediting our paperwork. *Osprey* was officially measured and a transit number assigned within a few days of our arrival. Not only did our enterprising cabbie rustle up ten old tires and rent four 120-foot mooring lines on our behalf, he also offered his services and those of his friend as line handlers for our canal transit. Our crew wrapped the tires in garbage bags and dangled them over the sides of our boat—hull protection to ward off the rough concrete canal walls or other boats bent on playing bumper cars with us.

On the appointed day at 0500 I fired up *Osprey* and we motored out to the Flats. A pilot boat roared up alongside and our advisor hopped aboard. Unlike the professional pilots assigned to the large ships, small yachts only rate pilots in training. If a transiting yacht can maintain a speed of six knots and if the advisor is willing, the normal two-day transit can be accomplished in one day. Our guy and his cohorts liked the idea of overtime so a one-day transit appealed to their entrepreneurial side. For us the one-day transit eliminated the hassle and expense of providing food and bunks for Carlos and his friend.

We were fortunate to be 'nested' with two other sailboats, which allowed us to raft together and travel as a team inside the locks. *Pacific Grace, Deviant,* and *Osprey* lashed together measured 45 feet long by 50 feet wide—a formidable but unwieldy motorized fiberglass island featuring three decorative flagpoles. As the center boat in our small flotilla, *Deviant* provided the motor. *Pacific Grace* and *Osprey* were the outriders and we were in charge of steering. Basically a spider web of lines positioned our floating island between the raw concrete sides of the huge locks.

An 800-foot freighter led the way as *Deviant* motored our nested entourage into the Gatun Locks. The massive ship dwarfed our modest sized sloops, as we were all up-locked 85 feet into Gatun Lake. After the forward gates of the lock were swung open, the enormous ship added to the heavy surge of incoming current as she ponderously gathered speed and cleared the lock. The accepted wisdom is never to untie a small vessel until the raging river of inflowing water into the lock has dissipated. Yachties who fail to pay attention can end up spinning around inside the locks and smashing into the unforgiving concrete sidewalls. Fortunately our trio of boats made it through the locks unscathed. We separated to make the 31-mile transit across Gatun Lake. As we motored through the lush tropical backwaters of the Banana Cut and past the Smithsonian Tropical Research Institute, I felt like Bogey on the *African Queen.* Our crew gaped at the resident alligators, parrots, and monkeys—the Banana Cut is definitely a notch above Disneyland's Jungle Ride.

Nick, our resident Panama Canal buff, pointed out that the Gaillard Cut, a nine-mile ditch blasted through tons of rock and shale, is a monumental example of ingenious engineering. The Cut is indeed awesome and it also straddles the Continental Divide, our official exit from the Caribbean. At the Pedro Miguel Locks, our trio of sailboats renested. We reenacted our spider web imitation, but this time at the front of the lock. The huge vessel that was our companion early on joined us again. After the ship was secured behind us, we were all down-locked 31 feet. Handily the behemoth transport now served as our blocker when a torrent of current swept in through the rear lock gates. The process was repeated at Miraflores as we down-locked another 54 feet into the Pacific Ocean. The world's largest ocean awaited us and, as promised, Panama City proved to be quite an upgrade compared to Colon.

The small store fronting the Balboa Yacht Club pier offers fuel, water, ice, and beer—all the essentials. As we stocked *Osprey* I noticed a couple of familiar faces aboard *High Drama,* a sailboat tied next to us. A few years prior PL and I had sipped sundowners with Jeff and Ann aboard their chartered sailboat in French

Polynesia. They were fascinated by our lifestyle and offhandedly mentioned that they dreamed of eventually cruising the world in their own boat.

In my experience relatively few people make the commitment to follow their dreams, but Jeff and Ann were doing just that. Rather than offer advice, I enjoyed sharing a few moments with like-minded voyagers. As we sailed back into the Pacific, *High Drama* entered the Panama Canal bound for the Caribbean.

37

Hanging Out in Central America

Many men go fishing all their lives without knowing that it is not fish they are after.

—Henry David Thoreau

The infamous windward slog from Panama to Seattle is said to favor sailors with a stoic disposition, good raingear, and lots of time. I figured it was doable so now we were testing the theory. The setting was spectacular—smoldering rays of the western sun highlighted the anvil head of a distant thundercloud as the Golfo de Chiriuis unfolded before us. The Panama Canal disappeared in our wake as *Osprey* caught the racing ebb outbound into the gulf. Lots of big iron, the heavy shipping traffic bound to and from the Panama Canal, merged just a few miles off our port beam as *Osprey* charged over the broad Pacific swells. Next morning Punta Mala slipped past our starboard beam and I changed our southerly course to a northwest heading. As we paralleled the coastline, the uninvited vanguard of huge ships tracked outbound over the western horizon. Now we were alone except for the pods of frolicking porpoise that crisscrossed our bow wave.

Since the entire gulf is only a few degrees north of the equator, the weather is usually hot, humid, and prone to thunderstorms—the doldrums of the Intertropical Convergence Zone. The pristine islands dotting the Pacific Coast of Panama are astonishingly untarnished and relatively unaffected by tourism. In a secluded cove on the northeast tip of Isla Parida, the jungle reclaimed the shattered remains of a Canadian couple's dream resort. Rusted ceiling fans, broken cupboards, unhinged doors, and overflowing cisterns diluted the tropical atmosphere. It was an unsettling commentary on the fickle nature of the tourist trade in remote tropical areas.

Isle Coiba, just over the horizon from the failed resort, features some of the world's best sports fishing. The island's infamous prison, now closed, is just a fading memory as ecotourists and big game fishermen have replaced the notorious convicts. Striking tropical birds, lethal reptiles, enormous sailfish, and huge sharks are heady ingredients in the region's extraordinary concoction of fascinating creatures.

One of our favorite places along the 300-mile route from Balboa to the Costa Rican frontier is Bahia Honda, a protected bight in the Panamanian mainland. A few scruffy cattle grazed on a bit of pastureland hacked from the encroaching jungle. A derelict shack was the only sign of a proposed "yacht club"—a futile attempt to transform the stunning cove into a destination anchorage for the cruising crowd. Wild rhododendrons and azaleas and bougainvillea infiltrated the unfinished foundation. Curious parrots and toucans peered down at us from towering coconut palms as we explored the place. The surrounding jungle resonated with all manner of exotic birdcalls. A battered concrete bunker turned out to be a functional, spring fed outdoor shower. Unlimited showers on a beautiful tropical beach brought a few smiles from my shower deprived, overheated crew.

We celebrated Halloween with the American ketch *Echelon*. PL and Joan whipped up some brownies while the four *Echelon* kids spent the day on the beach hacking away at reeds, gourds, leaves, and coconuts in pursuit of the 'right' costume. That evening the foursome, now transformed into fearsome natives wearing intimidating carved masks, came aboard *Osprey* to "trick or treat." It was definitely our treat.

Rounding Punta Burica, *Osprey* bashed through heavy seas and slashing rain as we pounded our way into Golfo Dulce and Costa Rica's territorial waters. By late afternoon a pale glint of sun popped through the washed out sky and the tortuous entrance to Golfito emerged out of the mist. Just after sunset we heard the roar of breaking surf as I was lining up the range markers for our ticklish entrance into the harbor. That was my first clue that perhaps the range markers were not all that they could be. I jammed the transmission in reverse and regrouped. Gingerly I plotted a new course disregarding questionable range markers and unlighted buoys. The locals must have scored a bargain on red paint since every buoy, regardless if it was to our port or starboard, was slathered in the stuff. No black or green for the folks in Golfito. As was our custom in the previous three-dozen foreign countries, our host country's courtesy flag flew from our starboard flag halyard. After five years only the courtesy flags for El Salvador and Guatemala were still unused.

Bruce, the harbormaster at Banana Bay Marina, treated us well despite the late hour. Customs, immigration, and the port captain were amiable guys who joined me in the bar and handled the paperwork as Nick, Joan, and PL headed for the hot showers. Bruce presented the gracious officials with a bottle of Scotch for their trouble. Our well-worn and heavily stamped international *zarpa* worked its magic again as the local bureaucrats nodded appreciatively. About the same time, one of our cruising sidekicks was presently stuck in El Salvador with no exit stamps from Costa Rica on his *zarpa*. Eventually the owner of Barillas Marina in El Salvador interceded on his behalf, but our friend initially faced the prospect of retracing his route to Costa Rica to beg for a missing signature and stamp. I did not need the aggravation.

Costa Rica is an eco-friendly place that boasts democratic institutions and a well-educated population. Unique to Central America, Costa Rica has no standing army. Ticos, a population of largely European extraction, make up 85 percent of the population and many expat Americans call the place home. In bygone days Golfito was a booming town thanks to the United Fruit Company, but the company synonymous with banana republics has moved on. Tourism in the forms of sport fishing, eco adventures, and a duty free shopping zone only partially fills the void.

Before Nick and Joan flew home, the four of us toasted our adventures at Mikes, a down home jungle steakhouse which rocked to juke box sounds from the '60's. Next morning a dusty, rusted out taxi wheeled up to the marina with a shy old Tico at the helm. The driver assured me that he was just the fellow to transport our friends to Golfito's small grass airstrip. Nick told me later that the route was convoluted at best. As the cab bounced along the narrow dirt road, the cabbie proceeded to pick up new riders along the way. The latest additions, crammed into the compact size cab, were local folks who needed a lift but had little money. In the end the driver delivered his friends to their destinations and he just assumed Nick would be more than happy to pick up the whole tab. As the evolution unfolded, the cab passed a small church. The driver unexpectedly slowed as he and the uninvited passengers made the Sign of the Cross and bowed their heads. Such gracious rural manners reminded me that civility and faith make the world a much better place.

My manners were tested the next day. As I flushed out our struggling refrigeration condenser, I accidentally splashed muriatic acid in my eye. I rocketed out of the bowels of the boat in record time, howling a few assorted profanities along the way. Listening to the racket PL figured I must not have been faking it. She grabbed hold of my head and dunked my face into a sink of water. The sudden wakeup call was another reminder that when it hits the fan, there is no substitute for a reliable mate who will see you through—it is love, and then some.

Bruce warned that the locals did not handle fresh fish well. He figured our best bet was to wait for the December sport fishing season when the high-end gringo sport fishing boats sold fresh yellow fin and dorado from their luxurious teak decked cockpits. Although our schedule did not allow us to dilly-dally in Golfito, Bruce was right about the great December fishing. My trusty green squid lure kept our freezer stocked with fresh fish all the way up the Central American coastline.

After rounding Peninsula de Osa, PL and I coast hopped past the Marenco-Corcorado National Park. Over 220 inches of rain a year pour onto the steaming jungle canopy and we got our share. Next up was the anchorage at Manuel Antonio National Park, an exquisitely beautiful place. Although there are dozens of national parks in Costa Rica, Manuel Antonio is the coastal gem. A starkly handsome rainforest framed the fine white sand shores of the coast. PL and I anchored *Osprey* and then swam ashore to enjoy the spectacular beach. The jungle is reportedly home to three-toed sloths, wild boars, coatimundis, and iridescent moths but we contented ourselves with the gymnastics of the local squirrel monkeys. Although advertised, no jaguars came to call.

Peace and tranquility…then the huge *Temptress Voyager*, an ecotourist boat from Honduras, had the audacity to anchor in our personal cove. The ship disgorged a fleet of inflatables and kayaks, and then hordes of passengers assaulted the previously deserted shoreline. By day khaki clad crewmen ferried lounge chairs to the beach bunnies; by night white uniformed waiters catered to the shipboard whims of the tourists. The harried captain stopped by to talk it over—he envied our adventure and would gladly swap jobs if given the chance. Around midnight the deep throb of powerful diesels and a grinding anchor chain fulfilled the skipper's promise to vacate our anchorage. The big steel floating carnival upped anchor and was out of there.

In the early '90's PL and I, as well as Kate and Tyler, flew to Costa Rica for a few weeks of family vacation. I recall how I wandered along Flamingo Beach and talked it over with a European yachtsman who had just pulled his dinghy ashore. As I longingly gazed at his beautiful sloop anchored outside the surf line, I peppered him with question after question. In the end I asked him if world cruising was all it was cracked up to be. My new friend nodded his head affirmatively. He insisted such an adventure was worth doing—he had no regrets. I treasured the anonymous yachtie's insightful comments for years and now as *Osprey* sailed past Flamingo Beach a decade later, his sage advice rang even more true.

Endangered leatherback turtles, resembling drifting bales of hay, bobbed along in the long Pacific swells. The big guys would eye us as they sedately paddled out of our way, sometimes with a blue-footed booby bird perched on their backs. They were methodically and instinctively returning to their Central American nesting grounds. An occasional bump against our hull announced a real slow mover—the flash of a primordial dining room table size shell and a few gurgling bubbles was its calling card.

Bahia de Culebra, named for the resident snakes, is the most spacious anchorage in Central America and the jumping off place for the passage across the notorious Gulf of Papagayo. Huge manta rays cavorted across the placid harbor and brilliantly colored sea snakes paddled by our boat. The Gulf of Papagayo was in a kind mood the next morning so we scooted north. With such a first-rate weather window to greet us, a good morning Costa Rican farewell snorkel at Bahia Murcielogos had appeal. The verdant rain forest gave way to dry scrub and parched rocky terrain. Although Murcielogos rates as one of Costa Rica's most spectacular diving destinations, PL and I considered it middle of the road. What the coral lacked in vibrancy was augmented by the brilliant colors of the Picasso (our favorite trigger fish), angelfish, and the coral chomping parrotfish. My mission was to rustle up a few of the barrel cactus from the slopes of Isla San Jose and supplement our on board Greek cactus collection. I waded ashore, transferred a couple of the prickly customers into a wide mouthed plastic jug, and then side stroked back to the boat with the jug held high. The trick was to keep our new Costa Rican cactus dry without drowning me in the process. A few vultures spiraled down for a closer look while a solitary osprey serenely took the whole thing in from his cactus perch.

The Pacific waters of Costa Rica, Nicaragua, El Salvador, Guatemala, and Mexico teem with porpoise, turtles, fish, and whales as well as an occasional sea snake or two. PL and I encountered relatively benign conditions from Panama to Mexico. Rather than coping with nasty weather, we simply enjoyed the stunning vistas and fascinating sea life. Mist shrouded mountains and enticing palm fringed shorelines birthed coke bottle green rivers. The runoff tinged the indigo blue coastal waters gunmetal grey. Frisky porpoise, nature's version of heat seeking missiles, streamed a trail of phosphorus as they homed in on our bow wave. The joyously inquisitive creatures would roll sideways to stare up at us as we peered down at them. Looking into the serene eyes of such a wonderful animal is a glimpse into the cosmos—an intimate moment of unbridled bliss.

38

The Overlooked Middle

Be kind for everyone you meet is fighting a great battle.

—*Philo*

Sailing across the Gulf of Papagayo can be a nail biting, exhausting trip through chaotic seas and wicked winds. Lucky for us it was calm as we rounded Cabo Santa Elena and beam reached across the gulf. Until recently most cruisers avoided the "Forgotten Middle" of Central America and hightailed it directly to southern Mexico, over 500 miles to the north. Numerous stories about unpleasant encounters with Nicaraguan patrol boats were all the impetus we needed to assiduously avoid Nicaraguan coastal waters. To the northwest, across the Golfo de Fonseca, El Salvador beckoned. It was just a matter of dodging hordes of fishing boats to get there.

El Salvador is the smallest and most densely populated Central American country. About the size of Massachusetts, it features over two-dozen extinct volcanoes as well as a few active ones. A brutal civil war racked the country for more than a decade until 1992. 75,000 people died and a quarter of the population emigrated. Free elections subsequently brought a new president to power. A couple hundred families now control the land and the subsequent destiny of the country's chronically poor populace.

After a night of evading rusting shrimp boats, PL and I spied Volcano San Miguel silhouetted by a breathtaking golden sunrise. The obscure headlands took on the color of burnished pewter as they emerged above the mangroves and palm trees. As we edged closer to the surf line of Bahia de Jiquilisco, our radio crackled to life. Barillas Marina advised us that a panga would be dispatched shortly to guide us over the tricky bar crossing at Lempa Shoals.

The rugged panga originated in Baja's LaPaz but is now the quintessential fiberglass skiff of Central America. Approximately twenty feet long, the outboard powered floating pickup truck has a range of power options usually dictated by the net worth of the owner. In this case well-funded Barillas Marina owned a virtual rocket sled and it showed up before we finished our morning coffee. Francisco the guide flashed a thumbs-up as Kreese, probably a frustrated hydroplane driver at heart, gunned the panga across the shoals and between the breakers flanking both sides of the very narrow bar entrance. PL and I prayed for deliverance as I hesitantly committed *Osprey* to a wild white-knuckled ride across the bar. We surfed over the shoals through sheets of spray as we blew past the foaming breakers.

Just inside the surf line the boys in the panga pointed out a jungle estuary that was virtually invisible from offshore. After we had meticulously weaved through a shallow 10-mile long mangrove lined canal, the Texaco Star rose out of the misty jungle like an apparition. But we were not dreaming—the petroleum icon was perched above the modern fuel dock at Barillas Marina. Dozens of substantial mooring buoys dotted the river front digs. A charming restaurant and an amazingly well supplied store serviced the heavily guarded compound, the brainchild of El Salvadorian entrepreneur Juan Wright. Internet access was only a download away at the modem outlet equipped, umbrella topped picnic benches. The marina, inaugurated less than a year before, provided transportation, complete with an armed guard, into the neighboring town of Usulutan.

Lewis and his shotgun toting guard drove us to the war weary town of San Miguel. The people, descendents from the Mayan and Aztec cultures, were shy but friendly. PL's blond hairdo absolutely fascinated the black haired local women. At the Pollo Comparo restaurant, the Latin American equivalent of Kentucky Fried Chicken, we met a couple that fled the gunfire in 1990. They had immigrated to the California, become US citizens, and started a successful landscape business—now they were back for a visit with their children.

Francisco assured me that his friend Santos was the guy to repair my outboard. The catch was that Santos lived a dozen miles upriver. Francisco and Lewis loaded me, as well as my unhealthy outboard, into their panga and proclaimed "No problem" as they torched off their huge engine and screamed upriver to a small riverfront village. In a dirt shack adorned with one light bulb, girlie calendars from the '50's, and dusty mounds of outboard motor parts, the chubby owner resurrected my outboard. He just chuckled when I showed him my store bought engine manual—the guy was into fixing, not reading.

By far our best dinner deal was dining at the shrimp boat repair facility next door to Barillas Marina. Archie Baldochie's Shrimp Boat Repair operation charged visitors $4 when they ate at his employee's cafeteria. Besides the good deal on eats, Archie ran a great repair operation. Louis, their refrigeration technician, flushed out my refrigeration system, fixed a leaky piece of refrigerant tubing, and recharged the system for $12. I liked the price of doing business in El Salvador.

PL and I were now ready to sail on to neighboring Guatemala. Heriberto Pineda, the Barillas Marina manager, graciously booked a room for us at Hotel Casa Santa Domingo in Antigua, Guatemala. Heriberto assured me Casa Santa Domingo was his favorite venue in Central America and that we would find the accommodations, service, and ambiance top notch.

In the wee hours Francisco and Kreese guided us back through the mangroves and into the more familiar and much deeper waters of the Pacific. As we sailed further north our VHF radio crackled to life again as Bahia de Sol, no more than a smudge off our starboard quarter, invited us to sail in and stay awhile. If we had not just cleared out of the El Salvador at Barillas Marina, we would have accepted the offer and followed their accommodating sport fishing boat across another bar and into their new marina complex.

El Salvador made international news a short time later when monstrous earthquakes obliterated entire communities. The tragedy was especially distressing for us since we had befriended Francisco, a local guide, and we had actually visited some of those same desperately poor villages a few months prior to the disaster. Canadian cruisers Malcolm and Jackie were in country during the earthquakes. Their description of the total devastation was sobering. We were deeply moved by their decision to stay behind and help to rebuild one of the hard hit neighborhoods.

There was no shortage of local color on our coastal cruise north to Guatemala. A booby bird decided to take up residence by riding on the horizontal aluminum spreaders that sprout laterally from our mast. At first we thought the interloper was sort of cute but the blue-footed hitchhiker wore out its welcome as bird droppings splattered on our deck. I returned the favor with a blast from our pressurized wash down hose. And then there was *The Green Flash*…somewhere off the west coast of Central America. After all those ocean sunsets PL and I finally saw the rare green glow linger for just an instant on the western horizon as the blazing orange sun dove into the far reaches of the Pacific.

Guatemala, Central America's third largest country, is infamous for its decades old civil war that began in 1960 and only recently ended in 1996 when a coalition of rebel groups signed a peace accord. The US State Department still issued consular warnings, but nothing we had not seen or heard before.

Puerto Quetzel is basically a quiet protected anchorage tucked into the Naval Base. PL polished up her Spanish to alert the navy officials that *Osprey* would be making a night approach. It was not difficult for them to track us. They just had to look for the sailboat dodging the huge motorized dredge that constantly worked the channel entrance. The courteous naval officials charged $150 for a five-day stay inside their very secure harbor. Mario was the lieutenant in charge of the largest patrol boat in the harbor. When I mentioned my ongoing hassle with a sick starting battery, Mario ordered his mechanics, Max and Eduardo, to come aboard and solve the problem. Although the accommodating guys were more than willing to tackle any mechanical problem, they only had to replace a frayed v-belt on the alternator.

Just as dogs seem to be an anthropomorphic image of their humans, the huge 220-foot salvage tug *Megaton* seemed to be a caricature of her burly no nonsense skipper. Captain Al gave us the tour of his massive 8000 horsepower vessel. Even the 'small' diesels that powered the gigantic fire fighting water cannons were ten times the size of *Osprey's* fifty horsepower putter. As one of the few large salvage tugs south of Seattle, Al handled emergency response for ships in crisis throughout the Pacific. If need be Al and his crew could steam for two months at a stretch. The big dredge at the harbor entrance did not look quite so imposing from the bridge deck of the monster tug.

PL and I joined Mike, our taxi driver and guide, for a grocery run into the nearby town of Escuintla. We savored our deliverance from wheeling dealing moneychangers as we marveled at the town's new ATM—then it swallowed our only bankcard. Mike nonchalantly knocked on the bank's barred door and explained the sad dilemma of his gringo clients to the sympathetic bank manager. The moneyman disassembled the new fangled contraption and retrieved our ATM card. The kindly banker turned us over to a teller for money exchange in the old fashioned, hands on way.

Although kidnapping foreigners seemed to be the newest cash crop in many Latin American countries, Mike assured us that travel in Guatemala was relatively safe. We teamed up with Jennifer and Bruce of *Jubula* to spend a few days exploring the Altiplano, the western high lands. The stunning beauty of the serene countryside with its mountain lakes, coffee plantations, and Mayan ruins made us forget that the local economy had been trashed by 30 years of civil war. Mike insisted that the unfortunate cremation of two Japanese nationals by Mayan tribesman was an isolated incident. We subsequently learned that the border between Guatemala and Mexico was a very dangerous place for the tourist crowd.

Lake Atitlan, one of the most astonishingly beautiful lakes in Central America, is renowned for its shimmering lapis blue waters. The enormous lake fills a volcanic crater more than ten miles wide and half again as long. In lakeside Panajachel our bungalow was hidden behind stonewalls draped with brilliantly colored bougainvilleas. A homey little café just down the winding road featured my definitive food pyramid—grilled jumbo prawns, frosty mugs of draft beer, and Cohiba cigars.

The eccentric owner of the local macadamia nut farm preached that if his macadamia oil did not cure what ailed you, your life had probably taken a decided turn for the worse. The Valhalla Macadamia Farm was a trip in every sense of the word. The experimental botanical station cultured four hundred varieties of macadamia trees—an attempt to achieve a sustainable, high quality forest product without slashing and burning the fragile rain forest. PL scored on a facial, manicure, pedicure, and waxing as the beauticians extolled the virtues of their macadamia nut skin products. I still have some of the macadamia wonder oil so if WD 40 ceases to exist, I am covered.

Although it is situated at the base of a volcano, the colonial Spanish city of Antigua has still managed to survive for the last four centuries. Herberto, of Barillas Marina fame, had definitely come through for us and Hotel Casa Santo Domingo was everything Herberto had promised. PL and I celebrated an elegant Thanksgiving dinner in the candle lit recesses and contemplative atmosphere of the hotel, originally a formidable monastery built in 1642. Our suite was so charming and cozy that we vowed to recreate the feeling someday assuming we made it back home. Our wandering ways taught us that impermanence is not such a bad thing. We had learned to let go of many attachments and it had set us free. Love permeated our lives so the rest of the extraneous stuff seemed to sort itself out.

39

The Mexican Riviera

One may not reach the dawn save by the path of the night.

—*Kahlil Gibran,* **Sand and Foam**

In 1848 General Santa Ana lost his war with the United States and subsequently Mexico lost more than half of its territory. No wonder that over the years relations have been strained as Mexicans envision what could have been had Texas and California stayed part of their traditional homeland. We sailed across Mexico's southern frontier on a moonless night. I had just staggered up on deck for my four-hour watch when PL muttered something about a fast moving radar target a few miles to the east. I could not make out what the fast mover was about, but I will always remember the blood red laser gun sight beam that flitted around our cockpit and then disappeared along with the radar target.

Our South African friends aboard *Jubula* were boarded and searched by military types when they sailed into the steamy backwater of Puerto Madero. The *Osprey* crew must have looked pretty straight because the intimidating black uniformed soldiers in the sinister looking charcoal grey patrol boats just waved at us. The Port Captain at Puerto Madero was a very accommodating fellow who proudly showed us his new baby, a relatively modern computer complete with Internet access to the latest weather reports. The Captain assured me that he would let us know when it was good to go across the Gulf of Tehuantepec, one of the most treacherous stretches of water on the Pacific Coast.

The valley at the Isthmus of Tehuantepec is a north-south gulch that cuts between two imposing mountain ranges. The gorge links the Gulf of Mexico with the Pacific Ocean as it transects mainland Mexico at its narrowest point. This geological channel is the breeding ground for many Mexican hurricanes. Hurricane alley racks the Gulf of Tehuantepec with gales, infamously known as

Tehuantepeckers, about 40 percent of the time. Since we were not into getting whacked by a gale, caution was the operative word. Basically the key to beating the system is to mind the weather and hug the beach with ten or so fathoms under the keel. Although an unexpected Tehuantepecker can still cause a lot of aggravation, the foot on the beach approach keeps a boat out of the middle of the gulf where huge violent seas can drive the unsuspecting skipper hundreds of miles out into the Pacific.

Wind races from high pressure to low pressure. The greater the pressure differential, the faster the wind blows. When the high-pressure in the Gulf of Mexico dissipates, the gale force winds screaming south across the Isthmus of Tehuantepec moderate and the critical eighty-mile passage across the Gulf of Tehuantepec between Punta Arista and Salina Cruz becomes much more user friendly. After a couple days of waiting for a good weather window, the Port Captain told us to go for it. Although the coastal shelf dished up a bit of short chop for us, PL and I only encountered a few hours of feisty sailing during our 200-mile dash around the periphery of the gulf. At sunrise lightning strikes miles off our stern quarter tore through mammoth columns of bruised cumulus clouds in the "Dragon's Mouth," but we were long gone. *Osprey* had the breeze under her skirts and the pressure was off.

Our reward for enduring this lumpy qualifying round was access to the Mexican Riviera, an idyllic cruising area that stretches from Huatulco in the south to Puerto Vallarta in the north. The stunning 600-mile coastline rates as one of our favorite tropical cruising destinations. Secluded strands of seemingly endless sandy beaches are tucked into the rugged, parched landscape of the Sierra Madre del Sur. Long gentle Pacific rollers and powder blue skies became our standard fare. Pelicans and frigates as well as turtles, manta rays, porpoise, and whales were along for the ride. Fishing was excellent—the best of our entire trip around the planet. Dorado and sierra mackerel favored our green squid lure and we favored fresh fish so it was definitely a win, at least from our perspective.

Even though it was a Mexican holiday celebrating the inauguration of President Fox, the port official at API (national port authority) in Huatulco graciously opened his office and issued our clearance papers. My tip was vigorously refused as our benefactor explained that corruption and bribes were embarrassing vestiges of old Mexico and his new president was out to change the national image for the better.

Just a day sail to the north, the snug anchorage and quaint village of Puerto Angel beckoned. Actually I came to talk it over with Papagayo, the Villa Florencia's resident parrot. Papagayo was famous for speaking three languages, but he had unexpectedly died. The hotel's manager wistfully recalled Papagayo's linguistic prowess, and then he whipped up a batch of incredible pesto pasta as sort of a tribute to the dearly departed parrot. After our Italian hit, PL and I agreed that we needed to work off the meal. As we tromped around the dusty streets, we were blissfully unaware of the little village's ongoing security problems. Just after our visit a couple of local thugs ransacked our friend's sailboat, apparently looking for drugs and money.

We ghosted north in the low western swell as the gentle sea breeze kissed our sails. The wild and surreal coastline of Oaxaca, less than a mile away, slid past our starboard bow. Some forty miles inland the Sierra Madre del Sur soared 12,000 feet into the cobalt blue sky. Air and sea temperatures mimicked each other with readings in the mid 80's. Suddenly a towering spray shot skyward from a glistening black hump just off our bow—maybe the lone humpback whale just wanted company. As the unhurried afternoon surrendered to twilight, the molten sun dripped flaming golden rain on the western horizon. By night the cool white glow of the waxing moon flooded the ocean surface with ethereal strands of refracted moonbeams. The comforting glow of ancient navigational stars served as sparkling guideposts throughout that impossibly beautiful night passage.

At the Acapulco Yacht Club, a 70 year old "dock boy" by the name of Edmundo took our lines and helped us jockey into a vacant berth. The folks at AYC have been in the yacht club business for over six decades and it shows. The club is nestled on a huge waterfront lot fronting the ten-kilometer horseshoe shaped expanse of Acapulco Bay. My logbook entry read like a travel brochure that could just as well have been describing Rio. The elegant yacht club is mated to an expansive tropical garden replete with multiple swimming pools and a fine restaurant. Attentive waiters served our poolside drinks and efficient staffers handled our check-in/check-out *zarpas*. The luxurious showers, reliable shore power, safe drinking water, and clean fuel spoiled us. But PL reminded me that she was overdue for a bit of pampering.

Our favorite haunt was at the Zocalo in Old Acapulco. The Feast of Our Lady of Guadalupe was in full swing in a carnival like atmosphere. Just up a steep winding road the Le Quebrada high divers swan dived off a 45-meter cliff just as they have every day since 1934. PL and I had come to enjoy these vestiges of old Mexico so an inland side trip seemed like a great idea.

Oscar Perez, our guide and driver, was at the helm as our van cruised into the picturesque old silver mining town of Taxco. Perched on top of an 1800-meter high silver veined mountain, the colonial hill town of Taxco boasts over 250 silver shops. Cobble stoned streets wind through a maze of alleys that house silver shops, art galleries, and cafes. The Baroque twin-towered Iglesia de Santa Prisca church dominates the town's skyline. Scores of VW bugs and vans, Taxco's unique taxi fleet, zipped through the labyrinth of narrow streets oblivious to interloping pedestrians. At a thriving outdoor market, a shriveled old lady proudly pointed out the wriggling contents of her gaily-painted jars. The wrigglers happened to be jumiles, the small beetles that migrate annually to the hills behind Taxco. The locals eat the crunchy beetles mixed with salsa and rolled in a tortilla. PL and I went ethnic, closed our eyes, and chomped on the very organic tortilla. For the record, jumiles do not taste like chicken!

Zihuatanejo, with its acres of palm trees and miles of sweeping beach vistas, has been a favorite vacation retreat for generations of Mexicans. Z-town is also a great cruising hangout—one of our favorites. The town retains much of its wonderful fishing village charm while supporting many good restaurants, shops, and markets.

At the new Commercial Supermarket, dozens of well-scrubbed personable local kids worked as bag boys and bag girls. Since these enterprising youngsters actually helped to support their huge families, a generous tip was very much appreciated. Although he spoke no English, our small bag boy took no chances with his gringo customers. On the front of the young lad's apron someone had obligingly stitched an unequivocal message: *I work for tips.*

The older embodiment of the entrepreneurial spirit was Ischmael. When anchored cruising boats radioed for basic supplies, Ischmael fielded the calls on his old VHF portable radio. In good time Ischmael and his helper would motor out in his battered panga to deliver diesel, water, beer, and pop. It was sort of an on call floating 7-11 operation.

Feliz navidad roughly translated means ordering a pint or two at Rick's Bar, the local yachtie watering hole. PL and I enjoyed a bit of small time celebrity status since we were within a couple hundred miles of completing our circumnavigation of the world. We presented a few talk shows, dragged out assorted memorabilia, and fielded questions from erstwhile voyagers. Questions became more interesting as the beer flow increased—my cruising guru veneer washed away in the froth of the free flowing suds. Old Mexican hands shared their stories about the fabulous cruising possibilities south of the US border. First timers sat bolt upright, like deer caught in the headlights, as tales of exotic ports and untamed seas bounced off the walls of the bar. I can shoot the breeze with the best of them, but sometimes the recollections and admonishments got mighty thick and threatened to drown our audience in a sea of the stuff.

I donated a copy of our cruising articles to the growing cruiser library at Ricks but as I looked through the library's offerings, I found our 1995 technology had been quantum leaped. Our vintage underpowered laptop, mail drops at AMEX, and scribbled chart notes were old news. The folks just heading out were equipped with lightning fast computers, sophisticated onboard email programs, and electronic charts. Although their boats were bigger and their equipment fancier, the neophyte voyagers would soon find that the fates have a way of leveling the playing field at the most inopportune times.

PL's sister Susie and her two daughters brightened up our holiday season by joining us for Christmas. Mark and Shannon joined us as well. In the finest tradition of visiting crew, bro Mark schlepped a duffel bag of spare parts to Z-town to satiate *Osprey's* lust for replacement parts. Mexican airport customs officials require each new arrival to push a button on a traffic light affair. A green light signals that you and your baggage are free to enter Mexico. A red light, supposedly only a random event, means that you and/or your luggage will be searched. Since the duty on imported marine parts is quite stiff, a red light can translate into a lot of hassle and expense. Fortunately Mark and Shannon got the green light as they strolled past the customs officials with my refurbished water maker tucked under Mark's burly arm.

A venerable local bus chugs back and forth over the hillside separating charming Z-town from glitzy Ixtapa. Although itinerant guitar players serenading passengers adds local color, we ended up donating a lot of pesos for questionable music. After spending a week at anchor off the beach at Z-town and having endured the bus ride once too often, PL and I decided to sail around the bend and spend some time at Marina Ixtapa.

Marina Ixtapa is a huge modern facility, but its Mexican heritage insures a quirk or two. The quirks just happened to be resident 6 to 12 foot crocodiles that liked to float in empty slips or sun themselves on the docks. The toothy critters also seemed to enjoy waddling through the stream that bordered the nearby golf course. Although the marina's "no swimming" signs warned about the huge reptiles, I did not see any signs that cautioned hackers to proceed gingerly when wandering through the rough at the golf course. All the hype did not faze the struggling Mexican divers scouring the bottoms of gringo yachts. Not only did the unfortunate guys have to put up with the crocs, but they also had to suck air through questionable air compressors that were designed to paint houses, not to sustain the life of a submerged diver.

Snorkeling with crocs was definitely not on our dance card so I fired up the dinghy for a visit to Isla Blancas, just a few miles west of the marina. Our old friends the Moorish idol, trigger, wrasse, angel, globe, puffer, and needlefish finned around in the clear warm water. A striped moray peered out from a rocky crevice. Pelicans, frigates, and boobies congregated on the jagged granite cliffs as if they wanted nothing to do with the homely vultures that aimlessly circled overhead.

The dazzling Michoacan coastline is a primal 190-mile stretch of rocky cliffs and dense jungle stretching from Z-town to Manzanillo. A few sheltered bights indent the rugged coast but they offer only marginal anchorages. The iffy anchorage at Muruata is renowned for its impressive setting. Since the weather was settled, we decided to drop the hook for the night. The long strand of sandy beach with its picturesque surf breaks and the gently swaying coconut palms lulled us into an afternoon siesta. Suddenly a barrage of rapid fire Spanish snapped us back to reality. Next to our boat was a panga with two distraught young fishermen aboard. The local boys had tangled their flimsy net in our anchor and things were looking dim for their team. I unleashed the *Finger of the gods* and gave the stricken boys thumbs up. PL and I did our thing and before long, the imminent catastrophe was sorted out. The net was free, our anchor was untangled, and the guys ended up with a clutch of cervazas and a stash of Marlboros for their trouble.

The Mexican Gold Coast stretches almost sixty miles from Manzanillo in the south to Camilla in the northwest. Manzanillo is famous for the resort complex of Las Hadas. Las Hadas is a fanciful collection of first-rate restaurants, swim up bars, and towering Moorish-style architecture. Scores of startling white sugar cube style hotel rooms are plastered on the side of a steep hillside. Some of the units were available as condominiums but the cracked walls and lifted sidewalks, indicative of a major earthquake hit, made us a little leery even if we had been in the market.

We were on the verge of completing our circumnavigation of the world, but our situation seemed to mimic the gleaming resort. PL and I put on a good face, but the shock waves generated by Tyler's death had left cavernous scars in the very foundations of our being. But now something new was miraculously repairing some of that deep wound. It seemed like our grand adventure was just the medicine we had needed to mend our hearts and move on.

40

Crossing Osprey's Outbound Track

If I knew what it was I was getting into,
I wonder if I would have had the courage to set out.

—Mark Twain

We officially completed our circumnavigation of the world as we crossed our outbound track at Bahia Navidad on January 7, 2001. The day was clear and warm with just a touch of sea breeze. The sapphire blue sky kissed a horizon that was laced with puffy white cumulus clouds. Anchor chain peeled out of our windless and soon *Osprey* was gently swinging on her hook in the shimmering waters of the lagoon. Chuck, a circumnavigator who had accompanied us through the Panama Canal aboard his yacht *Deviant,* blew us a salute from his conch horn. Almost 40,000 sea miles had slipped under *Osprey's* keel since we had sailed from Seattle in the summer of 1995.

As with most grand schemes, the finale was anticlimactic compared to the adventure itself. Our voyage allowed us to move on with our lives after losing our son. Rather than be engulfed in sorrow, we sailed into a huge world and an uncertain future. An insightful philosopher noted that anguish and heartbreak may not be distributed evenly throughout the world, but they are distributed widely. Over time we left not only many countries, but also our acute sadness in *Osprey's* wake. The pain of our loss had diminished but occasionally a rogue wave of sorrow still staggered us. We shook it off as best we could.

During our circumnavigation PL and I sailed into forty foreign countries and journeyed overland to a score more. One of the toughest parts of our trip was leaving. Packing it up and sailing off had been a huge leap of faith. Although we did not know it at the time, returning home would be just as challenging.

Unlike our first visit in 1996, Bahia Navidad now boasted a thriving Internet café operation—the ultimate hit for cruisers and backpackers. The ensuing years were not as kind from a bureaucratic perspective, since an overzealous Port Captain now dictated the movements of any foreign boats in or out of his port.

With a revitalized perspective and a lot more confidence, PL and I sailed north for Bahia Tenacatita. On our last visit five years prior, I was sweating about equipment and PL was stressed about provisioning. This time we could appreciate the moment. Now that we had experienced the challenges of offshore sailing and international cruising, introspection and a more minimalist philosophy was a much better fit than before.

Rio Boca las Iguanas empties into the northern anchorage at Bahia Tenacatita. Rather than blazing down the twisting narrow three-mile long mangrove lined slough at mach speed, this time around we just putted along enjoying the sights and sounds of the swamp creatures. After I tied up our dinghy, PL and I strolled down a long strand of sandy beach to enjoy lunch at a weathered palapa. The fresh fish tacos were great, the cervaza was cold, and the view of Punta Hermanos, framed by the lagoon's granite haystacks, was stunning.

"McHale's Navy" of TV fame was filmed next to the anchorage at Tenacatita. Now the classic tropical bungalow that was the headquarters for the PT boat guys is home to Restaurant Frances. Cruisers embraced the place because their food is inexpensive and tasty—the ultimate venue for a yachtie watering hole. Towards dusk folks broke out their guitars and harmonicas then the music got louder and the sea stories got bigger. PL and I gave a little spiel about our trip around the planet. After an evening of spinning yarns and reliving adventures, we almost had to wade out of the place.

Ipala, the little hole in the wall stop between Banderas Bay and the Mexican Gold Coast, was still the same. The surf thundered into the exposed outer walls of the anchorage, but the granite cliff absorbed the brunt of the breaking waves and shot the sheets of angry water to the sky. A timid local fisherman and his shy young son motored their panga out to our anchorage in hopes of being gifted with a few pencils and a tablet. We were happy to oblige.

The 500-foot spire of Cabo Corrientes, just north of Ipala, twists and spins potential hurricanes away from Puerto Vallarta and Banderas Bay. It was a little bit lumpy rounding the cape in the determined northerly, but Puerto Vallarta was in our sights and we were zeroed in on the bright city lights. PV was special to us because it was our hangout and staging area before sailing west in 1996.

We dropped our hook at the popular yachtie hangout of La Cruz de Huancax-tle, just north of PV in Banderas Bay. As the *Osprey* crew slowly acclimated to the crowds both afloat and ashore, a couple of the local expats tried to bring us up to speed. Puerto Vallarta, just to the south of us, was in one time zone while La Cruz was in another. I also learned that the downside of cruising present day Mexico is dealing with the local Port Captains. Each port in Mexico has its own Port Captain who is basically a god. No vessel moves in or out of a Mexican port without the Port Captain's blessing. Papers must be signed and fees must be paid every time a yacht leaves the harbor, no matter if the intended cruise is for a few hours or a month. Although the ham handed administrators can drive the unini-tiated gringo loco, Mexico is slowly unsnarling the entrenched bureaucracy.

Dick Markie, the harbormaster at Paradise Village Marina, presented us with a hand painted tamarind pod, cleverly painted with a special "welcome back," after we sailed into his beautiful marina. The marina, on the outskirts of Puerto Vallarta, is a bit on the extravagant side with its hot tubs, swimming pools, health spa, and restaurants, but PL and I adapted nicely. Since Paradise Village is the jumping off place for Coconut Milk Run across the Pacific, PL and I were sud-denly in demand for circumnavigation seminars. It felt strange to be back and watch the latest group of Pacific cruisers, the class of 2001, prepare for their off-shore initiation. Good memories came flooding back as we relived the voyage with a very appreciative audience.

Kate and Andrea, with their friend JoJo, joined us for a few days. Our crew managed to unload enough of our excess cruising gear at a yachtie swap meet to raise *Osprey's* waterline a few inches. Actually the unburdening process went much further than freeing our boat of superfluous paraphernalia. We had junked a lot of the expectations and attachments so much apart of our former life. Kate, ever the intuitive daughter, opined that we were on the right track.

41

Manana Land

After our visitors left town it was time for a bit of diversion. *Osprey* was left with the good folks at Paradise Village while PL and I joined Keith and Susan of *Cest Le Vie* for a road trip inland. Our foursome rented a tired Ford sedan and headed for central Mexico's high desert country—a land of parched badlands and expensive toll roads.

Guanajuato's unique underground highway system is a network of former mining tunnels that divert traffic away from the European-style plazas that lend the place so much charm. Like moles we hesitantly drove through the labyrinth of long darkened passages, and then uncannily popped up right in the center of town next to our hotel. The old world Spanish atmosphere of the charming town evoked memories of the Andalucia area of Spain with a vibrant mixture of tree lined plazas, outdoor cafes, and cobblestone streets. Teatro Juarez is ground zero for the sophisticated cultural life of Guanajuato. The opulent turn of the century theatre is a study in surreal lighting, flamboyant décor, and glamorous history. Our hotel, the delightful Posada Santa Fe, was handily just across the street.

A visit to the Don Quixote museum, the patron saint of this colonial mining city, renewed our admiration for the errant knight who tilted rainbows in his quest for truth and honor. During our trip around the globe I could picture myself as the deluded knight, transported from one encounter to the next by the faithful *Osprey*—I was still jousting dreams. The annual Cervantes Art Festival is a major Latin American happening. Local citizens take Don Quixote and Sancho seriously as they don medieval regalia to celebrate the timeless story of our favorite knight and his good friend.

San Miguel de Allende, one of our favorite Mexican cities, is a more relaxed and less trendy version of Santa Fe, New Mexico. The famous Instituto Allende, an art and language institute of world renown, hosts thousands of annual visitors for its art shows, theatrical productions, and musical performances. Attracted by the agreeable climate and the rural Mexico lifestyle, a sizable community of artists, authors, musicians, and expats has retired to San Miguel Allende. A cruising couple we met in Z-town enjoyed their San Miguel bungalow during the summer season, and then returned to their sailboat in the winter just as the Pacific Coast hurricane season was winding down. PL and I understood the draw of cruising, but once we savored the early morning strolls through the central plaza of El Jardin Square, the allure of San Miguel also made perfect sense. Our search for the ideal new home was proving to be an elusive goal. It occurred to us that perhaps it was not geographic location, but rather attitude that defines where a home should be.

PL and I eventually ended up in lively Guadalajara, the second largest city in Mexico. Actually we had checked the place out before—this time around our goal was to catch a ride back to Paradise Village in Puerto Vallarta. A super luxury first class ETN bus served as our wheels to PV, but octogenarians Lewis and Jean served as our latest role models. The spunky couple was on a road trip to Jean's condo in PV. Lewis swapped seats with PL so he and I exchanged assorted sea stories while PL and Jean enjoyed the scenery. By the time our bus wheeled into Puerto Vallarta, PL and I had invitations for dinner and go-cart racing. It turned out that Lewis, a product of the Midwest, bought a turbocharged Porsche without telling his children. The kids kept an eye on dad and his hot sports car when he was back home, but down in Margaritaville nobody was around to keep Lewis off the racetrack. Since a person can be judged or reprimanded when they stray outside the lines of life, Lewis simply moved the lines and established his own boundaries. Seemed like a very fitting commentary to me.

42

Hemingway Live

o o o o o o o o o o o o o o o o o o o o o o o o o o o o o o o o o o
Expect nothing. Be prepared for anything.

—*Samurai saying*

Official US policy does make travel to Cuba a challenge, but PL and I circumvented some of the officialdom by flying in and out of Havana through Mexico City. At the time the US stance utilized a fuzzy logic technique that allowed its citizens to visit Fidel land provided the visitor did not spend any money. "Don't ask permission, just ask forgiveness" was our motto and that of the AMEX travel agency in PV.

Cuba provides a fascinating glimpse into how it was in Hemingway's day. Vintage Chevys and Fords cruise the crowded streets of colonial Havana while thirsty tourists down frozen daiquiris at La Floridita, one of Papa Hemmingway's favorite watering holes in the '50's. Before Bugsy Siegel's Flamingo Hotel spawned the sin city of Las Vegas, Chicago mafia chieftains like Meyer Lansky favored Havana's casinos and its hedonistic offerings. It was way past our bedtime before the all-night partying at the local cabarets even got underway.

An orange slice picked PL and I up. Actually the huge fruit is a three-wheeled motorcycle contraption covered with an orange metal canopy and accommodating two passengers plus a driver. Our destination was Palador Los Cactus de 33, a beautifully restored mansion in the two square mile quarter of colonial Havana. Intimate atmosphere, exquisite food, professionally crafted drinks, and hand rolled cigars—it was definitely a Valentine's Day to remember for my sweetheart and I.

The state owns most enterprises such as taxis, hotels, and restaurants. Tourists provide the main source of Cuba's official hard currency, the US dollar. One of the harsh realities of Cuba's struggling isolated economy is the public transit system. Since fuel is scarce and new busses are virtually nonexistent for the locals, the *camello,* or camel, was created. A camel is an ingenious pairing of two old busses which are welded together, reconfigured as a fifth wheel trailer, and then towed around behind a tractor rig. Of course if you are a well-healed tourist staying at the International Hotel, government owned Mercedes taxis are at your disposal.

I had read about Hemingway Marina, so PL and I hopped a cab to the outskirts of Havana to check it out. While I was interrogating the driver about life in Cuba and the underhanded ways of the Castro's secret police, PL was jabbing my ribs and hissing that our driver was wary of making any derogatory remarks about a regime that controlled his life. The driver started to sweat and mumbled something about two undercover policemen riding on the motorcycle-sidecar rig in the next lane over. After our traumatized driver dropped us off at the marina and sped away, I noticed that Papa's namesake marina had seen better days. Crumbling concrete quays and tired shore side facilities torpedoed the government's futile attempts to create the ambiance of the Hemingway years. The few American cruisers complained about the bureaucratic shakedown for extra fees. As in many of the far corners of the world, the European cruising boats seemed right at home. PL and I always asked ourselves how many people could possibly be left in Germany, France, and Britain if they are all out cruising the world. The socialized economies of Western Europe may have their problems, but the generous hunks of vacation time and healthy retirement benefits enjoyed by the Euro yachties certainly encourage their wanderlust.

Rather than a rusty *camello,* PL and I rode a luxury tourist motor coach to the sandy peninsula of Veradero Beach. Our driver pointed out LaVigia, the home where Hemingway lived while he resided in Cuba. One of Cuba's most famous adopted sons, Hemingway penned *The Old Man and the Sea* and *Islands in the Stream* while in residence. Papa left Cuba in 1960 and returned to Ketchum, Idaho where he ended his life.

PL gauges a country on the quality and cost of a manicure, pedicure, and haircut. No stranger to questionable dos and primitive waxing techniques, PL is always in the hunt for just the right experience. At Veradero Beach a Cuban manicurist, in actuality a college-educated physiologist, gave PL the full treatment. Castro allocates approximately $15 per month per citizen regardless of their profession. Teachers, doctors, and taxi drivers all receive the same stipend. In order to improve their lot, many Cubans engage in covert forms of capitalism. As she was polishing my mate's nails, the manicurist happened to mention, "My real business is fine Cuban cigars." Since PL condones my occasional cigar, a box of fine black market Cohiba cigars came my way from the manicurist's secret stash.

I slipped into secret agent mode when a beach vendor discreetly passed me a piece a paper that directed us to a clandestine location—the home of a local family who served contraband lobster dinners. PL and I boarded a cab and cleverly, I thought, had the cabbie drop us a block from the intended rendezvous. Suddenly we were standing alone on a Cuban back road without a clue as to how the game was played. A few minutes later a mysterious young man motioned for us to follow him through a maze of alleys. As I mulled over thoughts of being mugged, or indicted as a political prisoner, a smiling Cuban lady pointed the way into her small house. Inside the tiny living room an oilcloth was draped over a small table and the dripping stub of a candle glowed. Although I am sure we missed many of the subtleties as she enthusiastically chatted away in rapid fire Spanish, PL and I were able to order a cerveza and assure her that we did indeed want her "special" dinner. It was a great evening and the secret police never came to call.

Despite its economic and political problems, Cuba overwhelmed us with its friendly people and historic monuments. Like an old snapshot, Cuba is a little frayed around the edges these days, but that has not stopped the influx of Euro tourists. When the Castro regime fades into history, Cuba is sure to become one of the most desirable vacation destinations in the Caribbean.

We took a chance when we visited Cuba, but the experience allowed us another glimpse into a different society. Each time we have exposed ourselves to unfamiliar cultures, it is like clearing away a bit more rubble from a hidden relic. PL and I have uncovered many such artifacts during our excursion of the world, but there are many more out there just waiting for us.

43

Sea of Cortez

○ ○

The matters of great importance we had left behind were not impor-
tant. We had lost the virus, or it had been eaten by the antibodies of
quiet. Our pace had slowed greatly; the hundred thousand reactions
to our daily world were reduced to a very few.

— *John Steinbeck,* **Log of the Sea of Cortez**

After spending a month moored in the brackish estuary of Paradise Village, *Osprey* did not seem to handle like her old self as we sailed north. In the middle of choppy Banderas Bay I discovered the problem. After diving over the side I found the prop, rudder, shaft, and thru hulls encrusted with barnacles—very reminis-cent of my Barcelona experience. I was one tired pup as I climbed back into the cockpit after sucking up a tank of air scraping the flora and fauna off the hull in the chilly 60-degree water.

As *Osprey* surfed into the narrow, constricted channel to Marina Mazatlan, the partially completed infrastructure spoke volumes about the economic realities of under funded marina projects. The town of Mazatlan seems better suited for col-lege spring breaks than a major cruising destination. Much of Mazatlan is a bit contrived and touristy for our taste, but we enjoyed the kindly fruit and vegetable vendors who chugged up to the marina gates each day in their overworked pickup. Mexican produce is as good as it gets and we got lots.

Since PL and I had thoroughly enjoyed the spectacular pageantry of Carnival in Trinidad, we figured the Mazatlan rendition would be a similar treat. Appar-ently our jaded perspective colored our appreciation for Carnival in Mazatlan even though the local press corps, gringo tourists, and itinerant yachties insisted it was the best around. As we came to find out during our slow, erratic and sometimes painful reentry into the brave new world of the twenty-first century, our view of things had changed but the world around us just continued on as before.

PL had hair issues. Word on the street was that Selena, a law student and hair cutter of renown, was the woman to see. The clear spring day was warm and sunny when the fabled hairdresser came aboard *Osprey*. PL perched in the companionway and Selena did her thing. As I watched the saga unfold, Selena merrily snipped here and there with a fierce determination. The clipping became more intense and the haircut took on that runaway lawnmower look. Not being an expert on the latest style in coiffures, I just watched the proceedings. When the emerging hairdo began to resemble the mop on Moe of Three Stooges fame, I suggested that PL might want to look in a mirror. PL was shell-shocked, Selena was clueless, and I was laying low. Selena's father, a local barber, responded to his daughter's frantic call and heroically salvaged the unsalvageable. PL resorted to a baseball hat and Selena wisely resumed her law career.

The disillusioned *Osprey* crew vamoosed and sailed west across the wide mouth of the Gulf of California, a 150-mile overnighter. Our landfall on the Baja Peninsula was Punta Los Frailes, a rocky headland punching up 750 feet into the clear Baja sky. From that point PL and I coast hopped north. By and by we crossed the Tropic of Cancer and officially sailed out of the tropics.

The Gulf of California, popularly known as the Sea of Cortez, is a 600-mile long gulf that separates the Baja peninsula from mainland Mexico. From its gaping southern mouth, the Sea is pinched to a mere 50 miles across at the northern Midriff Islands. Cruising the Baja is an event to be savored—the gulf is dotted with over a hundred fishing villages and scores of pristine and remote anchorages. Self-sufficiency is mandatory, since there are only a few harbors with moorage or diesel docks.

Five years prior we had skirted the Sea of Cortez as *Osprey* sailed directly from Cabo San Lucas to Puerto Vallarta. At the time PL and I were still dealing with the raw wound of Tyler's death and sightseeing was not on our mind. This time around the intense pain and profound sorrow had dulled with the years. Our quest now was to perhaps make sense of it all and what better place than an immersion into the languid pace of rural Baja.

PL and I were lost in our own thoughts as a companionable silence worked its magic. We became immersed in a land resonating with a compelling aura. Soaring sandstone mesas, streaked with dusty hues of slate and copper, rimmed the unspoiled blue waters of the gulf. Bizarre arroyos, sprinkled with cactus, carved deep fissures in the parched landscape as they coursed down to the gulf from the interior of the Baja peninsula.

Thousands of Pacific gray whales migrate to the shallow warm headwaters of the Baja Peninsula during their midwinter breeding and calving season. After the 5000 mile trip from the harsh environment of their Arctic feeding grounds, the gray whales probably enjoy the mellow Baja lifestyle as much as the tourists in Cabo. Humpbacks, finbacks, and even occasional blue whales share the Sea of Cortez with the huge gray whale population.

One afternoon a rampaging bus with an attitude rocketed out of the placid water not more than fifty yards off our bow. The breaching gray whale performed a monumental belly flop as it disappeared in a geyser of spray. Our encounters with humpback and gray whales of Baja ran the gamut from startling up close and personal breechings to just a vague glimpse of a puffy spout of vapor on the clear blue horizon. Veteran Baja cruisers regaled us with stories of whales accidentally, or maybe not accidentally, surfacing under the hull of a passing boat. As I sipped a cool one with another cruiser on the veranda of Marina La Paz, my new amigo was feeling in a rather expansive mood and I had to admit his whale story was a winner. A month prior he had been under power in his thirty-foot catamaran when a gray whale surfaced under his boat and lifted one of the catamaran's two pontoons out of the water. In the process the errant whale bent a rudder, dinged a propeller, and scared hell out of the owner. Apparently the dented whale just went on its way.

La Paz was my true reintroduction to the Mexican paperwork cha-cha. The bureaucratic boondoggle was an irritant in PV, but it was a downright hassle in La Paz. For a consideration of $25, Marina La Paz dealt with the Port Captain and filled out the endless paperwork—it was money well spent. The long time owners of Marina La Paz not only ran a cruiser friendly marina, but they also designed the quintessential third world skiff, the panga. PL and I liked the atmosphere of the place since it was the hub of the local yachtie community

The sharp winter gradient between the colder waters of the Sea of Cortez and the warmer waters south of Mazatlan precipitate the local Baja winds. Just to make it interesting the counter rotating lows over the desert landscape and the Sea of Cortez also contribute to the local climate. Calling the weather in the Sea of Cortez can sometimes be a crapshoot. But I was feeling lucky.

As the tidal current raced out of La Paz's narrow entrance channel, PL and I were intent on avoiding the shoaling sandbanks that lurked about on either side of the narrow harbor mouth. Suddenly *Osprey's* engine seized up and died, as if an unseen hand had ripped the pistons out of the engine block. Not good—now

I was not feeling so lucky. At first I assumed a drifting fishing net was wrapped around our prop. As our boat drifted helplessly along in the two knot ebb PL swung our swim ladder over the side. I popped on my dive mask, climbed down the ladder, and hung underwater on the bottom rung as the current tried to pry me loose from my perch. No problem with the propeller. I flopped back into the cockpit, regrouped, and then opened the forward engine compartment but I could not find any obvious problem. Finally I climbed into the cockpit locker to check out the back of the engine. There was the culprit—the engine driven refrigeration compressor had decided to pack it up. When the compressor seized up it was like asking our little diesel to keep running while a huge hand from the Jolly Green Giant gripped its innards. I cut off the seized compressor's v-belts and fired up the engine. Now our only issue was dealing with a lack of ice cubes as we headed up the Sea of Cortez.

A beleaguered sailboat had inadvertently run out of fuel and was drifting towards the rocks off Punta San Marcial when PL and I happened by. It was a hot windless Baja day so *Osprey* was pressed into duty as a rescue tugboat. We towed the hapless couple to Bahia Aqua Verde, tucked them into a protected cove, and then scoped out the surroundings. Above the shoreline the fading twilight brushed the free form sandstone boulders in desert hues from subtle peach to vibrant turquoise. Handsome cactus stretched their evening shadows across the hillside.

Next morning PL and I went ashore for a hike. We left our dinghy alongside an assortment of beached fishing pangas. Our trek wound up and over the hillside, and then into the parched desert on the leeside of the rocky cove's headlands. Eventually we followed a jeep trail and ended up in the small village of Aqua Verde, a few miles from our anchorage.

The only frisky inhabitants seemed to be the goats. The local residents had adopted the languid persona of desert creatures and were in no hurry. A small school, a score of ramshackle shacks, a tiny café, and a scruffy store shared the sparse stretch of Baja drainage. One of the young girls working the tienda sold us some shop worn local produce, but her entire extended family took an interest in our visit. From tiny suckling infants to tubercular hacking grandfathers, the tiny store was their home, business, and meeting hall all rolled into one.

Aqua Verde is not only popular with cruisers, but also with kayakers. PL and I talked it over with a group from Massachusetts who were camped on the beach outside the village. Their goal was to dig latrines for visiting kayakers. The concept made sense since rural Baja's standards of sanitation challenged any gringo's sensibilities.

We anchored at Honeymoon Cove in the lee of Isla Danzante. The immaculate nature preserve boasts clear turquoise water, picturesque slab sided cliffs, and cactus-studded plateaus. PL figured the small island, with its expansive views of the Sea of Cortez, was just the place to replant "the boys"—our seagoing cactus collection from Greece and Costa Rica. Our private garden was planted on a lovely north-facing slope, perched over a small rocky cove, and guarded by stoic Candelabra cactus. To the far west the great mesas of the Baja peninsula stretched north and south under the clear desert sky.

Since Baja has become action central for ecotourism, a number of kayak rental joints vie for part of the action. A group of bedraggled college kids lugged their rented kayaks ashore on Honeymoon Cove's secluded sandy beach just as we were hiking back to our dinghy. Over the past few days they had paddled from Loreto downwind to Isla Danzante. Now the young paddlers were cold, wet, and hungry. No matter what the tourist brochures said, it was still winter in Baja with cold northerly winds and chilly 62-degree water, a radical departure from the warm 80-degree water generated during the scorching summers. The handheld VHF radio the outfitter had loaned them was defunct and the kids were out of ideas. I fired up our radio and contacted their guy in Loreto. After we got it all sorted out, the youngsters arranged to meet the outfitter's van at Puerto Escondido, only a few hours away from a kayaker's perspective. PL, in her concerned mom mode, plundered *Osprey's* supply of goodies to feed the young kayakers.

Puerto Escondido, 115 miles north of La Paz, is the only true hurricane hole in the Sea of Cortez. Besides being a popular kayak drop off point, Baja yachties have favored the huge anchorage for years because moorage was free. But as with many good things, times and circumstances change. A recent hurricane trashed the place and Loreto's Port Captain, who is the ramrod on that section of the Baja, decided that a few fees might be in order. Puerto Escondido itself is basically a ghost town, an investors dream gone south. Streets are laid out, lampposts are erected, and huge concrete retaining walls poured. Boulevards travel to nowhere and abandoned concrete quays line the anchorage. Somebody threw quite a party but there were no takers. Maybe it was the vultures.

Since my liver was not up to the challenge of happy hour with the itinerant yachties who spend months at a time in the anchorage, PL and I hiked up to the Tripui RV Park. Tripui's operation was just off the main road coursing down the Baja. They offered a small grocery store, a modest restaurant, and email access—civilization in the sagebrush. But alas, a mysterious fire has since obliterated the place.

About 80 miles north of Puerto Escondido, on the western flank of the Baja Peninsula, lays Bahia Concepcion, a sea within a sea that measures over 20 miles long and 5 miles wide. Rimmed with steep volcanic slopes on the western shore and featuring dozens of protected anchorages, Bahia Concepcion casts a mesmerizing spell.

PL and I dropped the hook in the shallow waters off Playa Santispac. A standard offering of gringo RV rigs lined the sandy beach, but then we spotted the Green Tortoise. The Green Tortoise is actually a weathered charter bus, equipped with a galley and bunk beds, which makes the circuit between Seattle and Cabo San Lucas. The bus housed an interesting cross section of folks and we enjoyed talking it over with such fun-loving travelers. A dozen other Green Tortoise busses explore Alaska, Baja, Guatemala, Costa Rica, mainland Mexico, and the national parks in the USA. Turns out there is even a Green Tortoise hostel in Seattle. We really liked the whole concept.

Later on we trudged out to the paved road in hopes of hitching a ride into Mulege, a popular Baja town quite a ways north of our anchorage. An ancient Mexican farming couple in a battered Ford kindly gave us a lift and dropped us on the outskirts of the village. We enjoyed a very satisfying lunch and then PL decided to stroll through the local shops. My usual routine is to wait outside and let PL do her thing. As PL continued her exploration I encountered another bored husband. I blurted out "I think I know you" and indeed I did. Dick, a mentor from my dental school days, was patiently waiting for his wife Joanne who happened to favor the same shop as PL. After introductions were made we rode with them back to their vacation bungalow. Turned out that Dick and Joanne's winter retreat was on the beach just a mile from our anchorage. PL and I enjoyed their fine hospitality over the next few days and we were introduced to a number of rather fascinating expats who lived in the area.

Eventually we pushed further north and coincidently anchored off Punta Chivato just in time to celebrate St. Patrick's Day. The Punta Chivato Yacht Club had no yachts, but they did know how to throw a party. Jim and Mary of *Mooney Base* (as in Mooney airplane) invited us to the festivities. Punta Chivato's only connection to mainstream Baja is a long winding dirt jeep trail that eventually intersects with the paved north-south Baja two-lane highway. A number of well-healed expats built luxurious homes at the remote location and their deal seemed to be flying their airplanes and deep-sea fishing. Not a bad life, and according to our hosts, the price was right.

44

The San Carlos Saga

° °

Whatever you do will be insignificant, but it is very important that you do it.

—*Mahatma Gandhi*

After a lumpy sail across the Sea of Cortez we sailed into the tiny Mexican mainland port of San Carlos. Wedged into the edge of the Sonora desert in the northeast bight of the Sea of Cortez, San Carlos is renowned for being out of western Mexico's hurricane zone. We, as well as our insurance company, liked the concept. Marina San Carlos offers moorage and Marina Seca, its sister operation, offers long-term dry storage at their boatyard about a mile inland. Marina Seca houses hundreds of cruising boats perched stork-like on sturdy steel stands. Although the haul out area is basically a football field size hunk of the Sonora desert, a sturdy chain link fence and good security make it a popular storage facility.

Osprey was hauled out of the water on a huge flatbed trailer. Massive hydraulic arms supported the boat as a rugged CAT tractor slowly towed our rig down the village's main street to the desert boat yard. It was quite a sight to see our fully rigged sailboat riding piggyback on the octopus-like arms of a lowboy trailer. We had swapped *Osprey's* familiar blue water habitat for a parched setting of sagebrush and cactus.

After our well-traveled sloop was securely settled on top of a substantial steel scaffold, the local refrigeration guy slipped out of his manana mode just long enough to install a new refrigeration compressor—the replacement for the seized up compressor that aggravated me in La Paz. Since *Osprey* required a new marine survey for insurance purposes, I hired Francisco to do the inspection. The surveyor assured us that our boat was in Bristol condition but he kept eyeing our inflatable dinghy. Eventually Francisco related an involved story about how the dinghy on his boat had been stolen. We struck a bargain. Francisco became the proud owner of our old inflatable and I was not charged for the survey. Both of us were happy and now I had an excuse to treat *Osprey* to a new hard-bottomed dinghy on our return visit in the winter.

PL and I stripped off the sails, cockpit dodger, and other assorted bits and pieces. The intense desert sun, torrential rains, and occasional windstorms are tough on gear—it is best stored inside the cabin. We left buckets of water inside the cabin to add humidity and taped aluminum foil around the windows to reflect the heat. PL cleared out the canned goods so there was nothing to explode when the cabin temperature skyrocketed. After all the years of being afloat, *Osprey* was all set to dry out in the intense heat of the Sonora desert. I planned to wait until the June through November hurricane season had run its course before plunking our sloop back into the Sea of Cortez.

After we kissed our baby goodbye for the season, a little recreation was definitely in order for the crew. The pick of the litter was *Barranca del Cobre*. Better known as the Copper Canyon, the 2300-meter deep gorge cuts a formidable swath through the Sierra Madres. Mexico's Copper Canyon is a 23,000 square mile network of remote ravines and sparse bottomland that could swallow two Grand Canyons. It is also home to a reclusive band of 50,000 indigenous Tarahumara Indians.

A five hour marathon bus ride delivered us to the coastal town of Santa Anita and our waiting train. The Ferrocarril Chihuahua al Pacifico chugged out of the station right on time and lurched towards the far mountains. After a whistle stop at Los Mochis, the conductor yelled, "All Aboard." Our destination was the high mountains of the Sierra Madres.

The train rumbled onto a small mountain rail siding as the conductor pointed out a dusty jeep trail. We slung on our packs, stepped onto a battered wood platform, and waved goodbye to our train as it disappeared down the winding track. PL and I trudged along a twisting path that had been blasted across a rock face. As we rounded the next bend the charming Hotel Posada Mirador emerged from a huge sandstone outcropping. The small hotel is an exquisitely rendered lodge perched on the rim of the canyon. Our cliff side room was a cozy aerie commanding a fabulous view of the strikingly beautiful canyon. A maze of intriguing hiking trails coursed down to the floor of the canyon far below. We had no trouble whiling away a few days in our hideaway.

After our decadent lodge stay, we hopped aboard the next train heading to the small mountain town of Creel. Unlike our previous digs, Creel was a more realistic view of canyon life. Creel has a Mexican frontier town feel with an interesting cross section of humanity to match. Many Tarahumara people strolled the town in traditional dress while bundled up tourists poked around shops looking for Indian handicrafts. I rustled up a Tarahumara guide who assured us that his derelict 4x4 would easily negotiate the steep mountain trails and transport us to the ancestral hideaways of the shy Tarahumara. As the old truck bounced along the canyon roads, our driver proudly proclaimed that his people are famous for their long distance runners who can footrace for a hundred miles through the mountains. Sadly many of the secluded Tarahumara still live in caves and subsist on beans and maize even though the Mexican government provides some uninspired reservation housing.

It was nippy in Creel so the next day PL and I caught the next train heading back towards the coastal sun. As our train wound back down the long series of switchbacks cut into the steep mountainside, another small railroad station caught our eye. A short while later we found ourselves standing at that very station as the train continued on its way back to Los Mochis. We clambered into the back of a battered pickup and braced ourselves for a bouncy hour ride through the hinterlands. Our reward was the pastoral mountain settlement of Cerocahui. Hotel Mision was our own personal magic carpet back to the era of pioneering Jesuit missions and a simpler time. By day we strolled through the nearby orchards and vineyards of the friendly small village. The hotel's chef spoiled us with gourmet meals and his staff knew how to concoct the perfect Margarita. As night rolled around the hotel shut off their generator and a delicious stillness pervaded the cold clear sky. We cuddled in front of a flickering wood fire and read by the light of a kerosene lantern

The notion of a simpler life was now ingrained in our souls. The world might resist, but our lives had become an art form. Both of us had become passionate about gleaning some meaning out of all the chaos we had encountered. PL and I would no longer settle for our old lives—we envisioned a beautiful new world for ourselves.

45

Minimalist Reentry

I see a culture rich in materials for pleasure and excess communication, but poor in depth of feeling and imagination—dull and flat and rich.

—Robert Redford

As our circumnavigation unfolded, PL and I found ourselves living a dream that fired our imagination, simplified our lives, and expanded our horizons. Traveling became a rather pleasant addiction and meeting a world of fascinating people fueled our habit. Dropping back into the modern westernized culture was tough. The fast track life, which we enjoyed so much prior to our trip, had lost its appeal. The rampant consumerism and strong sense of entitlement synonymous with an affluent western lifestyle was diametrically opposed to our well-worn cruiser persona.

Reentry is an acquired taste—bitter at first but then acceptable in small doses. Even though the concept makes sense, things had changed for us big time. Our familiar circle of friends and acquaintances was not so familiar anymore. It was a long time coming, but PL and I finally realized the game had changed for us. We were an anachronism. At first we anticipated a few pats on the back, a lot of questions, and then a well-deserved assimilation back into the main stream. The hard reality slammed home rather quickly—very few people cared to hear about our circumnavigation, let alone relate to it. PL and I had "spit the bit" and it showed.

The world, as we had come to know it, had changed drastically while we were out and about. Living aboard a sailboat for a long stretch of time is charming and cozy, but the outside world just goes on about its business. The modern world is flattening—we need to run faster just to stay in place. Globalization, rather than international boundaries, seems to dictate the flow of commerce and technology. I suppose we were lucky not to sail off the edge of the planet.

Over the next six months PL and I tentatively reentered our former life. Cruisers call it "swallowing the anchor." Our collision with America's new millennium culture was jarring and messy.

46

Getting It Together in Baja

Vitality shows in not only the ability to persist but the ability to start over.

—*F. Scott Fitzgerald*

Since *Osprey* was living on a patch of desert, I was not too concerned about tenable anchorages and rogue waves, but the blazing desert heat and occasional flash floods concerned me. A December road trip to the Baja was the perfect opportunity to deliver a new hard-bottomed inflatable to *Osprey* and to reassure ourselves that she was ok after her six month stint of dry storage.

Our sailboat seemed to be doing just fine without us, so PL and I drove our 4x4 rig to the nearby port town of Guaymas. We boarded an aging ferry that would take us across the Sea of Cortez to Santa Rosalia on the Baja Peninsula. After the ferry left port, a Canadian expat befriended us. Bob was an old Mexican hand who was returning to Mexico to live out his days in Mulege.

Our ferry pulled into Santa Rosalia hours late because the captain decided to operate the lumbering ship on only one engine that day. In the wee morning hours we finally disembarked from the ferry, endured a search by the local military, and then drove thirty miles so Bob could spend the night in his beloved Mulege. Theoretically driving at night is not a good idea in Baja. I thought the prohibition had to do with avoiding collisions with wandering burros on the dark windy roads, but Bob, a hardened Baja veteran, pointed out the major mishap that could befall a gringo at night would be an unlucky encounter with corrupt *Federales*.

Driving on the Baja is an adventure in motoring. The long stretches of desolate desert, infrequent gas stations, military checkpoints, washed out roads, and ancient AARP retirees barreling along the narrow roads in behemoth motor homes can be unsettling.

The main purpose of our road trip was to spend time with our good friends Jerry and Gayle at their condo in Cabo San Lucas. Jerry and I fished every morning. There were scores of stray dogs scrounging around the fishing boat docks as Jerry, myself, and Jake (Jerry's dog) strolled down the gangway to the fishing boat. When I turned around to put Jake in the boat, a local mutt answered to the name and gave me a big lick of gratitude.

"You're not Jake," I yelled as I wiped off the drool.

Eventually Jerry and I tracked down Jake who must have decided that the Mexican dog gang had something to offer. As with most of us, Jake did not truly appreciate just how good his life was.

Our extended road trip wound north back up the Baja peninsula to Pasadena, where PL and I did our grandparent thing with Oliver and his folks. After our grandparent hit, we headed back to Port Orchard. PL opted to reacquaint herself with a land-based lifestyle. My goal was to sail *Osprey* home in the spring.

In late January I flew back down to San Carlos to recommission *Osprey*. I dragged a couple duffle bags jammed with spare parts and provisions off the plane, but nobody at the tiny Guaymas airport batted an eye. The customs officials at the rural airstrip were obliging folks who just waved me through—very unlike their big city brethren.

The clunky Ford taxi that delivered me to Marina Seca was older than the driver. The chain-smoking cabbie deposited my mountain of gear next to my dusty sailboat at about sundown. Although *Osprey* was nestled on a scaffold high and dry on the edge of the desert, the night was freezing. I kept warm by repeatedly climbing a spindly extension ladder as I transferred all my paraphernalia from the dirty haul out yard to *Osprey*'s cockpit ten feet off the ground.

Luckily the Marina Bar a mile down the road was having its own Super Bowl party, so I took the next day off to watch the witty commercials and momentarily forget about my long list of boat projects. This was a defining moment for me. Although I relished the idea of rekindling the flickering embers of my former cruising life, the work involved in properly refurbishing and refitting *Osprey* was staggering. I was disillusioned with the mundane offerings of life back home, but I was surprised at my negative gut reaction to all the work ahead of me in the boat yard.

Evies is a tiny local Internet café where I could get my java hit, chow down on delicious *juevos rancheros,* and stroll through cyberspace to my heart's content.

Since San Carlos is just a small Mexican coastal village, there are not many grin-gos about in the off-season. Fortunately a few other guys who also stored their boats at Marina Seca frequented Evies. Over the next few weeks our informal breakfast roundtable reignited my cruising passion. At that point my perception of the continuous boat chores and hassles was changed. I could once again reframe the problems, prioritize the work, and then just deal. Island time life was reemerging from my jumbled manic forays of the past six months.

Now that I was back in the hunt, my new plan was to spend January sorting things out and then launch the boat at Marina San Carlos. A number of friends volunteered to crew aboard *Osprey* en route back to Port Orchard. Stu would fly into San Carlos and then sail south to LaPaz. I would single hand around the East Cape of Baja to Cabo San Lucas. Bob signed up for the windward slog from Cabo to San Diego. From San Diego to San Luis Obispo, Don would lend a hand. At SLO Nick would come aboard for the ride to San Francisco. After a lit-tle diversion in Sausalito, retired USN Captain Bob was on tap for the coastal jaunt up to Newport, Oregon. Coming aboard at Newport, Bill would sail with me back to Port Townsend, Washington. The plan was tentative, but a combina-tion of ideal weather windows and accommodating friends eventually made it all work.

Jesus, the boatyard manager, and Luis, the bottom paint contractor, cracked the whip on their crews and things happened fairly quickly—at least by Mexican standards. Although there were not many bargains to be had at the commercial boatyard, local laborers restored my faith. Carlos spent days waxing *Osprey*'s hull and superstructure for about the price of a nice dinner and a good bottle of wine in the States. Paco, the patriarch of Hernandez Brothers Machine Shop in Guay-mas, resurrected a very pricey stainless steel guide arm on one of my winches at no charge just because I made a sincere but mangled effort to explain the problem in *espanol*.

As projects dwindled down I even found a wandering bottle of Scotch in the bilge—a souvenir from my major Scotch provisioning back in Darwin, Australia. An enterprising local in a jazzy yellow truck delivered fresh fruit, vegetables, fish, and meat to the boatyard and marina a couple times a week. Tito, my new amigo at the local fish taco stand, was the lunch guy. As I sat at his little roadside stand sipping a Negro Modelo, Tito grilled fresh triggerfish and shark. He wrapped the fish in homemade corn tortillas and presented it to me with homemade salsa. Life was good.

It finally felt right to be back in the cruiser mode again. The serenity of the lif-estyle promotes a more defining sense of self and a much more stimulating daily experience—expect the unexpected. Veteran cruisers do without many goods and services. They capitalize on trading their time and talent, instead of cash, to maintain an existence that is quite unique.

Debbie and Gary, lately of Colorado, had just built a new home on the bluff above San Carlos. They graciously introduced me to a local expat community renowned for its share of characters. Jim had spent 11 years on a single handed circumnavigation and then settled in San Carlos. Prior to his trip he circumnavigated Central America in his Cessna 210, but a drug dealer stole his plane. Paul, another Colorado boy turned yachtie, mixed killer cocktails for our gatherings.

Paul's sure-fire recipe for a Margarita on the Rocks:

3 fresh limes, ¼ cup Countreau, and ¼ cup tequila shaken together and then poured into a chilled salt-rimmed tumbler with an ice cube or two. For the sake of tender gringo stomachs, Mexican tap water is not used for ice cubes.

47

Breaking Free

o o o o o o o o o o o o o o o o o o o o o o o o o o o o o o o o

A mind that is stretched by new experience can never go back to its old dimensions.

—Oliver Wendell Holmes

A howling Blue Norther with gusts to 45 knots screamed down from the cold canyons of the distant Colorado River a day prior to our sail across the Sea of Cortez. The next day was stunningly beautiful as Stu and I beam reached towards the Baja in a light northerly. We logged much better time on our westward passage than the lumbering steel ferry that PL and I had ridden just a couple months prior.

Over the next ten days Stu and I enjoyed a good dose of lively downwind sailing. We sailed past the wind swept sand dunes of Punta Santa Domingo and reentered Bahia Concepcion. I revisited my friends Joanne and Dick while we gorged on the fantastic Coconut Shrimp at Ray's Café, a funky beach palapa not 200 meters from our anchorage.

Further south we tucked into Aqua Verde to renew an acquaintance with one of the most spectacular Baja anchorages. After retracing the hike that PL and I had taken a year prior, Stu and I were fired up. Stu decided to celebrate by whipping up his specialty, Pasta Carbonara. Unfortunately the presentation was unceremoniously sidetracked when the head (toilet) decided to back up. Marine heads notoriously exhibit their perverse nature and pervasive stench at the most inopportune times. After a long session of tearing apart odds and ends of the plumbing, we triumphantly extracted the 6-foot section of clogged rubber outlet hose. I banged hell out of that hose and eventually shook out all the offensive junk. As I tweaked the head back into operating mode, Stu tweaked our dinner back into eating mode. In the world of cruising, both evolutions are essential.

A stiff northerly fanned our coat tails as we screamed down some rather formidable wave crests en route to Isla San Francisco. As Stu and I tucked into the lee side of the scenic anchorage, handsome ospreys spiraled above the cactus-studded hillsides and crickets provided the background music. The cold silver dollar of the waning desert moon appeared to hang suspended in the dark twinkling vault of the Baja sky. All seemed right with our world.

I loitered in LaPaz for a few weeks after Stu flew home. The lobster tacos at the Baja Super Tacos, a gaily-painted trailer parked on a side street in LaPaz, were as good as ever. For a few bucks a clever eater can have a couple of tacos, a plate of fresh crisp vegetables, and a variety of rip snorting salsa. LaPaz's *malecon* stretches for miles so a brisk walk along the waterfront toned my old pegs and provided ample opportunity for people watching.

Mexicans are a family oriented culture and their interactions warmed my heart. Laborers would toil at their jobs during the week but on Saturday their kids would accompany them to work. The little guys sported hard hats and ate lunch with their dads. On Sunday no locals worked. The local Catholic Church packed them in for the morning, and then the entire family would spend the day together socializing with their neighbors and enjoying an afternoon feast.

Mary Kay and Jack live aboard their small sailboat in LaPaz during the winter and then returne home to San Lois Obispo during the summer. Their passion is to explore the ruins of all the old Baja missions, photograph the sites, and then catalog the findings along with the GPS coordinates. Their goal is to eventually donate their logs and pictures to the Mexican government and perhaps encourage the Baja officials to preserve some of the historic sites. Besides their constant exploration Mary Kay and Jack taught conversational English to local high school kids. I came to know students Ely and Jesus when they became frequent visitors aboard *Osprey*. The Mexican kids enjoyed practicing their English language skills, but they were very much homebodies who had no burning desire to travel outside their own little world. Mary Kay knew many well-educated Mexicans who eventually tired of the manic lifestyle in the States and returned to the much more easy going pace of Baja.

The manana attitude can be addictive to gringos. Many of the expat Americans living in LaPaz are bonded by a perverse kinship to booze and cigarettes. Disgruntled gringos are not the most inspiring companions, so I tried to steer clear of the chronic complainers. As in most of the other cruising ports of the world, there is no shortage of aspiring blue water cruisers. Even so, most of the boats never seem to make it past the breakwater let alone sail off into the sunset.

I planned to sail out of LaPaz on the shoulders of a westerly *Corumel*, but then a 35-knot northerly gale closed the port. After the gale blew out, the Port Captain finally reopened the port of LaPaz and I was out of there. LaPaz gets more than its share of nasty weather. Hurricane Marty subsequently tore through the Marina LaPaz a few years after my departure and virtually destroyed it.

I single handed *Osprey* south bound for Cabo with overnight anchorages on the East Cape at Muertes and Los Frailes. As the morning sun ignited the eastern sky, a sleek gray whale cruised by Punta Arena de la Ventana lighthouse not 100 yards from *Osprey*—magic. On a balmy morning, a few days after I sailed from LaPaz, Cabo San Lucas appeared on the horizon.

As I scoped out my landfall, a new target wandered onto the edge of my radar screen and my VHF radio crackled to life. A very familiar Aussie voice was asking about space availability at Marina Cabo San Lucas. The advancing radar blip materialized into *Dolphin Spirit*, a boat I knew very well from my South Pacific and Mediterranean days. The graceful cutter, with Laurie, Carol, and son Ryan aboard, was coincidentally arriving in Cabo within an hour of *Osprey*. The last time I had seen my Aussie mates was in the Mediterranean port of Rhodes.

Marina Cabo San Lucas is no bargain, so we opted to anchor outside of the inner harbor. After being separated by a couple of years and thousands of sea miles, both boats were soon bobbing alongside one another just outside the surf line at Cabo. Although the anchorage was quite tenable and the price was right, sometimes nature can exact a fee. The infamous Cabo San Lucas Storm of 1982 was a nightmare event when 27 cruising boats were washed up onto the very same beach and lost.

It was time to talk it over with my mates. Our lives should be a mosaic of experiences to savor, not to endure. Instead of fretting about our upcoming hop to San Diego, we reminisced about all the good times our families had shared. Now I had a bit of company as both boats waited for a decent weather window for our dash up the Pacific coast of Baja. Bob, a veteran of our downwind sleigh ride from Bonaire to the San Blas Islands, flew in to join me for the trip. He was ready for another adventure and so was I.

48

Taming the Baja Bash

Security does not exist in nature.
Avoiding is no safer in the long run than exposure.

—Helen Keller

Grizzled cruisers love to regale neophytes with hair-raising stories of the infamous Baja Bash. The Bash is renowned as a trying 800 hundred mile upwind slog from Cabo San Lucas to San Diego. Typically heavy winds and lumpy seas assault the northbound boats as they motor through the sloppy weather one hard fought mile after another. I figured it could not be any tougher than our six week thrashing in the Red Sea. Bob and I motor sailed out of Cabo San Lucas on April 1 and arrived in San Diego on April 8. Actually my onboard collection of seasickness remedies, such as ginger and scopolamine patches, remained untapped from the Sea of Cortez to Puget Sound. It was a testimony to just how mellow our excursion north turned out to be.

In company with *Dolphin* Spirit and with the Baja peninsula lying on our starboard beam, we punched north from Cabo. Although the wind and seas were a bit of a bother south of Cabo Falso, conditions rapidly improved by late afternoon. From that point on *Osprey* and *Dolphin Spirit* motor sailed north in light NW breezes and a low ocean swell. Because the wind and seas were unusually calm, we chalked up five overnighters in row. After five days of nonstop motoring, my trusty little diesel had drunk most of my onboard fuel supply—it was time to diesel up at Turtle Bay. Last time I had sailed into Turtle Bay, PL and I were just getting the feel of cruising. In the mid '90's the locals thought nothing of gouging gullible yachties with overpriced fuel metered by inaccurate fuel gauges. I still chuckle about our rookie introduction to Turtle Bay when our supposedly clean laundry was returned, neatly folded but still dirty. Now I was a little older and a whole lot cagier.

"Senor, welcome to Turtle Bay. What can we do for you?" At first I thought it was a crank call on the VHF radio but it turned out to be Benito, the new mayor of Turtle Bay. Benito must have been an honors graduate of a public relations course, or maybe I was just jaded after all my time in the Third World.

I anchored and the fun began. Our fuel source was Ernesto, the mayor's amigo. Ernesto and his helper drove a broken down pickup to the only gas station in town, filled a couple of huge jerry cans with diesel, lugged the jugs down to their skiff, and then motored out to us. Since Ernesto was not running a real high tech operation, his fuel transfer pump needed help. With no battery to call his own, the clever entrepreneur uncoiled a couple strands of wire and clipped one set of ends to his grimy fuel pump. He passed the other set of ends to me as he mumbled something about "...problem." Eventually the wires were threaded through a porthole and wound up clamped to my batteries. As the fuel pulsed into *Osprey*'s tanks Ernesto gave me a gap toothed grin as he continued the mayor's public relations campaign.

Isla Cedros, notorious as one of the windiest stretches of water in Mexico, favored us with a gentle westerly as *Osprey* reached up the coast from Turtle Bay. When boats are not quite as lucky, they become unsolicited members of the Cedros Island Yacht Club—a disparate group waiting days or weeks for a break in the heavy northerlies to continue their voyage up the Pacific coast of Baja. Next night we anchored just outside the reef choked entrance to San Quintin. From there it was an uneventful overnighter to San Diego. On April 8, 2002 *Osprey* sailed back into US territorial waters after being out of the country for more than six years.

The prevailing northwesterly winter winds on the Pacific side of Baja can generate steep, lumpy seas. Spring is the transition time and the transition weather is signaled when a seasonal low moves over Yuma, Arizona and effectively blocks heavy northwest winds from Baja. The seasonal low established itself for the first time of the year the day we sailed from Cabo. Although the low meant a "June Gloom" marina layer for Southern California and Baja, it meant smiling faces aboard both *Osprey* and *Dolphin Spirit* since we did not have to endure a frontal assault into heavy winds and seas—just a pleasant motor sail up the coast.

Whether it was because of the Mayan wind god Ehecatl, the Hindu god Siva, a dose of good karma, or just plain luck we arrived in San Diego cheerful and rested. Bob and I were feeling good. Even US Customs saw no reason to hassle us.

49

Graveyard of the Pacific

o o o o o o o o o o o o o o o o o o o o o o o o o o o o o o o o

I have had a great many troubles, but most of them never happened.

—*Mark Twain*

It behooves any cruiser to become at least a passable weatherman. Tracking barometric readings, plotting weather trends, and appreciating the subtleties of each region's unique meteorological trends makes life at sea more interesting and much safer. Weather fax downloads are quite helpful for analyzing weather patterns and the weather charts give a feel for how the forecasters reached their conclusions. Not all forecasts or forecasters are created equal. A favorable regional weather forecast does not guarantee the weather in a specific locale. Weather is a lot like politics—it is the local variety that affects you most.

Listening to tales of gloom and doom about the horrendous seas and brutal pounding yachts have endured on the northbound passage from San Francisco to Seattle is a bit on the non-productive side. To minimize the physical and mental fatigue, it is handy to have a bag of tricks. The key trick was not to be in a hurry. "Get homeitis" can be a dangerous affliction if nasty weather is coming down the pike. My basic northbound tactic on the Pacific Coast was to motor into a northwesterly if the weather was fair and sail downwind with a southerly if the forecast called for reasonable weather during a frontal passage. When in doubt, I opted to stay in the harbor. Since there was little to be gained by trashing *Osprey* or the crew, our forays north resembled more of a chess game than a frontal assault.

PL flew down to San Diego in late April for a few weeks of R & R with a gray-muzzled old sea dog she had not seen in four months. I definitely duded up for the occasion. Besides the chance to enjoy a holiday together and to soak up a bit of the Southern California lifestyle, PL and I were also invited to *Dolphin Spirit*'s circumnavigation celebration. The party was a great opportunity to relive the grand adventure with like-minded friends. As PL and I philosophized with Carol and Laurie, all of us agreed that reentry was just plain tough. I felt a part of my soul was still at sea. Although a circumnavigation may be an escapist notion, each of us had made the escape in our own way. Now if there were accounts to be reconciled, each of us had individual notions of how to define our place in the new world we had collided with.

PL jetted out of town about the time Don arrived for the next leg of *Osprey's* northbound journey. Don and I sailed out of San Diego's beautiful harbor on the first of May and started our harbor hop north up the blissful Southern California coast. Our destination was the Northern California town of San Luis Obispo. Along our intended route lay the coastal gem of Santa Barbara. The Santa Barbara region, tucked into a protected bight east of the Channel Islands, is the demarcation between the relatively benign conditions of the southern coast and the potentially blustery conditions of Northern California.

In light air and calm seas and without smoke or mirrors, *Osprey's* crew rounded Point Conception, "The Cape Horn of Southern California," at dusk in early May. We ghosted north under a blanket of stars. Port San Luis, our next port of call, is renowned for fog and we were not disappointed. Don and I tentatively picked our way into the anchorage early next morning as the comforting green blips of the harbor's entrance buoys painted on my radar screen. Since Port San Luis is a handy place for crew changes, I just relaxed and waited for Nick, an experienced *Osprey* hand, to arrive.

By the time Nick showed, a newly minted gale outside the breakwater was blowing itself out. After a great seafood dinner at the Olde Port Inn on the pier at Avila Beach, Nick and I decided to sail early the next morning. We slowly motored through a localized fog bank, and then burst into the brilliant morning sun. We enjoyed a beautiful day and fine sailing weather—typical of the conditions that follow in the wake of a fast moving cold front. San Francisco was our eventual destination, but after a couple of overnighters another gale was headed our the way so Nick and I ducked into Pillar Point at Half Moon Bay for a few days. Not only is Half Moon Bay a great place to ride a bike, there was also a circus in town.

After the harbor patrol lowered the two red gale-warning pennants, we moseyed around Pillar Point and continued our passage to San Francisco. Later that afternoon Nick and I sailed under the arch of the imposing Golden Gate and on to our anchorage in Richardson Bay. The shallow bay was jammed with derelict boats—a commentary on the liberal bent of Marin County. I was not excited about having *Osprey* T-boned by a poorly anchored scow.

Felix, the manager of the Sausalito Yacht Club and a true gentleman, came to our rescue. He listened attentively as I related my saga, and then he proclaimed that it would be SYC's honor to host *Osprey* and her crew. Felix graciously provided a gratis mooring buoy and assumed the role as our host for the next few days.

When I came ashore for the evening Bob, a longtime SYC member and all around good guy, offered me a fine Cuban cigar and a glass of magnificent Cabernet. As manager of a major winery in Napa, Bob knows his cigars and wines. I felt like a lifeline to the civilized life had just been tossed my way. One could do a lot worse than hanging around the Sausalito Yacht Club swapping lies with the genial members.

Captain Bob arrived in Sausalito to relieve the watch—he was piped aboard and Nick flew home. Our next weather window opened up within a day. Bob and I sailed on the ebb and pointed north once again.

Point Reyes, Point Arena, and Cape Mendocino (the highest bluff on the West Coast) were kind to us and actually gave us a free pass. Although we had been cruising just offshore past the exposed western edge of the Siskiyou coastal mountain range, things were going our way. There is 450 miles of exposed coastline between Northern California's Pt. Arena and Oregon's Cape Lookout. In southerly gales Crescent City is renowned as the only safe harbor in between those two landmarks that can be entered in any weather. After two overnighters *Osprey* and crew paid a sunrise visit to the diesel barge at Crescent City. After a quick stop for fuel we were on our way again towards the "Graveyard of the Pacific," the notorious 168 mile stretch from Cape Mendocino in California to Cape Blanco in Oregon.

Cape Blanco, the western-most point of the USA, proved to be a bit on the blustery side even though we timed our approach for the supposedly calm conditions of late evening. We tucked into the lee of Port Orford, threaded our way past the southern edge of Orford and Blanco reefs, and worked our way around the bend. After two more overnighters our tired crew arrived in Newport, Oregon.

We moored at Southbeach Marina in Newport since the staff was friendly and I needed to top off our diesel tank again. Actually the most compelling reason for our stop was the Rogue Ale Brewery and Pub, a very handy watering hole adjacent to the marina. After the skipper renewed the ship's beer stash, Bob said goodbye and my neighbor Bill came aboard. We sailed across the Newport bar on the slack tide next morning. Two more overnighters were notched on our belts as Bill and I sailed past Cape Lookout, Cape Disappointment, and Cape Flattery. The infamous capes were spectacular but benign landmarks as *Osprey* and her crew headed into the home stretch.

Osprey's 1200-mile passage from San Diego to Port Orchard was the culmination of our global cruise. Although the demons still haunted me from time to time, I had learned to stay focused and be mindful of feelings and thoughts that I would have discounted before. My spirit was rebounding after running on reserve for a long while. It was a time to feel magnanimous towards the world and to embrace the here and now. Over the years I have been humbled by the mercurial moods of the sea. I knew we were very fortunate to have enjoyed such a safe and uneventful passage up the West Coast. Although we had to dodge an occasional bullet from the North Pacific every now and then, *Osprey* shrugged it off and brought us back to where we started.

The contestants in the annual Swiftsure Yacht Race, a sailboat race originating in Victoria, B.C., were westbound in the Strait of Juan de Fuca as *Osprey* rounded the NW bend of Washington at Cape Flattery. In a flat calm, Bill and I motor sailed eastbound down the strait towards Puget Sound. Although the Swiftsure racers complained about the calm, settled conditions outbound in the strait, our inbound crew was not about to complain.

On May 27, 2002 Bill and I tied up at Pt. Hudson Marina in Port Townsend, Washington. The 800-mile harbor hop from San Francisco had taken only a week. PL was there to take our lines and relieve the watch. The following morning a new frontal system blew in from the ocean and a stiff westerly wind scoured our rigging. *Osprey* had sailed from Port Townsend seven years before in just such weather, bound for the western horizon.

50

The Osprey has Landed

Something is the matter with you! You are not the hobbit that you were! The hobbit was in fact quite content. Though few believed any of his tales, he remained very happy to the end of his days.

—*JRR Tolkien,* **Lord of the Rings**

The *Osprey* is back, at least for now. As with *Osprey's* namesake fish hawk, PL and I have become migratory. The word hawk comes from the Middle English word *hafoc,* to grasp or seize. We have chosen to seize not just a day, but a lifetime. To soar on broad wings across the sea brings with it new horizons and boundless opportunities.

Our osprey talisman served us well as we ventured into the uncharted reaches of our spirits. Although there were times when the exploration became exquisitely painful, we are introduced to mystical insights and philosophical paths that have revitalized our lives.

During the past decade PL and I have sailed across every degree of longitude on the planet. We have journeyed from New Zealand in the Southern Ocean to the Gulf of Alaska. In the process *Osprey* has crossed the equator twice. Those indelible memories are the ultimate heirlooms.

I have been blessed with a wonderful family and fine friends. Without the support of a loving mate, my dream of sailing the world would have been a hollow accomplishment. Besides cutting a swath through the world's oceans, we have also carved away some of the deep bruises from our hearts. Our souls are at peace and our days are good.

The *Osprey* crew prior to sailing south from Puget Sound in 1995

Tyler & Ashley at college graduation in 1995

Basic transportation in the Indian Himalayas

Underway repairs somewhere in the Pacific

Advanced journeling technique adapted to trade wind sailing

Family outing in French Polynesia

The latest fashion statement in Papeete

Dentist-at-large in Bora Bora

Shopping for just the right basket in Bali

Osprey anchored off Komodo Island in Indonesia

The *Osprey* crew making social calls in the South Pacific

Crossroads of the Pacific in the Cook Islands

The ancient port of Suwakin in the Red Sea

First lesson in Camel Driving 101

Transiting the Suez Canal

Nile River tugboat

Andrea and Kate in Istanbul

Another member of PL's fan club

Vintage motorcyclist and his ride in rural Turkey

Motor scooter outing in the Greek Islands

The *Osprey* crew prior to crossing the Atlantic in 1999

Master mariner determining *Osprey's* position in the mid-Atlantic

A goodwill ambassador with his multi-functional Frisbee

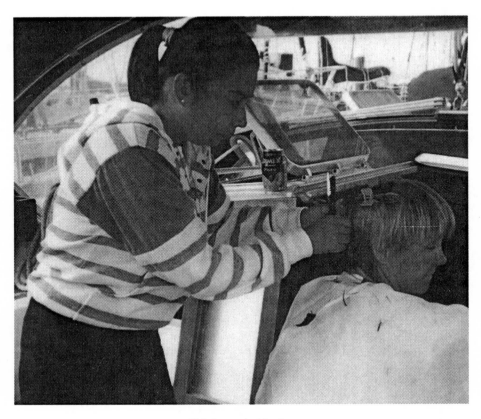

Hair issues in Mexico